Fragments of Truth

D1607759

FRAGMENTS OF TRUTH

Residential Schools and the Challenge of Reconciliation in Canada

NAOMI ANGEL

Edited by Dylan Robinson and Jamie Berthe

DUKE UNIVERSITY PRESS
Durham and London 2022

Designed by A. Mattson Gallagher
Typeset in Garamond Premier Pro by
Westchester Publishing Services

Library of Congress Cataloging-in-Publication Data
Names: Angel, Naomi, [date], author. | Robinson, Dylan,
editor. | Berthe, Jamie (Film scholar), editor.
Title: Fragments of truth : Residential schools and the challenge
of reconciliation in Canada / Naomi Angel ; edited by Dylan
Robinson and Jamie Berthe.
Description: Durham : Duke University Press, 2022. | Includes
bibliographical references and index.
Identifiers: LCCN 2021054701 (print)
LCCN 2021054702 (ebook)
ISBN 9781478015932 (hardcover)
ISBN 9781478018575 (paperback)
ISBN 9781478023173 (ebook)
Subjects: LCSH: Truth and Reconciliation Commission of
Canada. | Off-reservation boarding schools—Canada— History
—20th century—Sources. | Indigenous children— Education—
Canada—History—20th century—Sources. | Indigenous
children—Crimes against—Canada—History— 20th century
—Sources. | Documentary mass media—Canada. | Psychic
trauma and mass media—Canada. | Collective memory in mass
media. | BISAC: SOCIAL SCIENCE / Ethnic Studies /
American / Native American Studies | HISTORY / Canada /
Post-Confederation (1867–)
Classification: LCC E96.5 .A54 2022 (print) | LCC E96.5
(ebook) | DDC 305.23089071—dc23/eng/20220201
LC record available at https://lccn.loc.gov/2021054701
LC ebook record available at https://lccn.loc.gov/2021054702

Cover art: 215 pairs of children's shoes set up in Vancouver as
tribute after residential school discovery. Photograph by
Anadolu Agency / Getty Images.

This book is for Nate, because everything is.

Contents

Preface
Tracing Memory in Naomi Angel's Archive

JAMIE BERTHE AND EUGENIA KISIN

I am left with the feeling that reconciliation is an act of creation. It is about new conversations and discussions, about creating new archives, producing artwork, dialogue and new relationships.
—NAOMI ANGEL, tracingmemory.com, October 3, 2012

Canada's Truth and Reconciliation Commission (TRC) on Indian residential schools (IRS), the inquiry that this book chronicles, released its final report in 2015. A massive archive of trauma, affect, and resilience, it testifies to Indigenous peoples' experiences of the brutally violent residential school system in Canada. The release of the TRC's *Final Report* was accompanied by ninety-four "calls to action": recommendations for transforming—indeed, reconciling—settler and Indigenous publics across the nation now known as Canada, primarily via changes in institutions of law, medicine, and higher education. That spring, performative and collective readings of the calls proliferated widely across art institutions in Canada, helping to amplify the recommendations. They have been echoing ever since, intertwined with strong Indigenous critiques of the TRC and its outcomes, as the settler state of Canada continues to reckon with what it means to acknowledge genocide and Indigenous survivance simultaneously.[1]

Naomi Angel, the author of this book, died in February 2014, before the commission had completed its work. She did not live to hear the calls to action or to witness the recent iterations of decolonization and indigenization of the academy—profound, incomplete, and full of friction—as generations of Indigenous activism were magnified by the cultural and moral weight of the TRC's findings. Less than five years later, in 2019, the

National Inquiry into Missing and Murdered Indigenous Women and Girls (MMIWG) produced its own final report and calls for justice.[2] Starting in spring 2021, the unearthing of unmarked graves on the grounds of several former residential schools—increasingly recognized as crime scenes and sites of mourning—continued to bring the TRC's findings into focus for the larger public. None of this is to say that Indigenous movements and communities required validation through the curious nonjudicial inquiry that was the TRC; rather, we wish only to gesture toward the profound and cumulative effect of the years since Angel's passing for shifting the conversation in the public sphere toward Indigenous justice.

Angel left us as a young mother and brilliant early-career academic, her research and ideas yet unfolding, her work still unfinished. The manuscript she left behind remains vital and relevant nonetheless. As friends and colleagues who have been affected by her intellectual legacy, our intention in this preface is as much a task of translation as one of framing. We want to explain the significance of *Fragments of Truth* as we understand it, to underscore the manuscript's most salient contributions as seen from our vantage point writing in 2021, seven years beyond the end of her life and six years out from the conclusion of the TRC. In working with the text, it quickly became apparent that we would not simply be able to "update" her research or bring it into full conversation with the still-unfolding events of the traumatic present, given that we cannot possibly know how Angel's singular mind would interpret everything that has happened in the TRC's wake. Instead, we want to suggest that engaging with Angel's interpretation of events, made at a particular moment of the TRC, can augment our collective understanding of present conditions, specifically with respect to conversations about how to shoulder the "burden of reconciliation" and decolonization's complex and layered subjectivities.[3]

This project feels particularly fraught in the present moment. In 2020 the Canadian federal government's denial of established Aboriginal land titles and the Wet'suwet'en hereditary chief's objections to a proposed gas pipeline route in British Columbia generated a full-blown political crisis. For much of early 2020, rail transit and trade across the country were shut down by protests in solidarity with Wet'suwet'en, bringing together Indigenous and environmental activists against the state police's violent attempts to push the pipeline through by attacking and dismantling the land defenders' encampment. Work continued on the pipeline throughout the COVID-19 pandemic; indeed, protesters reported continued pipeline work by Coastal GasLink employees even amid the province's declared state

FIGURE P.I Two hundred fifteen children's pairs of shoes placed on the steps of the Vancouver Art Gallery as a memorial to the 215 children whose remains were discovered at the Kamloops Indian Residential School in British Columbia, May 28, 2021. The Canadian Press/Darryl Dyck.

of emergency and on-hold negotiations. Given this ongoing struggle, it is important to attend to the wrenching declaration of Wet'suwet'en land defenders who—after witnessing the government's failure to honor its agreement of free, prior, and informed Indigenous consent for resource-extraction projects (signed on to in the United Nations Declaration on the Rights of Indigenous Peoples)—declared reconciliation dead (and revolution alive).

Then, in May 2021, on the heels of this crisis, the remains of 215 Indigenous children were uncovered on the grounds of the former Kamloops Indian Residential School in British Columbia (see figure P.I). Members of the Tk'emlúps te Secwépemc First Nation had known about the burials and missing children for many years but were able to confirm the locations of the bodies only after bringing in specialists who were able to locate the remains with ground-penetrating radar. In late June the Cowessess First Nation undertook its own search and confirmed 751 unmarked graves at the site of the Marieval Indian Residential School in Saskatchewan. Several days later, in Cranbrook, British Columbia, another 182 graves were confirmed at St. Eugene's Mission School. These grim findings—which are likely to be the first of many as communities continue to search other school grounds—led to an outpouring of public grief and political mobilization on both sides of the US-Canada border. In the United States, Secretary of the Interior Deb Haaland (Pueblo/Laguna)—the first Indigenous woman to serve in this position—has, in explicit response to these events, commissioned a federal investigation to examine the sites of former residential schools on US territory. In an op-ed published by the *Washington Post* on June 11, 2021, Haaland expressed the need to bring this trauma to light in radically personal terms, for both of her grandparents were survivors of boarding schools: "Many of the boarding schools were maintained by the Interior Department, which I now lead."[4] Haaland's words point to the ways that these histories are alive and resonant through time and across borders. The proposed federal investigation, and even Haaland's complicated relationship to state power, echo some of the tensions that animated the TRC, pointing to both the political anger and the sense of hope that national, state-sponsored attention can bring to the process of collective reckoning.

In dialogue with this present, Angel's manuscript suggests that if there is anything to be salvaged from Canada's project of reconciliation, returning to the TRC's earlier moments offers one potential way to recover some of those fragments—particularly through images, testimonies, and gatherings—and to understand their revolutionary portent. Angel set out to examine how various, often conflicting, notions of "truth" were deployed and mobilized by the IRS TRC, focusing in particular on the role played by visual media in the reconciliation process. Compelled by the affective pull, ideological instability, and provocation of a wide variety of visual phenomena—including archival images, Indigenous artwork and films, the national gatherings, and the physical structures of former residential schools themselves—Angel sought to consider the historical pathways that have been traversed by disparate visual artifacts and technologies, as well as their potential trajectories into unknown futures. Most importantly, she noted how visual culture troubles and complicates the authority of state discourses, suggesting a different set of criteria for evaluating reconciliation's efficacies. This is especially visible in her analysis of the national gatherings as sites for Indigenous communities to reconcile within themselves and to rediscover the shared connections that have animated many forms of pan-Indigenous activism in both the past and the current moment.

Over the course of her research at the TRC national gatherings, libraries, and archives, Angel kept a blog, *Tracing Memory*, as a public repository of her witnessing of the TRC's unfolding and concurrent Indigenous cultural activism. She used the blog as a place to work through thoughts and impressions that didn't quite fit into her dissertation chapters, to write more publicly and immediately about the landscape of the TRC, and, at times, to reflect on what coming to terms with historical responsibility meant to her. As a Jewish-Japanese-Canadian woman, Angel approached her work consciously, closely attuned to how the weight of these multiple identities shaped her understanding of historical trauma.[5] She was also deeply uncomfortable when well-meaning archivists and librarians read her mixed-race appearance as Indigenous, prompting a thoughtfulness about what it means to be a subject of desire to do right and about the complicated demands of allyship.[6] Writing of a reconciliation event in Sault Ste. Marie, Angel's revelations come after "most of the academics packed up to leave," while artists stayed on to "work through many of the points of conversation (and contention) that were raised throughout the few days of the event." Angel writes about being drawn to this idea, of "collaborative creation" as both a method and an outcome of the TRC, one that is not necessarily the purview of the academy. It is significant that we do not know from her story whether Angel left or stayed; either way, she makes space for collaborative creations to be the outcome that matters.[7]

In her public and scholarly writing, Angel followed both an intentional and inadvertent ethics of being a vulnerable observer.[8] She was pregnant for much of her research and later sick from the genetic breast cancer that declared the Ashkenazi heritage living through her body.[9] Following her diagnosis, she started a new blog, *Everybody Hearts*, documenting her treatment and providing updates to her many friends and colleagues. "I used to write a lot: short stories, a personal journal, academic papers, and I enjoyed it. But I was always somewhat nervous about sharing my writing," Angel explains. "When I was diagnosed with breast cancer in December, this fear began to fade away. (It was, unfortunately, replaced with plenty of other fears.) I had always wanted my writing to be as *polished* as possible before sharing, now I just want it to be as *honest* as possible."[10]

This simple statement might be read not only as a paring-down response to illness but also as a trace of the practice of writing about truth in conversation with Indigenous interlocutors that clarifies her idea of creative collaboration. Indeed, an important aspect of calls to make space for Indigenous critical thought in the academy and to "decolonize mastery" has to do with honoring affect that isn't particularly polished and with valuing honesty over other conventions of academic style.[11] Dylan Robinson, Stó:lō ethnomusicologist, one of Angel's research collaborators and coeditor of this manuscript, has written eloquently of the dangers of transforming Indigenous anger into an aesthetic resource for performance studies.[12] For Robinson this aestheticization risks both an extractive relation to research—mining experience to perform an academic function—and missing the everyday texture of social movements as they are lived. It is this kind of honesty, we argue, that Angel was after in her practice as a writer and researcher, evincing a sensitivity to the material that is deeply felt.

After an introduction that orients readers to the book's primary themes and questions, chapter 1 of *Fragments of Truth* looks at how Canada has been framed as a "nation of tolerance" and at how this narrative can be seen to intersect with the history of both the Indian residential school system and the IRS TRC. Illustrating how the IRS system was initially framed as part of the state's project of "benevolent assimilation," Angel explores how photographs, illustrations, and films worked to normalize, justify, and perpetuate both the existence of and the horrors wrought by the schools. Having made the relationship between colonial regimes of representation and genocidal practice explicit, Angel argues that any call for reconciliation must also be understood as a call for a profound shift in relations of looking.

In chapter 2 archival photographs produced by and in the IRS system serve as the point of departure for reflecting on how visual representations were used by the Canadian state to further the imperatives of empire. However, the inherent instability of meaning that infuses every image archive unsettles this top-down story, and Angel also insists on the evocative power and complicated entanglements of these photographs to highlight the various ways that Indigenous communities have returned to and reclaimed these archives as their own: "While image archives should be recognized as having been produced through certain contexts and within specific constraints, they are also productive, cultural spaces in and of themselves, where narratives form, coalesce *and* change."[13] Although the IRS images were born from a logic of control, containment, and colonial violence, Angel gestures toward the ways that former IRS students, Indigenous artists, activists, and community members have subverted this logic by reclaiming and resignifying the imperial image archive.

The interrelated acts of witnessing and offering testimony, and the role played by both at the national gatherings for the IRS TRC, constitute the focus of chapter 3. As the most public aspect of the commission's work, the national gatherings, Angel tells us, "were in many ways grandly staged performances where 'embodied culture' played an important role in producing meaning and negotiating memories of the IRS system."[14] Angel focuses on what she calls the political affective space engendered by these events, arguing that "by sharing their IRS experiences at these National Gatherings, survivors often manage[d] to create a space where the public display of affect [became] a powerful mode of political intervention."[15] Weaving together her field notes from the Winnipeg and Inuvik IRS TRC events with survivor testimonies, the work of Indigenous scholars, performances by Indigenous artists, media narratives, and historical texts, this chapter opens up a conversation around the complicated dynamics of embodied reconciliation work, which, as Angel shows, can be both a contested and contestatory practice.

Chapter 4 moves away from the official work of the IRS TRC and examines the physical sites of several former residential schools as a provocation and invitation to consider how local communities have engaged in their own processes of reconciliation. Here Angel considers these sites as archives in their own right, spaces that evidence their own specific kinds of logic, histories, and memories, spaces where reconciliation is being negotiated in myriad ways. As remnants (and sometimes ruins) of the IRS system, the sites push Angel to ask whether or not it is possible to hear the "stories told by these structures" in order to construct a narrative of relationships between memory and place.[16] Putting the material structures in conversation with various other voices—including literature written by Indigenous authors, testimony of survivors, cinematic representations of the schools, her own field notes, media narratives, and interviews with individuals who lived and worked in proximity to the sites—Angel wrestles with the complexity of what it means to unearth silences embedded within the physical structures of the schools themselves; to do so, she appeals, in part, to notions of spectrality and haunting. Acknowledging both the potential within and limitations of such an approach, Angel encourages readers to consider what it might mean think about reconciliation as "a ghostly encounter." Although it is a theme that spans the entirety of the manuscript, in this chapter Angel is acutely concerned with the ethical quandaries and the sometimes uncanny experience of bringing into presence those who are no longer alive to tell their stories. It is worth noting that in editing the book on her behalf, and in writing this preface, the resonance of these ideas has a very peculiar kind of potency.

In concluding *Fragments of Truth*, Angel tells us that her writing and research are not meant to be understood as definitive declarations but rather are meant to gesture toward both a past that needs more attention and a present that continues to unfold. For Angel the most critical question left unanswered by her research is to know whether or not the labors of

reconciliation will lead to meaningful action concerning redress and restitution for Indigenous communities. It is unfortunate but not surprising that
years after the publication of the commission's *Final Report*, this question
remains as urgent as ever.

In spite of its ongoing relevance, there are several silences in *Fragments
of Truth* that require a response from the present moment in order to let
readers in on how the TRC's legacy has continued to evolve in the public
sphere. Most pressing, we believe, are the Missing and Murdered Indigenous Women and Girls inquiry and the Idle No More social movement. In
September 2016 the newly elected Liberal prime minister Justin Trudeau
launched a national inquiry into the disproportionate number of Indigenous
women and girls—sisters, mothers, granddaughters, aunts, partners, wives—
who had disappeared without explanation or been killed. The inquiry
was not Trudeau's compassionate invention; rather, it responded to years of
pressure from community organizations, activists, and scholars to investigate
the structural settler violence perpetrated against these "stolen sisters," the
earlier moniker for MMIWG that emphasized injustice and kinship. Cultural
production was also an extremely important space for organizing political
response.[17] In one of her final research blog posts, Angel drew her readers'
attention to an ImagineNATIVE film festival project that displayed short
films about the Stolen Sisters Initiative on Toronto subway platform screens.
Her interest suggests that she was already drawing connections between the
TRC and what would unfold with the MMIWG inquiry, even if these ideas did
not make their way into the pages of this manuscript. The pan-Indigenous
Idle No More social movement started in 2012 to protect land, water, and
sovereignty. It grew out of opposition to a proposed piece of Conservative
budget legislation that threatened environmental protections. Although
Angel documents the initial part of the movement in this text, she did not
anticipate how rapidly it would grow over social media as the #IdleNoMore
hashtag inspired new generations of activists across Turtle Island in the years
that followed. Despite these gaps, we are nevertheless struck by Angel's
prescience about the mediated quality of activism, something that her close
attention to visual culture allowed her to see and that keeps her work relevant
in the contemporary moment, particularly with respect to her analysis of
the schools themselves as archives. These kinds of insights continue to tie
her work quite explicitly to cultural memory in present-day media worlds.

In editing the book for publication, Dylan Robinson and Jamie Berthe
aimed to preserve Angel's voice and the integrity of her ideas while updating
the text wherever possible, particularly in ways that they believed would

align with Angel's approach and perspective. In some instances this simply meant revising language to reflect the outcome of the IRS TRC, but in other instances it meant incorporating references that were obviously pertinent but that had been published after Angel's passing. For Robinson, contributing to this book was an opportunity to continue the dialogue that he and Angel had initiated at the TRC events they attended together, formative conversations that also included Elizabeth Kalbfleisch, Peter Morin, and Pauline Wakeham. By returning to Angel's work, Robinson found a way to extend this dialogue, in particular by integrating some of the unpublished writing that he and Angel had exchanged about the national gatherings. In streamlining Angel's original manuscript for publication, Berthe also approached her contribution as a dialogic process. Berthe and Angel started doctoral studies together in 2007 and were both working at the intersection of visual culture and colonial histories; they also lived through the experience of being pregnant, and then new mothers navigating academia, in tandem. The two had spent countless hours discussing their ideas, research, and lives; therefore, editing the manuscript gave Berthe the chance to pursue a new form of creative collaboration and intellectual growth with Angel. Both Robinson and Berthe recognize that if Angel had lived to see the conclusion of the IRS TRC and the subsequent evolutions of the reconciliation process in Canada, this book would be a very different piece of writing; still, they are equally confident that *Fragments of Truth* remains entirely Angel's book and that it represents a significant contribution.

The book both theorizes and is an example of the fragmented truths produced by the reconciliation process. But in its refusal to draw hard conclusions and resolve its own tensions, the text offers readers different kinds of insight. Angel was acutely reflexive about her subject position and how it compelled her to share the weight of what many Indigenous intellectuals in Canada have started referring to as the "burden of reconciliation," which entails serving as a subject called to heal the wounds of the settler state while resisting the tokenism of superficial indigenization strategies that amount to liberal inclusion rather than political transformation.[18] We can see in Angel's work a compassionate refusal to always need to know more; she frequently makes such refusals, along with her struggle to engage with them on their own terms, explicit in her writing. Speaking to the experience of being told not to photograph a particular moment she was witnessing at a gathering, Angel tells readers: "It was also a reminder that there were barriers to what I was allowed to access, that I could not understand everything happening here."[19]

In the passage that opens this preface, Angel suggests that "reconciliation is an act of creation," that the process is "about new conversations and discussions, about creating new archives, producing artwork, dialogue and new relationships." These ideas undergird and illuminate the insights of *Fragments of Truth*, and as her creative collaborators we would suggest that it is not in spite of, but rather by virtue of, the book's situated scope that her work makes an important and inimitable contribution to the literature on reconciliation—"fragments of truth" brought together in small gestures, edges, and silences that cannot be reconciled.

Acknowledgments

MARITA STURKEN AND FAYE GINSBURG

This book, *Fragments of Truth*, has had a particularly long and complex journey to its publication. It has involved extraordinary efforts from a group of people who labored with love and determination. We are deeply grateful to see it now fully realized.

This book's author, Naomi Angel, was a promising young scholar and much-beloved person whose life was cut short by breast cancer in 2014 at the age of thirty-seven. Naomi had been very brave as a researcher, and her bravery was in full force in her confrontation with the challenges of her illness. When she defended this work as a dissertation in August 2013, in the Department of Media, Culture, and Communication at New York University, everyone celebrated her multiple triumphs. She had survived cancer, and she had, while undergoing treatments, written a powerful, insightful, and pathbreaking manuscript, one that would go on to win a dissertation award. She was grateful to be an Andrew W. Mellon Foundation postdoctoral fellow in the humanities at the Jackman Humanities Institute at the University of Toronto. When, soon thereafter, it became clear that her cancer had returned, it was a terrible blow. At that point, her dissertation committee and her friends became determined to see her work eventually published. As faculty who worked closely with Naomi, the two of us, Marita Sturken and Faye Ginsburg, facilitated and oversaw this process together in the years that followed.

We would like to thank Dylan Robinson, Stó:lō scholar and Canada Research Chair in Indigenous Arts at Queens University in Canada, who graciously served as an outside reader on this dissertation and then undertook the complex and arduous task of editing, updating, and expanding the work of the original manuscript, bringing in Naomi's words from other contexts and revising the manuscript with great sensitivity and wisdom. Naomi's close friend Jamie Berthe, also a scholar of visual culture and imperial histories, worked tirelessly to streamline, edit, and finalize the manuscript with great intelligence, determination, and perseverance. For Jamie in particular, this was a labor of love, doing much of the work that Naomi herself would have done to bring her scholarship into book form. Jamie and Eugenia Kisin, another close friend of Naomi as well as a colleague at NYU's Gallatin School who works with Indigenous artists and activists in Canada, wrote the preface, skillfully situating Naomi's work in relation to how the context in Canada has changed since the finalization of the TRC. Doctoral student Matthew Webb did a careful and thorough job bringing together the images for the book with tremendous skill and resourcefulness. Naomi's close friend and colleague Kari Hensley was an important part of the initial process of bringing the book together. The input from several reviewers for the press was enormously important to bringing this project to its full potential.

We would like to thank the Department of Media, Culture, and Communication (MCC) at New York University and its chair, Rodney Benson, for funding to support the book's revisions. Thanks to the NYU Center for the Humanities, which provided us with a grant to fund image permissions and research, and to Tracy Figueroa, Danielle Resto, and the staff at MCC for facilitating these funds. We are grateful to Ken Wissoker at Duke University Press, whose support for this project and deep engagement with the challenges it posed were crucial as well as generous. At Duke University Press, Joshua Gutterman Tranen has been a vital resource, Susan Albury shepherded the book through production, and Donald Pharr provided excellent editing.

Naomi's husband, Mitchell Praw, has been a stalwart and patient advocate of this project. Naomi dedicated her dissertation to "survivors of the Indian Residential School system, and for survivors of many kinds." It is tragic, of course, that she did not survive, but we hope that this book will be one of her legacies. She also dedicated the work to her son, Nate, who was two at the time of her death and who she considered to be her most important legacy. It is thus to Nate that the book is dedicated. What follows are the original acknowledgments for this work in Naomi's own words.

This dissertation would not have been possible without the help, encouragement, and support of many people. I am grateful to the people who publicly shared their experiences of the Indian residential school system. Their strength and courage in speaking about often difficult times were both humbling and inspirational. I would also like to thank those people who took the time to elaborate on these experiences and answer my questions. In particular, I am grateful to Eric Large and the staff at the Blue Quills First Nations College, Harvey Youngchief, Charles Wood, Barb Esau, Robert Peters, Ruth Roulette, Petah Inukpuk, and Jules Koostachin. I am indebted to them for their generosity. Archivists at the National Archives, Anglican Church Archives, Presbyterian Archives, United Church Archives, North Vancouver Archives, and the Saskatchewan Archives Board provided much-needed information and clarification on key documents. Representatives from the Squamish Nation and Coqualeetza Archives were also generous with their time and knowledge.

My committee's insights greatly strengthened this project. Marita Sturken, my chairperson, provided a steady source of support. Her skill in pulling out salient issues for further analysis has been invaluable in shaping my scholarship. Throughout the PhD program, she encouraged me to ask difficult questions and to draw out difficult answers. Arvind Rajagopal also contributed important feedback, suggesting critical paths to pursue, and his scholarship on post-colonial visual culture inspired me to look at my research through a different lens. Faye Ginsburg suggested critical readings and helped me to understand the international contexts of this research. This project was greatly enriched by her scholarship and her approach to research. I have been inspired by my committee's enthusiasm for the project and their commitment to their students. For their early feedback, I am indebted to Nicholas Mirzoeff and Gabriella Coleman. Dylan Robinson and Diana Taylor, as external readers, also contributed valuable insights to this research. They also helped me imagine the ways in which this research may develop in future iterations, and for that I am grateful. Mary Taylor has also helped to make my experience at NYU a positive one. Her skill in navigating administrative issues, and her ability to facilitate scholarship from afar, were a great help.

My cohort at NYU, Solon Barocas, Jamie Berthe, Kari Hensley, Paul Melton, Nadja Millner-Larsen, and Magda Sabat, comprised an amazing family of scholars without whose humor, candor, and support the doctoral process would have been far less productive and much less fun. Starting a family while a doctoral student would have been more daunting without the laughter shared with Jamie Berthe about navigating academic life with a baby in tow. I will forever be grateful for Jamie Berthe and Kari Hensley's presence during a very difficult health emergency. Both their words and physical presence during this time helped me to remain optimistic in the face of a challenging situation. To my other colleagues at New York University (particularly Zenia Kish and Eugenia Kisin), I am grateful for your insight, feedback, encouragement, and laughter. Kaitlin McNally-Murphy, Lee Douglas, Danielle Roper, and Nathalie Bragadir formed a self-selected cohort that was the source of many productive conversations and adventures. I am thankful to call these people my colleagues and friends. I look forward to future collaborations.

The members of the Aesthetics of Reconciliation in Canada Research Group contributed to my understanding of the complex dynamics of artistic representation of the IRS system, especially as represented at the TRC's national gatherings. I am thankful to Dylan Robinson and Keavy Martin for inviting me to be a part of this research group. I would also like to thank Pauline Wakeham and Robyn Green, researchers who shared their approaches to the reconciliation project in Canada in ways that deeply influenced my own approach in navigating and negotiating the TRC's national gatherings.

I would also like to thank the doctors and staff at Princess Margaret Cancer Center, particularly Dr. Christine Elser, Dr. David McCready, and Dr. FeiFei Liu. I would like to extend a very special thank-you to my nurse, Shelley Westergard, whose capacity for empathy and strength in supporting others continues to inspire me.

The Social Sciences and Research Council of Canada provided funding that allowed me to attend several crucial events across Canada. Funding from the Department of Media, Culture, and Communication, the LeBoff Research Grant, and the Alice E. Wilson award (administered through the Canadian Federation of University Women) also provided invaluable assistance. The Hemispheric Institute of Performance and Politics and the Irmgard Coninx Foundation provided funding to present my research in Bogotá, Colombia, and Berlin, Germany, respectively.

I would also like to express gratitude to my family, without whom I would not have been able to embark on a doctoral degree: Saeko Tsuda, Leonard and Susan Angel, Bernie and Annie Praw, Ken Angel, T'ai Rising-Moore, Jason Praw and Pam Kolker, Robbie Praw and Lauren Povitz. The friendship of Nicole Kapos and Steven Dam has enriched both my scholarship and my life. For my husband, Mitchell, whose encouragement kept me afloat in moments when I thought I would drown in the dissertation, thank you. In the last year of the PhD, you saved me, many times over.

And last but not least, I would like to thank Nate, who came into this world as I worked on this dissertation. This dissertation is for Nate, because everything is.

Reconciliation and Remembrance

I can hear Eric Large flipping through the dictionary over the phone. "Nope, no word for *reconciliation* in here," he says. "No Cree word that means that." We had been talking on the phone for about twenty minutes at this point, discussing the Canadian Truth and Reconciliation Commission: "The TRC is looking for truth and looking for reconciliation. What does that mean anyway? Whose truth? And *to reconcile* would mean to return to some common, peaceful state in the past. When was that?" Large is a former student of the Blue Quills Indian Residential School who now works as a resolution health support worker in his community. As such, he provides information and counsel to other survivors of the Indian residential school (IRS) system. We met at a conference in Montreal titled "Breaking the Silence: International Conference on the Indian Residential School Commission of Canada" in the fall of 2008.[1]

The Canadian TRC, also known as the Indian Residential Schools Truth and Reconciliation Commission (IRS TRC), was established in June 2008 and focused on the mistreatment and abuse of children in the IRS system. Run by the government of Canada and the Presbyterian, Anglican, United, and Catholic churches, the system was in place for more than a century (1876–1996). It separated Indigenous children from their families and placed them in 139 recognized Indian residential schools across the country.[2] Children at the schools were forbidden from speaking their traditional languages and practicing their cultural and spiritual beliefs. When parents objected to having their children taken, their children were often forcibly removed. Many former students have spoken out about the physical, emotional, and sexual abuse that took place at the schools, both prior to and following the IRS TRC. The IRS system is now recognized as one of the major factors in the attempted destruction of Indigenous cultures, languages, and communities in Canada. The last school closed in 1996. Many of the schools have cemeteries where the marked and unmarked graves of the children who died there remain as traces of this troubled history (see figures I.1 and I.2).

The Montreal conference was a revealing glimpse into the dynamics at work in the process of reconciliation between Indigenous and non-Indigenous people in Canada. Over the course of the two-day conference, roughly sixty people participated in conversations about the IRS system and its legacies. From the start of the first day it was clear that this conference would be unusual in both the mixture of academics and nonacademics in attendance and in the forms and discourses of knowledge shared. The day began with a welcome prayer offered by Delbert Sampson from the Shuswap Nation, Salmon Arm, British Columbia. Throughout the day, participants spoke different Indigenous languages (Cree, Anishinaabe, and Inuktitut), often left untranslated. (Simultaneous translation was offered for French and English only, Canada's two officially recognized languages.) Although the panelists generally followed a recognizable academic format (Power-Point presentations, the use of specific terminology, the asking of rhetorical questions, etc.), audience members also disrupted conference expectations by claiming the space as one for the telling of stories and sharing of experiences.

At noon on the first day of the conference, an organizer announced that it was time to convene for lunch. Donna Paskemin, a member of the audience who was standing at the microphone at the time, refused to table her comments. "Can I ask the panel a question?" she repeated several times. Like many participants from the audience, she began by speaking a few words in her Indigenous language (Cree), and then she went on to share her story and her concerns about the loss of languages in Indigenous communities. Toward the end of her question, she was reminded again that the conference was running late and told to wrap things up. For many people there, this created a moment of significant tension and was representative of one of the potential problems with the reconciliation process. Ms. Paskemin wanted to speak about her experience at that moment, in that space, and in her own way. The conference organizers wanted to keep things running on schedule. There was an obvious discomfort created among audience members by this confrontation. As we left the hall for lunch, I overheard the conference organizer being reprimanded by audience members for cutting off a participant, particularly one whose family had attended an Indian residential school.

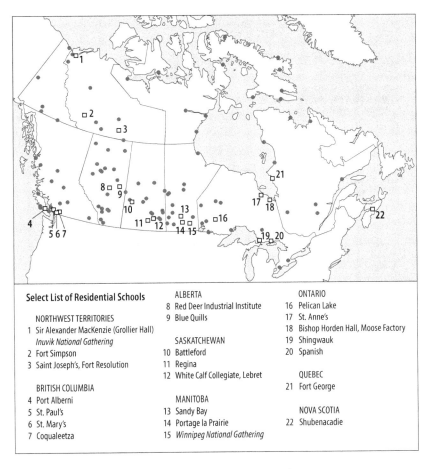

FIGURE I.I Select List of Residential Schools of Canada, 1831–1996. Dots represent all the schools; named schools are discussed in the text. Source: Truth and Reconciliation Commission of Canada.

The dynamics at the conference signal some of the challenges of reconciliation in Canada. Although everyone at the conference agreed on the importance of a greater understanding and awareness of the oppression faced by Indigenous peoples, the way in which that knowledge has been elicited and shaped remains controversial.[3] Critics have questioned how reconciliation in the shape of a truth commission could provide more than a temporary forum for much larger issues facing Indigenous communities. Following the conclusion of the TRC in 2015, concerns have continued to

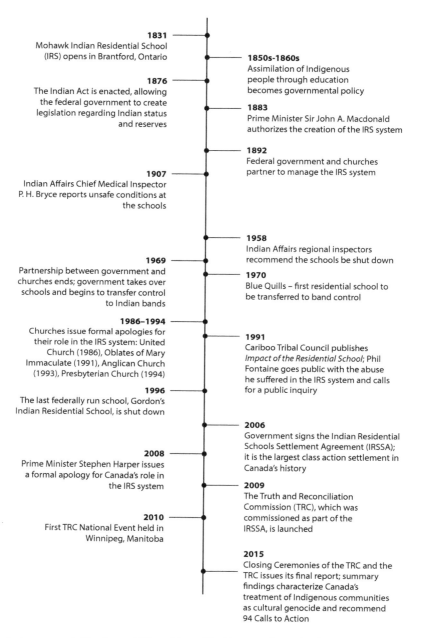

1831
Mohawk Indian Residential School (IRS) opens in Brantford, Ontario

1850s-1860s
Assimilation of Indigenous people through education becomes governmental policy

1876
The Indian Act is enacted, allowing the federal government to create legislation regarding Indian status and reserves

1883
Prime Minister Sir John A. Macdonald authorizes the creation of the IRS system

1892
Federal government and churches partner to manage the IRS system

1907
Indian Affairs Chief Medical Inspector P. H. Bryce reports unsafe conditions at the schools

1958
Indian Affairs regional inspectors recommend the schools be shut down

1969
Partnership between government and churches ends; government takes over schools and begins to transfer control to Indian bands

1970
Blue Quills – first residential school to be transferred to band control

1986–1994
Churches issue formal apologies for their role in the IRS system: United Church (1986), Oblates of Mary Immaculate (1991), Anglican Church (1993), Presbyterian Church (1994)

1991
Cariboo Tribal Council publishes *Impact of the Residential School*; Phil Fontaine goes public with the abuse he suffered in the IRS system and calls for a public inquiry

1996
The last federally run school, Gordon's Indian Residential School, is shut down

2006
Government signs the Indian Residential Schools Settlement Agreement (IRSSA); it is the largest class action settlement in Canada's history

2008
Prime Minister Stephen Harper issues a formal apology for Canada's role in the IRS system

2009
The Truth and Reconciliation Commission (TRC), which was commissioned as part of the IRSSA, is launched

2010
First TRC National Event held in Winnipeg, Manitoba

2015
Closing Ceremonies of the TRC and the TRC issues its final report; summary findings characterize Canada's treatment of Indigenous communities as cultural genocide and recommend 94 Calls to Action

FIGURE I.2 A Condensed Time Line of Indian Residential Schools and the IRS Truth and Reconciliation Commission. Sources: https://nctr.ca/exhibits /residential-school-timeline; http://education.historicacanada.ca/files/619/Resi dential_Schools_History_and_Heritage_Education_Guide_FINAL.pdf; and www.ahf.ca/downloads/condensed-timline.pdf.

arise about the fact that pressing health, welfare, education, and land issues have been obscured and overshadowed by the focus on the more abstract issue of reconciliation. Many Indigenous communities face higher rates of unemployment, drug and alcohol abuse, incarceration, and youth suicide. Members of these same communities were and continue to be called upon to participate in a reconciliation process that seems to have done little to address or alleviate these challenges.

Through an analysis of archival photographs from the IRS system, testimony taken at TRC gatherings, and popular representations of the IRS legacy in media and literature, *Fragments of Truth* confronts the complicated terrain of reconciliation in Canada. In particular, the book examines how concepts of nationhood and ideas of indigeneity were deployed through the IRS TRC, how visibility and invisibility were negotiated by different groups and actors, and how the dialectical relationship between remembering and forgetting came into play through the reconciliation process. Much of the scholarly research on truth commissions has focused on the genre of testimony as a way to heal and to come to terms with the past.[4] But these commissions circulate "truth" in other forms as well. In the Canadian context, media representations, images (old and new), and the revisioning and rebuilding of former schools have also played key roles in the processes of national reconciliation. Taking this diversity of forms and practices into account, *Fragments of Truth* looks at the normative, disciplinary orders of remembrance as dictated through the IRS TRC and at how individuals and communities resisted, rejected, and reframed those imperatives, often through visual tactics. Bringing together a wide range of theory from Indigenous and settler colonial studies, as well as from visual and memory studies, *Fragments of Truth* examines the visuality of "truth" and "reconciliation" in the Canadian IRS TRC context.[5] To do so, it engages a diverse array of visual forms and media: the visuality of tolerance that gave rise to and worked in conjunction with the assimilationist policies undergirding the residential school system; various visual traces of the residential school system, including photographs, film, visual art, and even the infrastructure of schools themselves; and the relationships that have been forged between these visual traces and IRS survivors, Indigenous communities, and members of the non-Indigenous public (such as myself) who participated in TRC national events. The book explores how the residential school system and the ongoing processes of reconciliation can be understood from an embodied and sensory orientation, focusing on visuality's affective impact on members of both Indigenous communities and the non-Indigenous public.

Contested Terms of Identification

Before delving into the residential schools' history and the visuality of reconciliation, it will be useful to provide some background regarding the identificatory terms of indigeneity and settler colonialism that this book engages. Identity categories are far from straightforward, and using the terms *Indigenous* and *non-Indigenous* or *Aboriginal* and *non-Aboriginal* to discuss the ways in which one approaches research can be problematic. At worst, the usage of these overarching terms gives a false sense of cohesive world-views or epistemologies, masking the exponentially layered, intersectional realities and differences that exist between Indigenous and non-Indigenous communities across the lands now known as "Canada." One thing that the TRC made clear was that residential school histories and survivor experiences are as diverse as the more than six hundred distinct First Nations whose lands and waters are occupied by Canada.[6] Consequently, I use such identity markers with the understanding that, while necessary, they are imperfect descriptions. For Indigenous peoples, such terms also have different affective impacts and signal affiliation, belonging, and disidentification.

In Canada, where the term *Aboriginal* has frequently been used to identify First Nations, Métis people, and Inuit, a significant refusal of this government-defined term has been taking place across the country. Indeed, for many Indigenous people across the lands now known as Canada, as a term applied by the Canadian government the label *Aboriginal* carries with it a long history of government imposition. As Taiaiake Alfred and Jeff Corntassel note, the term upholds a "political-legal relationship to the state rather than ... any cultural or social ties to ... Indigenous community or culture or homeland."[7] Although the 2006 census calculated that 1.4 million people identify as "Aboriginal," Indigenous peoples across the country are also shifting the politics of identification by returning to nation- and community-specific terms in their languages.[8]

Although the term *First Nations* has no legal definition, it is widely used in Canada to denote Indigenous peoples and to distinguish them from Inuit and Métis people. It is alleged that Solomon Sanderson of the Chakastaypasin Cree First Nation proposed the term as an alternative to the word *Indian* in 1981 while serving as elected chief of the Federation of Saskatchewan Indian Nations.[9] Identifying as "First Nations" also prompts a reevaluation of the foundations of the Canadian nation, often imagined as French and British, and brings issues of Indigenous sovereignty to the fore. Yet this term has also elided the specific histories of Inuit and Métis people when it is misapplied as a larger framework to speak of all Indigenous peoples across Canada. Although Inuit have traditionally occupied northern regions of Canada, particularly in the arctic and subarctic regions, there are growing urban Inuit populations in cities across the country.

The identifying term *Métis* also has a contentious history. Some who have non-Indigenous and Indigenous mixed ancestry identify as Métis, but there has been significant debate (particularly in the Quebec context) about the ways in which this definition has worked to elide the sovereignty and distinct cultural history of Métis people.[10] In using *Indigenous* as an umbrella term, I do not wish to flatten the differences among Inuit, Métis, and First Nation cultures. Rather, I use the term, as well as the specific names of nations and communities, to follow the choices made by Indigenous peoples themselves in the act of self-determined identification.

I will also be using the contested identity categories *settler* and *settler colonialism* throughout the book. The vast majority of non-Indigenous Canadians do not identify as "settlers," but an increasing usage has resulted from the ongoing activism and decolonizing efforts that have in large part resulted from the work of the TRC. Although usage of the term is more predominant in activist, academic, and other institutional settings, it has begun to gain some purchase within the general Canadian public. *Settler*, in its simplest conception, describes someone who came and never left. As Patrick Wolfe has written, settler societies are those where the colonizers have "come to stay," where "invasion is a structure, not an event."[11] In Canada the colonial project continues to unfold; it "is not a singular historical event but an ongoing legacy—the colonizer has not left."[12]

In this broad definition, *settler* encompasses all non-Indigenous people: those whose families were among the original settlers, those who have more recently immigrated, and even Indigenous peoples who have relocated to lands other than their own. For this reason, scholars have noted the tendency of the term to reify subjectivity within an unmarked, white, heteronormative framework.[13] The singular identification of *settler* thus tends to elide the important work of identifying how specific histories of immigration, coalitional relationships, and cultural values, gender, sexuality, and class intersect with histories of colonization (and residential schools in particular) and their ongoing legacy. Other scholars have critiqued the term's minimal affective impact and the lack of accountability it tends to effectuate. For example, Annie Coombes notes that "the term 'settler' has about it a deceptively benign and domesticated ring which masks the violence of colonial encounters that produced and perpetrated consistently discriminatory and genocidal regimes against the Indigenous people of these regions." Coombes and others have called for a casting off of this "benign" mask as part of an acknowledgment of the violence upon which these countries were founded and that they continue to inflict on Indigenous communities.[14] Indeed, in the increasing uptake of the term since the conclusion of the TRC, one might also question the extent to which *settler* has become a nonperformative term that, when used as mere acknowledgment, stands in for individual reckoning with one's responsibility in the ongoing work to redress the legacies and ongoing effects of the residential school system for Indigenous people. Despite these valid criticisms, my sense is that the term holds potential value in drawing attention to the "relational terms of our settlement" as an ongoing process enacted by individuals rather than by institutions.[15]

International Context

The Canadian TRC took place in a historical moment that found many nations undertaking similar processes. Indeed, reconciliation has become a dominant mode for engaging with troubled national histories—so much so, in fact, that the United Nations declared an international year of reconciliation in 2009.[16] The negotiation of violent and contested pasts can take many shapes and forms, and discourses of reconciliation, forgiveness, and healing resonate differently, depending on nations' specific histories. In the interest of situating the specificity of the Canadian TRC, it is useful to provide a brief overview of the larger "culture of redress" in an international context.[17]

Perhaps the closest comparison to the context of the residential school system in Canada and the subsequent government apology is seen within the Australian history of the "Stolen Generations." This is the name given to the thousands of Indigenous children in Australia who were taken from their homes and families and placed in boarding schools and Native settlements. As in Canada's residential schools, students were forbidden from speaking their languages and taught to forget their traditions and cultures. The oft-cited goal of these schools was to bring "civilization" to these children.[18] In 1991 the Australian parliament created the Council for Aboriginal Reconciliation (CAR). The legislation acknowledged the need to address issues of land, housing, heritage, education, health, infrastructure, and employment in Indigenous communities, but it did not discuss redress for the Stolen Generation.

Major criticisms of the CAR process have included its neglect of the legacy of the Stolen Generation and its deflection of other contemporary Indigenous issues. As one critic, Damien Short, writes,

> Australian reconciliation was born out of a political desire to deflect the growing campaign for a treaty in the 1980s. Indeed, far from providing the basis for nation to nation treaty negotiations with indigenous peoples of equal terms, Prime Minister Paul Keating and the CAR positively promoted an overt nation building agenda which aimed to cosmetically legitimize the settler nation, by the inclusion of previously excluded Aboriginal people, while at the same time indigenizing settler culture and effectively restricting indigenous aspiration to participation "within" the political and cultural confines of the nation state.[19]

In addition to the official reconciliation project, Australia embarked on several public events in regards to its treatment of Indigenous people. These included a "National Sorry Day" to commemorate the official apology of 2008 and the publication of the "Bringing Them Home Report."[20] Although the ritual of an annual day of apology may bring awareness to the legacies of the Stolen Generations, it does not give back land or language taken from Indigenous people in Australia.[21] Likewise, the report and the discourses resulting from it sparked "the history wars," where Australian history became a battleground for revisionist and reactionary versions of the past.[22]

Although there is great diversity among the stated goals and practices of TRCs, there are several commonalities that bind these quasi-juridical bodies together. Historically, and in contrast with the Canadian version, TRCs have become commonplace in transitional or postconflict societies as a means by which to come to terms with violence and oppression that was both inflicted and then denied by the state. The TRC has generally been seen as a way to mobilize public memory in order to begin to deal with these injustices. Priscilla Hayner has identified several key components of truth commissions, including a focus on the past and an emphasis on prolonged or repeated abuses that were sanctioned by the state. Hayner argues that the aims of truth commissions revolve around the discovery, clarification, and acknowledgment of these abuses. The commissions often provide recommendations regarding accountability for the individuals involved, and they help to determine the level of responsibility for governmental and nongovernmental institutions. In short, Hayner contends that the overarching goal of a truth commission is to "reduce conflict over the past."[23]

Most truth commissions have taken place in Africa (including Uganda, Zimbabwe, Chad, Burundi, Nigeria, Sierra Leone, and South Africa) and in Central and South America (including Argentina, Chile, El Salvador, Guatemala, Bolivia, Ecuador, and Uruguay). Others include Sri Lanka, Haiti, Nepal, and Germany.[24] Some of these were not considered truth commissions in their own time but have since been incorporated and subsumed into the larger discourse. Some truth commissions focus on establishing long-denied facts. Others highlight the need for further action, which may involve prosecution of persecutors or new legislation to prevent further abuses. Still others are generally recognized as ineffectual or impotent.[25]

Although "truth" and "reconciliation" are often paired, the concepts do not necessarily go hand in hand, nor does one always imply the other. In fact, the commissions of the 1970s and early 1980s generally stressed "truth" without much mention of "reconciliation." For example, the commissions set up in Chile and Argentina focused largely on establishing the facts surrounding the disappearances of loved ones. Because the silence with regard to "the disappeared" was so deafening, simply allowing the details to be discussed in public was considered a significant step forward. Although reconciliation may have been implied, the arduous task of documenting the lost history of state violence was seen as an important starting point. How reconciliation was to take place would in many ways depend on the facts established. In the case of Argentina, the documents created in and by the commission were later used to prosecute the perpetrators involved.[26] In Canada's IRS TRC, which did not involve legal proceedings to prosecute perpetrators, my experience of the proceedings was that the process of establishing truth was less aligned with a singular and exclusive conception of fact and, instead, embraced the multiplicity of experiences as "truth."

Like truth, reconciliation can have a myriad of meanings and imply a range of processes.[27] Which groups are being reconciled? Is a person being reconciled *to* something or reconciled *with* someone? In relation to one of the most well-known and celebrated TRCs, the South African example, Antjie Krog raises the issue of defining reconciliation: "The dictionary definitions of 'reconciliation' have an underlay of restoration, of reestablishing things in their original state. The *Oxford* says: 'to make friendly again after an estrangement; make resigned; harmonize; make compatible, able to coexist. …' But in this country, there is nothing to go back to, no previous state or relationship one would wish to restore. In these stark circumstances, 'reconciliation' does not even seem like the right word, but rather 'conciliation.'"[28] As Krog notes, reconciliation implies a state of previous harmony. In most cases, however, this privileged state of peace is itself a myth. Instead of returning to a state of preconflict, the process of reconciliation actually results in new relationships and new dynamics of power.[29] In the Canadian TRC context, Métis artist and critical arts writer David Garneau has shared his thoughts about the word *reconciliation*:

> [It] imposes the fiction that equanimity was the status quo between Indigenous people and Canada. It is true that for many generations after contact the Indigenous majority had good trading relationships with some Europeans as individuals rather than nations. The serious troubles began when the visitors decided to become settlers, when traders were replaced by ever-increasing waves of colonists, when invading nations decided they would rather own the well rather than just share the water, and they reached a crescendo when these territories became Rupert's Land and then Canada without consultation with the original inhabitants.
>
> The problem with the choice of the word reconciliation over conciliation is that it presses into our minds a false understanding of our past and constricts our collective sense of the future. The word suggests that there was a time of general conciliation between First Nations, Inuit, and Métis people and Canada, and that this peace was tragically disrupted by Indian residential schools and will be painfully restored through the current process of Re-conciliation.[30]

As evidenced by my conversation with Eric Large—whose words open this chapter—similar criticisms and questions were also raised by other Indigenous community members.[31] In attempting to rectify the violence of colonial policies, the IRS TRC confronted the question of whether a process of reconciliation can truly destabilize long-standing, extant structures of power. Particularly in the context of nations that are not going through large-scale political transitions (such as Australia and Canada as opposed to nations such as South Africa), are truth commissions a process of decolonization, or do they simply work to reinscribe existing hierarchies and legitimize the disproportionate power of the state? Although many critical voices, including those of Indigenous and settler scholars alike, have examined the Canadian IRS TRC as an inherently flawed process that frequently revictimized survivors through the renarration and reliving of trauma, others have sought to understand its limitations while also acknowledging the IRS TRC's decolonial potential. Reflecting the complexity of the histories and stories at stake, the IRS TRC enacted a process that was at once highly flawed in its orientation toward confession and the expression of trauma but also frequently useful for survivors in healing, in the expression of their histories, and in strengthening kinship and community.[32]

Approaching the Research: Reflexivity and Relationship

Positioning oneself in relation to one's research when working with Indigenous individuals and communities is often about trust and accountability. Maori scholar Linda Tuhiwai Smith has discussed the conflicted relationship between scholars and Indigenous peoples, highlighting how academic research is itself a site of struggle, enmeshed in the power dynamics that it often purports to challenge: "Research is not an innocent or distant academic exercise; [it is] an activity that has something at stake and that occurs in a set of political and social conditions."[33] In Canada these political and social conditions include the unevenness of power relations, the discounting of Indigenous knowledge, and the systematic oppression of Indigenous populations. It is with an acknowledgment of these conditions—and a desire to engage and disrupt them—that I have developed my approach to this research.

For Indigenous researchers, stating one's nation, community, or treaty affiliation can itself be a political act. For populations that were faced with oppressive and violent forms of forced assimilation (such as the IRS system), asserting that one is Anishinaabe or Cree makes clear the failure of such attempts at assimilation and undermines myths that circulate about Native Canadians and Americans as a "vanishing race." "Location is more than simply saying you are of Cree or Anishinaabe or British ancestry; from Toronto or Alberta or Canada," write Kathy Absolom and Cam Willett. "Location is about relations to land, language, spiritual, cosmological, political, economical, environmental, and social elements in one's life."[34] For these reasons I have included information about Indigenous authors' backgrounds where appropriate.

Although my own identity category (mixed Japanese-Jewish-Canadian) has helped me, at least to a certain extent, understand some feelings of marginalization within the spectrum of Canadian multiculturalism, I recognize that as a non-Indigenous Canadian I face complicated ethical challenges and relations of power involved in being an "outsider" conducting research with Indigenous people. Taking a cue from the many people I have met while undertaking this work, I believe that sharing my personal story can help to elucidate how my own location has shaped my work on and interest in the IRS TRC.

I was born in Japan in the small town of Kochi, but I grew up in Vancouver, daughter of a Japanese mother and Jewish-Canadian father. Although I was born in Japan, because only one parent was Japanese, I was not granted Japanese citizenship. And because Judaism is passed through the matrilineal line, I was not considered Jewish either. It is from this position, of not quite belonging to these two cultures, that I came to see Canada as my home. Before I embarked on this project, my research revolved around cultural memory and sites of memorialization, and I was particularly interested in how traumatic pasts get represented in museum spaces. Memorials built in response to the atomic bombing in Hiroshima and the various museums dedicated to remembering the Holocaust had been my primary foci. Because of my own hybrid ethnic background, these two histories—of the atomic bombing and its aftermath in Japan and of the Holocaust in Europe—resonated with me personally. It wasn't until Canadian prime minister Stephen Harper's official apology for the IRS system in June 2008 that I began to feel myself being pulled toward trying to understand the reconciliation process in Canada.

Following Harper's apology, I wanted to read everything I could find on the history of the residential schools. Having been brought up in the Canadian educational system, I was surprised not to have heard even a whisper about this past during my own schooling. High school history classes contained little more than short tangents or reductive sections about Indigenous histories and cultures, and even these generally focused on pre-confederation-era practices and interactions. After the apology, I realized that as a Canadian and as a settler I was implicated in the history of the IRS just as much—if not more—than in the histories of Hiroshima and the Holocaust.

Early in my research, I came across Thomas King's "Coyote and the Enemy Aliens," a short story about a coyote that becomes involved in rounding up "enemy aliens." The piece is set during the internment of Japanese Canadians during World War II. As the definition of *enemy alien* changes in the story, King illustrates the fickle nature of dividing people into categories of "us" and "them."[35] While growing up in Vancouver, I had closely watched the process of redress for Japanese Canadians. Although my immediate family was not directly affected by the internment, the reverberations of those histories and events were ever present in the Japanese Canadian community. Having been stripped of property and possessions in 1942 in British Columbia, Japanese Canadians were moved into internment camps in the interior. Once the war ended in 1945, the interned were given the option of moving further east or being repatriated to Japan. The internment deeply damaged once-vibrant communities, and the subsequent relocation and repatriation tore families apart. After years of lobbying by Japanese Canadians and their supporters, the government of Canada offered a formal apology in 1988 as well as a reparations package to those who had been interned.

As I became increasingly familiar with the Canadian process of reconciliation, I often wondered if it would be possible to relate these two experiences (of Japanese Canadians and Indigenous peoples) to each other without erasing their important differences. King uses the character of the trickster coyote to tie the two historical narratives together, offering his readers the following explanation for his strategy:

> I know the story of the Japanese internment in Canada. I know it as most Canadians know it.
>
> In pieces.
>
> From a distance.
>
> But whenever I hear the story, I think about Indians, for the treatment the Canadian government afforded Japanese people during the Second World War is strikingly similar to the treatment that the Canadian government has always afforded Native people, and whenever I hear either of these stories, a strange thing happens.
>
> I think of the other.
>
> I'm not suggesting that Native people have suffered the way the Japanese suffered or that the Japanese suffered the way Native people have. I'm simply suggesting that hatred and greed produce much the same sort of results, no matter who we practice on.[36]

King's story opens up a way of creating a particular type of Canadian narrative, one that allows for a relationship between intimacy and estrangement, where the two are allowed to coexist.[37] It provides a space for many voices, maintaining ties to an Indigenous mode of storytelling while also working to close a gap between seemingly disparate histories and drawing attention to similarities rather than differences.[38] For King, memories of distinct traumatic pasts need not be framed as competitive. Rather, they can be seen as related sites of negotiation.

In his work on "multidirectional memory," Michael Rothberg explores the idea of a noncompetitive realm of shared, public memory. Memory, Rothberg argues, is often understood as occupying a "zero-sum space" where the act of remembering one event somehow threatens to displace the memory of another. In contrast, he proposes a shift away from competitive memory to multidirectional memory. In doing so, Rothberg conceptualizes memory "as subject to ongoing negotiation, cross-referencing, and borrowing; as productive and not privative."[39] By understanding public memory as multidirectional, *Fragments of Truth* seeks to frame the reconciliation process as an ongoing negotiation, one that is situated within the broader context of both national and international discourses of redress. It places my own experiences of the TRC and research on residential schools in relationship with those experiences of survivors and intergenerational survivors. By doing so I hope to remain accountable to an ethics of witnessing without seeking to center my own settler subjectivity within the narratives I tell.

To understand the constellation of conditions that gave rise to the IRS TRC and to explore how reconciliation took (and continues to take) shape, the research for this book required a range of methodological approaches: interviewing survivors and intergenerational survivors; undertaking research in archives across Canada; observing and volunteering at TRC hearings, gatherings, and events; and engaging in close readings of visual and archival artifacts. In Canada the archives of religious institutions have often been ignored by the academy, and this privileging of secular sources has left some of the material held in denominational archives out of IRS narratives.[40] In contrast, my work focuses on both government (the National Archives in Ottawa and the North Vancouver Municipal archives) and church archives (United, Anglican, and Presbyterian archives in Toronto), while also taking into account those archives collected by Native peoples (at Coqueleetza and Portage la Prairie). These archives house a wide array of materials, including old photographs, daily rosters, financial records, postcards written from staff to their families, press coverage of the schools, and personal diaries of former staff. Following Ann Stoler's lead, I sought to read these materials both *along* and *against* the grain of the archive in order to understand the conditions in which the repositories were created and cultivated and also the conditions in which their materials are now read.[41] Archives are not simply produced; they are productive. In line with Stoler's insights, I have tried to remain cognizant of the fact that archives generate both knowledge and anxiety and that they must be read as sites of contestation with the potential for resignification.

Because my research also considers what may be forgotten during the reconciliation process, the book also examines some of the material and infrastructural traces left behind by the residential system. This took the form of traveling to several sites of former residential schools that have been shut down, demolished, and/or abandoned, and to other sites that have been converted into community centers and even new schools. Visiting schools that had been abandoned or were waiting for demolition allowed me to engage with sites of absence, where disuse and disrepair could be read as an important part of a larger historical context. Walking through the halls of these former schools, speaking with local community members, and seeking out former students who still lived or worked near the schools offered me invaluable insights into how the memory of the IRS system continues to be negotiated through the specificity of place, even if only through the forgotten histories etched into the physical structures of the schools themselves.[42]

In several of her public speaking engagements, IRS TRC commissioner Marie Wilson spoke about the necessity of being personally engaged in the reconciliation process. To illustrate this engagement, she would recount an anecdote that began with a spelling error.[43] In quickly writing or typing the word *reconciliation*, she explained, it is easy to leave out one *i*. Wilson used this observation to remind the audience that the reconciliation process is personal and requires an *i* to be present. Of course, *reconciliation* requires several *i*'s, and it involves multiple levels of engagement: personal, communal, scholarly, and artistic, to name only a few. With this in mind, and particularly in chapter 3, where I write about the use of testimony, I lean heavily on the technique of reflexivity and use the first-person voice frequently. In working with the testimonies given by Indigenous peoples, I did not want to appropriate their voices. By incorporating field notes and first person into my writing, I have sought to make my own voice and perspective more apparent to readers.

In the many months I spent traveling across Canada, I came to expect feelings of unease or confusion when participating in or watching traditional ceremonies. As an outsider to Indigenous cultures, I learned to take the lead from others, sometimes quietly observing, sometimes actively participating (when called upon). I engaged in conversations and asked questions if it seemed appropriate but tried to also see listening and silence as contributions. And at times the research process has been uncomfortable. In negotiating this discomfort, I have often thought of Paulette Regan. In positioning her own research to reconciliation in Canada, Regan has remarked that her "own deepest learning has always come from those times when [she] was in unfamiliar territory—culturally, intellectually and emotionally. . . . As members of the dominant culture, we have to be willing to be uncomfortable, to be disquieted at a deep and disturbing level—and to understand our own history, if we are to transform our colonial relationship with Indigenous peoples."[44] My research has often involved navigating new customs and protocols of which I had limited understanding. Among other things, I learned about the complicated dynamics of what can be seen and what is meant to remain hidden, about when pictures could be taken and when photography was forbidden. I also learned to take my lead from others, and in the process I came to understand that knowledge is passed on in several ways and forms.

In 2008 I started a research blog (tracingmemory.com) as a way to share and engage with a public outside of academia, to be part of the active and ongoing dialogue about reconciliation. The content I posted included field notes, travel reports, book reviews, and personal reflections. In some cases, unexpected lines of communication were created through this site. Sometimes survivors or their family members would reach out to say that they attended the school I had just written about and that they wanted to know more. Sometimes individuals were interested in the photos I took or the people I met. One man left a comment about his father; another mentioned that their mother was a teacher at one of the schools. These exchanges—discussed further in chapters 3 and 4—would not have occurred if not for the blog. In this way, blogging became at once a tool for extending what I had come to know and a method for learning more about how the histories and legacies of the IRS system continued to reverberate.

Structure of the Book

My work on the IRS TRC led me to engage with discourses of nationhood, visual culture, and memory—exploring their entanglements and drawing attention to their various mechanisms and technologies. I paid close attention to how an imperative to remember was prescribed, represented, and interpreted by the movement for reconciliation. At the same time, I sought to explore how individuals and communities took up, negotiated, and pushed back against that imperative. In this way the goal of the book is twofold: I wanted to understand the context for the IRS TRC, of course, but I also wanted to recognize and create a space for the important ways that reconciliation took (and continues to take) place outside of the TRC. Given that this study was completed before the commission concluded its work in 2015, the results of the TRC and its subsequent final report are not the primary concern of *Fragments of Truth*. Instead, the book examines and illuminates what the commission activated, in ways that draw attention to both its failures and successes.

Chapter 1 focuses on the history of the IRS system and the vexed relationship it has with ideas of Canadian national identity, which has traditionally been framed as "benevolent" and "tolerant." In chapter 2 I explore the relationship between the process of reconciliation and the archive. Here my exploration draws specific attention to both the demands for recognition and the silences engendered by the Indian residential school photographic archive. The role of affect and the uses of testimony and performance at IRS TRC events in Winnipeg and Inuvik are the central concerns of chapter 3, where I argue that by sharing their IRS experiences at these national gatherings, survivors often managed to create a space where the public display of affect became a powerful mode of political intervention. Finally, chapter 4 focuses on the politics of place with regard to both the IRS system and the process of reconciliation. In particular, I explore the discourses of haunting produced at and through the sites of former schools. Throughout the book, in discussing the IRS system through the lens of visual culture, I argue that any call for reconciliation is also a call for a profound shift in collective ways of seeing.

In my engagement with the work of reconciliation in Canada, I found that even when constraints were placed upon the forms and modes of memory called upon, former students were able to claim the reconciliation process for themselves. In this way the reconciliation process was (and remains) generative of new discourses. It can shift one's understanding of Canadian history and draw attention to the importance of restitution as well as reconciliation. And by unearthing old memories, the reconciliation process also engendered new ones. In arguing that visual culture played (and continues to play) a crucial role in this process, *Fragments of Truth* seeks to draw attention to the importance of Indigenous practices of self-representation and to how colonial images of indigeneity are being renegotiated and reframed by Indigenous artists and communities.

This book is but one engagement with the complex project of reconciliation in Canada. In many ways the IRS TRC expanded and challenged the way that truth commissions were understood. Because it did not mark a moment of radical change in government, it offered a unique opportunity to observe how techniques of transitional justice can be mobilized in settler nations as they work to excavate their colonial pasts and address historical injustices. The TRC itself concluded in 2015, but the work of survivors, intergenerational survivors, institutions, and settler individuals that has followed in its wake continues to expand and transform the TRC's findings, even as it undoubtedly falls short of the calls to action identified in the commission's *Final Report*. Nevertheless, the repercussions and reverberations of the IRS TRC constitute an important legacy, one that will ideally result in the strengthening of Indigenous kinship, community, and culture for generations to come.

1

Reconciliation as a Way of Seeing

*The History and Context of the Indian
Residential School System*

*Our objective is to continue until there is not a single Indian in Canada that
has not been absorbed into the body politic.*
—DUNCAN CAMPBELL SCOTT, deputy superintendent of Indian Affairs, 1920

During his tenure as the deputy superintendent of the Department of Indian Affairs (1923–32), Duncan Campbell Scott made the intentions of the Indian residential school system clear. The IRS system was designed as a tool of assimilation, and the body of the Indigenous child became the imagined terrain of colonial policy. "The happiest future for the Indian race is absorption into the general population," Scott would later elaborate, "and this is the object and policy of our government."[1] Indigenous children were seen as subjects to be first molded and then absorbed into a Canadian public.

Although Canada portrays itself as a leader in issues of human rights and frames itself as a nation of "tolerance" (as will be discussed shortly), critical examination by observers such as Eva Mackey reveals that Canada's history is, in fact, a story of how the concept of tolerance has been mobilized to subjugate and incorporate difference in service of the nation-state. As I show in this chapter, even before the accommodation of difference was enshrined within governmental policies of official multiculturalism, the values of tolerance and benevolence were precisely what allowed the emerging nation-state of Canada to justify the destructive IRS system. The aim of this chapter is first to chart the history of reconciliation in relation to the "national memory" of Canada as a tolerant and benevolent nation and second to show how national values of tolerance, the assimilationist policies of the Indian residential schools, and the ideals of reconciliation have deep resonance with one another by examining how these phenomena have manifested across different visual media.

So foundational is the myth of tolerance to Canadian identity that even now, years after a composite picture of residential school system history has emerged through the IRS TRC, the image of Canada as a tolerant nation persists. In spite of countless testimonies, writing in the popular press and in academic publications, and the memorialization of residential school histories in public monuments across the country, there remains ongoing skepticism about and resistance to reckoning with the atrocities committed through residential schools. In 2017, for instance, two years after the TRC proceedings concluded, Conservative senator Lynn Beyak announced in the Canadian Senate that the record of "good things" that happened at residential schools had been overshadowed by discussions of "the horrible mistakes" that occurred there:

> I speak partly for the record, but mostly in memory of the kindly and well-intentioned men and women and their descendants—perhaps some of us here in this chamber—whose remarkable works, good deeds and historical tales in the residential schools go unacknowledged for the most part.... The fathers and sons and family members of the nuns and priests, to this day, have to bear the reputation as well, and nobody meant to hurt anybody.[2]

Beyak's focus on the "well-intentioned good deeds," where no one intended to cause harm, reveals how the myth of Canadian benevolence emerges even in the face of what is now an incontrovertible and overwhelming "record" of abuse and negligence. It is worth noting that mere years before the TRC began, the frame of reconciliation was itself irreconcilable with the perception of Canada as a benevolent state, as evidenced by the jacket cover from *Dilemmas of Reconciliation: Cases and Concepts*:

> How can bitter enemies who have inflicted unspeakable acts of cruelty on each other live together in peace? At a time in history when most organized violence consists of civil wars and when nations resort to genocidal policies, when horrendous numbers of civilians have been murdered, raped, or expelled from their homes, this book explores the possibility of forgiveness. The contributors to this book draw upon the insights of history, political science, philosophy, and psychology to examine the

trauma left in the wake of such actions, using, as examples, numerous case studies from the Holocaust, Russia, Cambodia, Guatemala, South Africa, and even Canada.[3]

The word *even* is used to qualify Canada's inclusion in the authors' list of case studies, pointing toward the imagined reader's potential incredulity when it comes to acknowledging Canada's history of genocidal policies.

Intent on assimilation, the IRS system constructed normative subjectivities and projected model Canadian citizens. The project of "benevolent assimilation" that animated the logic and impulse behind the residential school system often took shape through visual representations. Examining photographs, illustrations, and films that have been used to further this assimilative project reveals how colonial regimes of representation have contributed to policies such as the Indian residential schools in Canada. It also illuminates why reconciliation requires confronting these visual legacies and rereading the moments they represent. Indeed, any call for reconciliation must also be understood as a call for a profound shift in relations of looking. Many of the images that helped construct and define Indigenous and non-Indigenous communities in Canada positioned Indigenous peoples as lacking or inferior, as subjects that needed to be shaped, transformed, and absorbed. Reconciliation requires that Indigenous people no longer be seen as passive subjects in need but rather as active agents, particularly with regard to self-representation. In order to fully understand how the visual legacies of colonialism continue to resonate in the contemporary moment, it is necessary first to return to the past.

Reframing the Tolerant Nation

A central aspect of the fate of being a Canadian is that our very existing has at all times been bound up with the interplay of various world empires. One can better understand what it is to be Canadian if one understands that interplay.
—GEORGE GRANT, "Canadian Fate and Imperialism"

Our people look on with concern when the Canadian government talks about "the two founding peoples" without giving recognition to the role played by the Indian even before the founding of a nation-state known as Canada.
—HAROLD CARDINAL (CREE), "Buckskin Curtain"

The terrain of Canadian history is a site of contestation.[4] There has been a tendency to conceptualize Canada as a new country, one without much of a historical narrative. "If some countries have too much history," stated Canada's then prime minister, William Lyon Mackenzie King, in 1936, "we have too much geography."[5] King's message reveals two important issues with regard to Canadian history: it is often said to begin with settlement, and it is deeply enmeshed and entangled with relationships to land. Because Indigenous communities in Canada have largely relied on oral histories as a way to pass down information and knowledge about the past, many Canadians have dismissed the idea of Indigenous history.[6] This denial has served the purposes of colonial conquest. Conceptualizing Indigenous peoples as those without history made "settling" the land an easier task and allowed what happened before "discovery" to be deemed unimportant.[7] The history taught within the Canadian educational system consolidated this narrative and continues to disregard the founding presence of Indigenous peoples—along with their beliefs, religions, and cultural and political systems—confining their histories, quite literally, to the margins of textbooks.

The issue of Canadian national identity has long plagued the cultural, economic, and political discourses that permeate Canadian popular culture and academic discourse. "Everywhere, Canadian identity is seen as crisis-ridden," writes Eva Mackey, "as a fragile and weak entity constantly under attack and in need of vigilant defense. Some people say that Canada has no identity at all, or at least not a real one."[8] Despite the difficulties in constructing a unified national identity, as I have noted, there is one recurrent theme that tends to arise with reference to Canada: tolerance. Indeed, highlighting the nation's role in international peacekeeping and its promotion of human rights, depictions of Canada as a benevolent nation-state, coupled with a misguided belief in a relatively untroubled past, have helped to frame Canada—both in the eyes of Canadians themselves and for the rest of the world—as a nation of tolerance.

But this conception of Canada as a tolerant nation obscures a foundational part of Canadian history: the state's violent oppression of Indigenous peoples. And this historical absence does not simply work to conceal; it actively creates other kinds of narratives as well. In other words, the idea of Canada as a tolerant nation is not just reductive; it is also *productive*. For instance, it might easily be argued that the concept of tolerance can be linked to the idea of a civilized, compassionate people. By contrast, intolerance might evoke notions of callousness and barbarism. The concept of tolerance here serves as a powerful political tool, then, and in the case of the IRS system it has often implicitly worked to demand the assimilation of and to justify the state's violence toward Indigenous peoples.

As with the "Sixties and Seventies Scoop," in which Indigenous children were taken from their families and placed into foster and adoptive care through the child welfare system, the IRS system was welfare-based cultural genocide framed as a benevolent gesture.[9] The underlying conceit of the system was that it would help "civilize" a racialized population in need. Ironically, given what we know now, this framing allowed the IRS system to contribute to the idea of Canada as a tolerant nation, which also helped to keep criticisms of the schools at bay. The TRC and the ongoing reconciliation process have challenged this understanding of Canada to some extent, but given that the IRS TRC is frequently pointed to as evidence of the Canadian state's benevolent, tolerant nature, it also risks reframing and further entrenching these narratives. Thus, one of the challenges of reconciliation has been to resist this gesture of entrenchment and to allow new ideas and images of Canadian history and subjectivities to emerge.

Imag(e)ining Settlers and Indigeneity

As Benedict Anderson has written, a nation can be thought of as an "imagined community" in which fellow citizens feel kinship with other citizens even if they never actually meet them.[10] However, concepts of nationhood are always in flux. Macarena Gómez-Barris writes that although "national subjects are conditioned to view the nation as fixed, nations are in fact phantasmatic and inherently unstable productions."[11] Official narratives of Canadian history focus on a "grand narrative of pioneers and waves of immigrants birthing a peaceable nation from a vast, untamed landscape."[12] Indigenous peoples have often been depicted as part of this "untamed landscape," an unfortunate inheritance of "discovery." Representations of Indigenous peoples have tended toward two extremes: the Indians as violent, primitive peoples or as noble savages, still primitive but innocent and in need of paternalistic care. These two stereotypes were represented in and consolidated through the written word (correspondence, poetry, prose, and newspapers, for instance) and other visual technologies such as photography and film. Emma LaRocque (Plains Cree Métis) writes of the damage the savage stereotype has caused Indigenous peoples:

> Should anyone wonder still why the "savage" has caused us extreme aggravation, it is important to remember that most of us first met the savage visually, not only abstractly in print. Many of us first saw the savage Indian image in comic books, in school textbooks, and in movie theatres. It was

my experience with the pictorial image as much as with written material that drove me to research and resistance. Graphic, colourful, larger-than-life presentations of the lurking, crouching, tomahawk-swinging, scalp-taking, painted, naked, howling savage (who was rumoured to be my forefather) left a profound and lasting imprint on me. And, as my subsequent research has confirmed, on so many other Native peoples as well.[13]

In contrast to these images of lawlessness and savagery, settlers were generally depicted as fair and just. One of the popular symbols of Canadian civility is the Mountie (the colloquial term for an officer of the Royal Canadian Mounted Police). In his red uniform and the hat of an outdoorsman, the Mountie has symbolized Canadian (and, by extension, British) fairness and justice. Daniel Francis explains the centrality of the Mountie image to Canadian identity:

> Canadians are the only people in the world who recognize a police force as their proudest national symbol. For a hundred years the Royal Canadian Mounted Police has occupied a special place in our history and our imaginations. The story of how they drove out the American whiskey peddlers and pacified the West is familiar to every school child. Their frontier exploits have been romanticized in decades' worth of movies, books, and television shows. They stand on guard at our national buildings; in gaudy scarlet coats and stiff-brimmed hats, they are present at all our important national ceremonies. They project just the right mixture of stern rectitude and pleasant helpfulness which Canadians like to think we all possess.[14]

Francis goes on to note that "the Mountie is the face [Canadians] turn to the world.... So widely known and well regarded is our national police force that in 1995 the Disney Corporation recognized its profit potential by purchasing a license to control the marketing of the force's image."[15] The Mountie is also used as a counterpoint to the US symbol of the cowboy. Whereas the cowboy embodies American expansion westward through rugged lawlessness, the Mountie represents Canadian colonial expansion through rugged lawfulness and moral fortitude.[16]

A popular and well-circulated image representing the national myth of tolerance is the meeting of Chief Sitting Eagle and a Mountie (figure 1.1). In the image, which also circulates as a postcard, Chief Sitting Eagle and a Mountie face each other, shaking hands. In her book *The House of Difference:*

FIGURE 1.1 Mountie and Indian Chief Sitting Eagle, 1955. Image courtesy Williams & Harris Shared History Centre, Calgary Public Library pc_1836.

Cultural Politics and National Identity in Canada, Eva Mackey uses this photograph to open up a discussion about Canadian history and what she calls the "Benevolent Mountie Myth." On the surface, the image can be read as representative of "collaborative cultural contact," where both colonizer and colonized engage in a "friendly, peaceful and collaborative pose."[17] But Mackey asserts that reading the image this way neutralizes the force of the state behind the Mountie, obfuscating the power differential between the Mountie and the chief. For Mackey, the image represents one of the central myths of Canadian nationhood, that of a tolerant, peaceful, and inclusive society. She also perceives an implicit comparison between the histories of Indigenous peoples in Canada and those in the United Sates. The image projects the idea that collaboration reigns in Canada, whereas it is well known that antagonism has defined the relationship between Indigenous and settler populations in the United States.

Although Mackey's reading focuses on the Mountie and the possible values he can be seen to embody, Chief Sitting Eagle remains undertheorized in her text. She explains that he stands in for the "minority culture" and the colonized, but surely there is much more to be said.[18] Indeed, perhaps the first thing that one notices about this image is the contrast between the two costumed figures: the Mountie appears cheery and youthful, but the chief looks weathered by time. The discrepancy in their life experience is visible. Both men are clad in uniform, but the Mountie wears the color of Canada, red, and the chief is dressed in traditional regalia and headdress. With their exchange of looks, each man respectively represents aspects of settler identity and indigeneity. As Mackey notes, the two men are in a collaborative pose, but Chief Sitting Eagle's stoicism seems to reveal a sense of skepticism about, even suspicion toward, the colonial figure in front of him.

The image might even be read as a representation of the reconciliation process itself: the Mountie, with a slightly forced smile, offers an outstretched arm to make amends. Still, he remains in a position of power even when apologizing for the nation's mistakes. In the photo's caption, Chief Sitting Eagle is named while the Mountie remains anonymous. Indigeneity is named. The settler is anonymous. Looking this unnamed figure of the state in the eye, Chief Sitting Eagle holds his regard with earnest suspicion, mirroring the distrust that so many Indigenous people have felt and continue to feel toward the Canadian government.[19] In reading the postcard as a representation of the reconciliation process, we might follow the gazes of the Mountie and Chief Sitting Eagle as they graze past each other. In his refusal to connect, Chief Sitting Eagle rejects the symbolic offering of an outstretched arm, which does nothing to address the material reparations that remain to be made—in particular, the return of land.

Just as a cursory glance at this image risks oversimplifying the complex histories and individual subjectivities it represents, official reconciliation has been criticized for the way it has tended to reduce complex historical relations and personal experiences in problematic ways. For instance, some critics of the TRC's structure have drawn attention to the commission's apparent focus on residential schools as an "Aboriginal" issue, with numerous survivors pointing to the fact that they want to hear testimony from perpetrators, government officials, and clergy members who were involved in running the schools. Ronald Niezen's *Truth and Indignation* explores the way in which the "victim-centric" focus on Indigenous perspectives in the IRS TRC worked to obfuscate the complexity of the system's history, pointing to various occasions in which "other" perspectives—of the church or those with benign memories—were marginalized or condemned.[20]

As an image and as a story, then, "Mountie Meets Sitting Eagle" works to obscure many painful aspects of Canadian and Indigenous histories. Canada's past is neither straightforward nor without its fair share of abuse, mistreatment, and oppression. But the Canadian state has been relatively successful in projecting an image of benevolence. Until quite recently, in

fact, the schools were held up as part of this facade. It is only because Indigenous peoples have fought for and continue to mobilize for redress that
these stories have begun to change.

Foundations of Assimilation

The Indian residential schools became official policy in Canada in the late
nineteenth century, but the foundations for the system were laid long before
this time. In the century before Canada's confederation in 1867, interaction
between Indigenous and settler communities ranged from violent encounters to peaceful coexistence. Trade heavily influenced these relationships,
as did several important battles and wars, and struggles over control of land
and resources. Tracing the changes in these relationships—as reflected in
official policy—reveals several important shifts in colonial ways of thinking
about Indigenous peoples. For example, in the Royal Proclamation of 1763,
there was a clear articulation of the "separateness" of Indigenous peoples
and support for self-governance. The proclamation put forward a "policy of
civilization" in which skills in agriculture, commercial fishing, and industrial
training for work in saw and grist mills were to be provided to Indigenous
communities. The logic was that a modern economy would develop and
allow these communities to become self-sufficient. The proclamation was
meant to establish the authority of the British over the French, but it also
recognized some rights to land for Indigenous peoples. In doing so the proclamation, as several thinkers have argued, "instanced a radical beginning."
Its "assertion of the British crown's sovereignty over the former territorial
claims of New France also acknowledged the national and territorial rights
of the Indians, an unprecedented and singular formulation of sovereignty
that underlies both the constitutional concept of the treaty rights of aboriginal peoples today and the legal concept aboriginal title, both of which
have been crucial to First Nations' contemporary struggles."[21] Although it is
recognized today as an important foundation for Indigenous claims to land,
the original intent of the proclamation was to more effectively manage both
French and Indigenous populations and to further secure British power.[22]

In 1857 the Gradual Civilization Act ushered in an important shift in
policy. It was during this period that the concept of "civilization" was increasingly seen to be in conflict with Indigenous self-governance.[23] As a
result, the official policy approach toward Indigenous people moved from
that of self-governance to assimilation. To the colonial administrators, previous attempts to "civilize" the native population appeared to have failed,

so efforts were refocused and redirected toward educational policy. Indigenous adults were viewed as a lost cause; therefore, the focus became their children. With confederation in 1867, the country's unity took precedence over diversity, and Indigenous peoples were seen as an impediment toward a harmonized and modern national identity. The Indian residential schools were imagined as one way to achieve more unity. As a result, the Canadian government passed a series of acts that granted power and control to the Department of Indian Affairs. Through these acts (in 1876, 1880, and 1884), the project of assimilation continued to take shape, and the state gained several forms of control over Indigenous communities. Historian John Milloy explains how the acts began to redefine all aspects of Indigenous life: "Aboriginal traditions, ritual life, social and political organization or economic practices could be proscribed as obstacles to Christianity and civilization or could be declared by Parliament, as in the case of the potlatch and sun dance, criminal behavior."[24] It was during the late nineteenth century that day schools were deemed insufficient to the project of assimilation. Residential schools, which could more fully separate children from their parents, communities, and cultures, became the new norm.[25]

The Indian Act of 1876 was particularly restrictive and outlined the government's attempts to control all aspects of Indigenous life. As Sunera Thobani writes, "Aboriginal peoples were relegated to an infantilized status as wards of the state."[26] It is important to note that there were attempts to resist these colonial policies. Peter Kulchyski has pieced together important pieces of this story of resistance: "while these acts came over time to articulate a host of repressive government policies, it is possible to read in the traces of policy and lawmaking the lineaments of resistance. when the indian act banned two indian ceremonies by name, then a few years later amended the legislation to ban them by description, one needs little other evidence to know that the former legislative problem was overcome by practitioners simply using a different name for the same ceremony."[27] Kulchyski's work illustrates that Indigenous resistance to assimilation, though often present, requires a type of reading that goes against the grain, for its traces don't always make it into written records.[28] By considering what is implied by amendments to the Indian Act, Kulchyski offers a reading of implications and imbrications where Indigenous people can be seen to play an active role in interpreting and opposing colonial policy.[29]

The rules governing attendance at the Indian residential schools constitute sections 114–122 of the Indian Act. For example, section 119(6) states that "a truant officer may take into custody a child whom he believes on reasonable grounds to be absent from school contrary to this Act and may convey the child to school, using as much force as the circumstances require." Following Kulchyski's lead, a similar interpretation can be offered for the amendments to the act that governed compulsory attendance at the schools. From 1894 to the 1920s, several amendments were made that required attendance at the schools. The need for each subsequent amendment suggests that parents—despite the threatened use of force to compel them to send their children to residential schools—continued to resist these policies.[30] Further, through the TRC's work and survivors' personal narratives, more nuanced histories of resistance have been revealed in the commission's findings.[31]

From the beginning of the IRS system in the nineteenth century, the Anglican, Presbyterian, Catholic, and United churches were generally put in charge of the day-to-day operations of the schools.[32] Section 118 of the Indian Act shows how both the government and the churches took an active role in deciding where Indigenous parents would be required to send their children to school: "Every Indian child who is required to attend school shall attend such school as the Minister may designate, but no child whose parent is a Protestant shall be assigned to a school conducted under Roman Catholic auspices and no child whose parent is a Roman Catholic shall be assigned to a school conducted under Protestant auspices, except by written direction of the parent."[33]

Although Section 118 includes a provision for parents to let their wishes be known by written direction, it also makes clear that the minister of Indian Affairs and the churches played roles in this decision as well. And it suggests that the ultimate decision was left to the government minister. The churches and the government were aligned in their ambition to civilize: a project that was seen to go hand in hand with converting Indigenous peoples to Christianity. Sam McKegney elaborates: "The historic partnership between the federal government and the churches was thus borne out of complementary goals: the churches desired first and foremost to create Christians, but to do so they would first need to make Canadians; the government desired to obliterate Native nationhood and consume the Native populace into Canada at large, while sharing the churches' view that 'for the betterment' of Native people, they must first be converted to Christianity."[34]

The role of the churches in the IRS system was felt all across the country, but their respective forms of administration depended on a diverse set of factors, including "rivalry among creeds, financial adversity, and, in some instances, Indian resistance."[35] In general, scholars working on IRS history have relied more heavily on government archives when constructing their

Do Indian Young People find prejudice among employers?

Yes, they do, because Indians have the reputation of not staying with the job. This is due to their cultural background and their lack of concern for the morrow. Training and association with non-Indians will overcome this.

Are Indians lazy?

Culturally, Indians of the plains were hunters and the routine work was done by the women. Indian men are capable of great exertions but in the past employment has been away from their families, and when enough was earned for immediate needs, they had a natural incentive to return home. Some Indians are now holding steady jobs in the city and have adopted the white man's attitude towards thrift and industry. Given the opportunity of living with their families and holding steady jobs, it is believed that every Indian can acquire similar habits.

How is our Church helping Indian Young People to adjust to City Life?

Indian young people are reticent and it takes time to win their confidence and friendship. As a result, when they come to the city, they are often lonely and sometimes make the wrong kind of friends. The Anglican Church of Canada has appointed three young women as friendship workers in Vancouver, Winnipeg and Toronto to

needs to the non-Indians, helping them to meet other Indians, to find places to live where they will have the benefit of Christian home life, and to help them become established in local parishes. An important part of this work is to make Church people aware of the presence of these young people and of the need to extend to them a warm, understanding, patient friendship. For further information, friendship workers are: —

Vancouver —
   Miss Irene Rau, 309 East Cordova St.,
   Vancouver 4, B.C.

Winnipeg —
   Miss Ruth Hall, 939 Garfield St.,
   Winnipeg 3, Man.

Toronto —
   Miss Helen Gough, 11 Trinity Sq.,
   Toronto 1, Ont.

The Indian young people with us are citizens of Canada, and they should be given the same opportunity as other Canadian young people.

The Missionary Society
of
The Anglican Church of Canada
Church House, 600 Jarvis Street,
Toronto 5, Ontario
75-61

YOU WERE ASKING...

FIGURE 1.2 "You were asking" pamphlet, circa 1961. Image courtesy General Synod Archives 6575-104, box 137 9-14.13.

narratives. "In the increasingly secular atmosphere that has prevailed in Canada since the middle of this century," J. R. Miller explains, "a tendency has developed to ignore religious figures, their actions, and their records."[36] This has resulted in neglect of a rich and diverse body of documents that offer tremendous insight into the day-to-day routines at the schools. But this is not to say that these records are unproblematic. Voices of the students are predominantly absent from such records, and even when they are present, they are filtered through the lens of the church. Images of students often remain unnamed. But the materials nevertheless reveal important details about how the IRS system both reflected and perpetuated the existing discourses surrounding Indigenous people. They were seen as "savages" and "uncivilized," they were framed as the "Indian Problem," and the residential schools were said to be part of the solution.

Couched in the language of benevolence, the rhetoric of the early and middle twentieth century spoke of educating Indigenous people as part of a path toward betterment. For example, one Anglican Church pamphlet (circa 1961) elaborates on the putative benefits of education and assimilation through a series of questions and answers (figure 1.2). One section begins with the question "Are Indians lazy?" The response is as follows:

Culturally, Indians of the plains were hunters and the routine work was done by the women. Indian men are capable of great exertions but in the past employment has been away from the families, and when enough was earned for immediate needs, they had a natural incentive to return home. Some Indians are now holding steady jobs in the city and have adopted the white man's attitude towards thrift and industry. Given the opportunity of living with their families and holding steady jobs, it is believed that every Indian can acquire similar habits.

The following page asks "What of their future? Are the Indian young people capable of acquiring skills which will help them to take their places in Canadian life?" The response: "A sufficient number have proved themselves capable of being excellent mechanics and tradesmen to show that, given the basic education and training, thousands of others would similarly qualify. Unfortunately, only an insignificant percentage has received education beyond the elementary grades. More is being done now but the proportion receiving such educational opportunities is not in ratio to the increase in their numbers." The pamphlet contains illustrations which also suggest that Indigenous children require help and support from the government and churches of Canada. These kinds of documents worked to advance an image of the Indigenous individual as primed for absorption into the national body politic. In one picture a man stands outside his home with two kids and a dog running toward him, projecting the idea of a normative Canadian subject, someone who aspires to being head of the family, to home ownership. A puff of smoke streams out of the chimney suggesting that a wife is at home, tending the hearth.

The pamphlet then implores its readers to consider working at one of the Anglican Indian residential schools, stating that an applicant "should have a sincere love of children, the ability to work well with them, and be prepared to give of her best in the service." Applicants are rarely pictured in these pamphlets. Rather, it is the subject of the transformation—the Indigenous subject—who is figured and represented.

In some ways the image of the man and house in the pamphlet advance an aspirational picture of success, of a career, of house and family, of a happy home life, and of memories in the making. In settler colonies the family was one site where the ideology of civilizing projects was centered.[37] In other words, "family ideology would become civilizational ideology," where the rules of hierarchical and gendered notions of the family structure became one way to exert colonial power.[38] The pamphlet projects not only an image of the normative Canadian subject but also of a normative Canadian family.

Given the history of the schools and how they worked to sever familial bonds, this image is particularly troubling, for in the Canadian case the authority of the law was also enacted to strip away parental rights from Indigenous people, disallowing them the possibility of caring for their own children. This violation resulted in damaging reverberations throughout communities. Although the last school closed in 1996, the aftermath of the Indian residential school experience still pervades these communities, touching generations that, even without firsthand experience of the schools, remain deeply affected.[39]

Memory and "Postmemory" of Residential School Experience

While Indigenous communities were being devastated by the IRS system, the greater Canadian public was either unaware of or indifferent to the abuses at the schools. Many Canadians simply believed, following dominant ideology, that the schools worked in the service of the greater good. But former students tell a very different story. Many have spoken of the constant hunger they felt within the walls of the schools, both emotional and physical. In *Indian School Days*, Basil Johnston writes that "food was the one abiding complaint because the abiding condition was hunger, physical and emotional. Food, or the lack of it, was something that the boys could point to as a cause of their suffering; the other was far too abstract and therefore much too elusive to grasp. But food was a reality that boys could understand; it was a substance that could not only allay hunger but also bring some comfort to a desolate spirit and soul."[40]

Indeed, the Truth and Reconciliation Commission's research has revealed that food shortages and nutritional deprivation were commonly experienced by students and were even documented and recognized by school administration and the federal government.[41] One former student, identified as Sheni7 in *Behind Closed Doors: Stories from the Kamloops Indian Residential School*, shares his story of hunger: "If you said you were hungry they would probably starve you even more, take you away from your supper table, take you from your breakfast, you know. It was endurance between us and them. Maybe it was a way of breaking us down even further, trying to break that spirit we had in us, of who we were. I would never bow down to let them be winners."

Sheni7 later recounts the fate of the students he knew there: "They're all gone now and whether it's drinking, or suicide, or drugs, or whatever the case may be, it could have been because of this school." A great number of students also suffered from physical and sexual abuse or other forms of mistreatment at the schools. One student (listed as "Anonymous") writes simply: "Loneliness is a killer, it kills everything inside of you, you become absolutely nothing."[42] Expressing a similar sentiment, former IRS student Marlene Starr writes that "people suffered in silence and isolation, believing they alone had been singled out for hell on earth."[43] Some families hid their children from Indian agents sent to take them. Others, having attended the schools themselves, were resigned to sending their children to the institutions. The schools regulated interactions with family members, leaving many children feeling alienated and isolated. Alice Blondin-Perrin, who attended Saint Joseph Indian Residential School in Fort Resolution (Northwest Territories), has written about how the school controlled and limited the means of communication between parents and students:

> I never got a letter from my parents. They could not write, but they both knew all the Dene languages in the region, and I learned years later that Dad had people write us, and sent money as well. But not one letter reached me or my siblings in all the years we were there. I felt heartbroken and abandoned. All communication was cut off. My parents did not receive one of my letters either, that I wrote along with all the other girls. We wrote at least once a month, which dwindled to once a year when we received no reply. We were brainwashed to think that our parents did not care for us.[44]

Other students have written about the regimented nature of daily life in the schools. Basil Johnston describes how each day began at Spanish Indian Residential School in northern Ontario:

> 6:15 a.m. Clang! Clang! Clang! I was nearly clanged out of my wits and out of bed at the same time. Never had anything—not wind, not thunder—awakened me with quite the same shock and fright. … "You deaf? You no can hear? Hmmm? You like sleep? No?" Father Buck asked as he stood beside Simon Martin's bed. He rang the bell even harder. There was no sign of movement from the still form. "Sooo! You won't get up, Simon!" And Father Buck seized one side of the mattress and lifted and overturned Simon, bedding and mattress together.

But Johnston also writes of the camaraderie between some of the students and the support they were able to give each other:

> At Smith's Lake the boys dispersed, friends gathering in small clutches and knots to exchange tales of injustice, recount humorous incidents that

had occurred during the past week, or scheme how best to get revenge on a prefect or relive the last baseball game. ... Our sole aspiration was to be rescued or released (it didn't much matter which) from Spanish, and to be restored to our families and homes. That was the sum total of our ambitions.[45]

Children of survivors—who sometimes identify as "intergenerational survivors"—experienced the aftermath of the residential-school era through their parents. Children of former students have written about the legacies of violence and trauma passed down from generation to generation: "I am a victim of Canada's residential school system. When I say victim, I mean something substantially different than 'Survivor.' I never attended a residential school, so I cannot say that I survived one. However, my parents and my extended family members did. The pain they endured became my pain, and I became a victim."[46]

In writing about children of Holocaust survivors, Marianne Hirsch coined the term *postmemory* to describe "the relationship that the generation after those who witnessed cultural or collective trauma bears to the experiences of those who came before." It is a term that may also be pertinent in the case of intergenerational survivors of the IRS system. As Hirsch writes, the structure of postmemory involves being "shaped, however indirectly, by traumatic fragments of events that still defy narrative reconstruction and exceed comprehension."[47]

Some students ran away from the schools and perished trying to return home, whereas others persevered at school but had difficulty returning home.[48] In the documentary *Remembering Inninimowin* (also discussed in the book's conclusion), David Okimaw recounts his desire to return home.[49] When he was a young boy, Okimaw's family taught him how to trap, and he learned to live off the land. But at ten years old, he was sent to residential school. In grade ten, Okimaw told his mom that he wanted to come home. His mother, though, told him that he would no longer fit in. Having lost his trapping skills, he would have very few options as part of the community, she said. He recounts her words: "It's hard living. And the trapping business is coming to an end. Stay in school. Forget about coming home." Such experiences were common. Even with a desire to return home, with traditional knowledge and languages forbidden and forgotten while at school, returning to their own communities became increasingly difficult for students. The experiences of survivors after leaving residential school vary as greatly as do their experiences while they were in the schools. Some survivors went home anyway and tried to carve out lives for themselves; others moved to cities and towns to find work. Some turned to alcohol and substance abuse, whereas others still found their voices through politics, becoming involved in activism and calls for change—calls that would eventually help to bring down the residential school system—while also pushing for reparations and redress.

Building toward a Truth and Reconciliation Commission

Like the establishment of the Indian residential schools, the movement toward reconciliation in Canada took many years to unfold. By the 1970s, the churches had been phased out of the system, and the government took over the day-to-day administration of the schools. As I will discuss in chapter 3, it was also a time when several communities attempted—often with success— to take back their schools. The 1970s also saw significant changes in Canada's cultural landscape. In 1971 Prime Minister Trudeau announced plans to adopt an official multicultural policy. The concept of a national multicultural mosaic has since played an important role in the construction of Canadian identity. Meant as a policy of inclusion, official multiculturalism was also a way to assuage and manage both immigrant and Indigenous populations who were agitating for more rights. The policy further contributed to Canada's international reputation for tolerance. "The adoption of multiculturalism," writes Sunera Thobani, "enabled the nation's self-presentation on the global stage as urbane, cosmopolitan, and at the cutting edge of promoting racial and ethnic tolerance among western nations."[50]

Indigenous people have had a troubled and unique relationship with these policies. Though purporting to work via principles of inclusivity and a celebration of cultural difference, Canada's multicultural policies have often simply helped to further entrench the idea of the French and British as the nation's two founding cultures.[51] When Indigenous issues are discussed as part of the national dialogue, they are generally framed in terms of cultural rights, without much discussion of Indigenous sovereignty. In other words, the incorporation of Indigenous people into the umbrella of multiculturalism works to erase "their unique political status and rights under the precedence of international law."[52] For these reasons the discourse of multiculturalism obscures the underlying tensions (and the source of much conflict) with regard to land and resources that have troubled relationships between Indigenous and non-Indigenous communities throughout Canada.[53]

Because of the way that official multicultural policies in Canada situate Indigenous people as one cultural group among many that can agitate for more rights, Indigenous people have an uneasy relationship with the state (the governing bureaucratic body) while maintaining a central space in relation to the nation (the constructed identity of a people).[54] The legal rights of Indigenous peoples (largely defined through the Indian Act of 1876 and the subsequent amendments to the act) confine them as subjects of the state. At the same time, Indigenous cultural symbols remain central to the ways in which Canada represents itself on a global stage. Indigenous peoples' struggle for sovereignty and self-government sits in striking relief with the state's role in the construction of Canada as a nation—an "imagined community"—in no small part defined in relation to Indigenous cultural imagery and values.[55] Indigenous people are both defined as central to the myth of the Canadian nation but still labeled as Other, demonstrating a "doubled ontological centrality."[56] Their Otherness and the continuing need to define and redefine this Otherness places Indigenous people both at the center of Canadian self-definitions and at its margins. The reconciliation process brings this "doubled" relationship to the forefront of Canadian politics and highlights the ways in which the construction of nationhood is constantly in flux. Exclusionary and inclusionary practices of the state, including immigration policies, land claims, rules of citizenship, truth commissions, and colonial policies of assimilation such as the Indian residential schools, define who gets to belong to the national body and who does not.

The 1980s and 1990s marked a significant shift in awareness of Indigenous issues—both in Canada and on the international stage. In 1989 the city of Oka, Quebec, planned to expand a luxury golf course onto disputed Mohawk land. In July 1990 the police force, and later the military, were locked in a standoff with Mohawk protestors, who occupied a part of the Kanesatake forest known as "the Pines." The crisis lasted seventy-eight days and resulted in the death of Corporal Marcel Lemay.[57] As it turned into a national media event, the Oka crisis became an important moment for the renegotiation of Canadian national identity.[58]

During the standoff, the image shown in figure 1.3 was splashed across television screens and the front pages of newspapers and magazines all over Canada, a sort of visual shorthand that represented the growing conflicts between Indigenous and non-Indigenous populations. In many printed versions of the image, only the military officer, Patrick Cloutier, is named, whereas the Indigenous protestor is often identified simply as "a Mohawk Warrior." The protestor in the image is in fact Brad Larocque, a student from

FIGURE 1.3 Canadian soldier Patrick Cloutier and protester Brad Larocque come face-to-face in a tense standoff at the Kanesatake reserve in Oka, Quebec, September 1, 1990. Photo: The Canadian Press/Shaney Komulainen.

Saskatchewan. Cloutier has been called "baby-faced," and several scholars have noted that only Larocque appears to be carrying a gun.[59] In reality, both sides were armed, and the Canadian police and military forces greatly outnumbered the Mohawk activists. So even though the Canadian government was the trespasser, the media painted the Mohawks as the aggressors. Moreover, there is a striking similarity between the settler-to-Indigenous encounter shown in this image and the image of the Mountie and Chief Sitting Eagle discussed earlier. It could be argued that Cloutier's "baby face" here continues to depict the benevolent face of the state, in contrast with what could be read as the "uncivilized" aggression of Laroque. But regardless of who is portrayed as the antagonist, the image works to disrupt the persistent belief that Canada's past is without violent conflict.

In the year following this standoff, an important step toward the establishment of the Canadian TRC was made: in August 1991 the Royal Commission on Aboriginal People (RCAP) was established. This marked a period of very strained relationships between Indigenous people and settler Canadians. The year before, the Oka crisis had been receiving daily media coverage. And that same year, Elijah Harper—chief of the Red Sucker Lake

FIGURE 1.4 Elijah Harper holds his eagle feather and votes "no" on the Meech Lake Accord. Photo: Wayne Glowacki/ Winnipeg Free Press.

First Nation and member of the Manitoba legislature—had launched a filibuster to block the Meech Lake Accord, a series of constitutional amendments seeking to quell the Quebec sovereignty movement. Harper believed that Indigenous peoples had not been properly consulted in the matter. Phil Fontaine—Manitoba regional chief for the Assembly of First Nations at the time—helped to orchestrate a blocking of the accord. Winona Wheeler elaborates: "Fontaine and Harper stressed that while they did not oppose special status for Quebec, they were angry that special status for First Nations was not also recognized in the Meech Lake deal. According to Fontaine, of 'particular concern was the big lie that Canada was made up of two founding nations, two official languages.'"[60] These years and these events produced some of the most iconic images of Indigenous resistance to emerge from Canada in the latter half of the twentieth century, including the image of Elijah Harper holding his eagle feather as he votes "no" on the Meech Lake Accord (figure 1.4). The circulation of these images helped to catapult the struggles facing Indigenous communities into the national and international spotlight.

And it was in this context that the RCAP undertook its inquiry, which lasted for 178 days. During that time, seven commissioners worked with ninety-six Indigenous communities, conducting interviews, reviewing historical documents, and examining past inquiries. The commission produced five volumes of work (published in 1996), including recommendations for future courses of action.[61] Although the RCAP was not set up to address the IRS system, the IRS legacy was continuously raised as the commission traveled across the country. It became clear that the destruction of culture and community that had been inflicted through Canada's policy of assimilation was of the utmost importance to Indigenous communities. In response to the information and recommendations put forward by the RCAP (including redistribution of land and resources, improvement to the education system, improvement of employment conditions, and the establishment of an Aboriginal peoples review commission), the Canadian government released *Gathering Strength: Canada's Aboriginal Action Plan*. The plan included provision for a residential schools unit in 1996 by the Department of Indian and Northern Affairs. In 1998 Jane Stewart, the minister of Indian and Northern Affairs, issued an official statement of reconciliation and announced the creation of a $350 million "healing fund." This fund was allocated to the Aboriginal Healing Foundation, created in the same year to aid Métis, Inuit, and First Nations in the healing process.

In May 2006 the historic Indian Residential Schools Settlement Agreement was approved by all parties involved in the lawsuit. The case was brought against the Canadian government for abuses inflicted under the IRS system; it was the largest lawsuit in Canadian history, with eighty thousand claimants.[62] The agreement included financial compensation for IRS survivors and called for a national truth-telling commission to bring greater awareness to the history and legacy of the IRS system. Through the Common Experience Payment (CEP), each student would receive C$10,000 for the first year they spent in an IRS and C$3,000 for each subsequent year.[63] Students who were physically or sexually abused at the schools could apply through the Independent Assessment Process (IAP) for further compensation.[64] The settlement also stipulated the creation of a Truth and Reconciliation Commission, which was allotted a budget of C$60 million to complete its projected five-year mandate. This was the first time a truth commission arose out of a judicially mediated agreement, as opposed to through legislation or decree. The objectives of the TRC included hosting seven national gatherings to promote awareness, creating an accurate public record, publishing a report at the halfway point of the five-year mandate, and establishing a resource center.[65] The IRS TRC fell into the category of "historical truth commission," one that was not established as part of a political transition but rather was focused on rectifying absences in national historical narratives.[66] Its goal was to create public awareness of the IRS system in both Indigenous and non-Indigenous communities.[67]

Within its first year, the Canadian commission faced considerable obstacles. The commission began under the leadership of Justice Harry LaForme (Ojibwe), a judge who (in 2004) became the first Indigenous person to sit on any appellate court in Canada. The other two commissioners were Claudette Dumont-Smith (Kitigan Zibi), who had a long career in Indigenous health, and Jane Morley, a lawyer and mediator who worked with First Nations communities in British Columbia as a child and youth officer. But on October 20, 2008—less than six months after the commission's start—Justice LaForme stepped down. In his letter of resignation, LaForme communicated his disappointment in the administration of the commission and in the two other commissioners, Dumont-Smith and Morley. LaForme believed that, as chair, he was entitled to be the decisive force with regard to the commission's course; to his mind, the other commissioners were simply there to provide input. Morley and Dumont-Smith did not share this view.

LaForme also expressed discomfort with how the relationship between "truth" and "reconciliation" was being defined through the IRS TRC: "Unlike mine, [Morley and Dumont-Smith hold] a view that leaves much of the work of reconciliation for another day."[68] LaForme wanted the TRC to focus on reconciliation in the present and future, but Morley and Dumont-Smith wanted to focus on gathering the truth about the past. With his statement, LaForme raised important questions about the concept of reconciliation as it relates to truth, and he disrupted any easy coupling of the two terms. The process of gathering and establishing "truth" about the past does not necessarily lead to reconciliation in the present or future. Justice LaForme's remarks underscored what he perceived as a need for the TRC to go beyond a focus on the past, to engage with the present and future as well.

A few months after Justice LaForme's resignation, the remaining commissioners also stepped down. Morley and Dumont-Smith stated that Justice LaForme's resignation and the controversy it stirred up had tainted the commission. They believed the commission needed a fresh start, so a search for three new commissioners began. In June 2009, one year after the first commission had been established, a new commission was announced. Justice Murray Sinclair (Ojibwe), Manitoba's first Indigenous judge, was named the chair. Marie Wilson, a former journalist and Canadian Broadcasting

Corporation (CBC) North regional director from Yellowknife, and Chief Wilton Littlechild (Cree), Alberta regional chief of the Assembly of First Nations, filled the other two positions.[69]

A National Duty to Remember

To forget, and—I will venture to say—to get one's history wrong, are essential factors in the making of a nation; and thus the advance of historical studies is often a danger to nationality.
—ERNEST RENAN, "What Is a Nation?"

In the process of nation building, a unifying collective history is one of the key ties that bind disparate peoples and communities together. As Ernest Renan remarks, in order for the illusion of unity to take hold, there must be a certain amount of collective forgetting. But as the process of nation building continues, collective memory plays a role as well, revealing a dialectical relationship between remembering and forgetting.

Although the academic study of memory is by no means new, recent decades have witnessed a coalescing around the idea of "collective memory" and a recognition that issues of memory do not reside solely within the domain of the individual. In the early twentieth century, Maurice Halbwachs's research on the social aspects of memory marked an important shift in both psychology and sociology.[70] But it wasn't until the latter half of the twentieth century that the social aspects of memory were widely taken up. Several historical moments, including the end of World War II, the fall of the Soviet bloc, and the spread of decolonization, radically refashioned the stakes and politics of memory discourses, highlighting the ruptures and entanglements of history and memory. Transitioning nations had to deal with contested and contentious pasts in ways that would allow for new articulations of the future.[71] The area of collective memory became recognized as one rich for theoretical and practical work. The concept of memory, and the recognition of its ephemeral, fragmented nature, made it an important, if imperfect, tool for both supplementing and challenging official historical discourses.[72]

Truth commissions further complicate the relationship between memory and history. In forcing a collective reckoning with the past, they can potentially allow new narratives to be integrated into national histories, thrusting stories of historical oppression into both the national and international spotlight. At the same time, a call to memory can also be used to mask contemporary injustices. For these reasons, and others, the politics of memory has a complex and sometimes contradictory relationship to questions of social justice.[73]

The Indian residential school system was, among other things, an explicit and devastating assault on cultural memory. It directly aimed to stop the continuity of traditions and languages across generations. It was an exercise in forced forgetting. Children were forbidden from speaking their own languages, so they began to forget them.[74] Beliefs and traditions, once familiar and natural, ceased to make sense. This attack on memory was also an attack on Indigenous communities and traditions, whose stories were intentionally suppressed and excluded from Canada's historical narratives.

Scholars have called this kind of suppression or denial "nonmemory," "willful amnesia," or "induced amnesia."[75] *Forgetting* implies a sometimes unconscious slipping away of memories. It can occur simply with the passage of time, or it can be willed. However, *amnesia* suggests a difficulty or inability to remember. Furthermore, *amnesia* implies that trauma may have acted as a trigger to block painful events from memory. When the state is engaged in this process, it often works actively to replace these old memories with new ones. As Marita Sturken has written, "The 'culture of amnesia' actually involves the generation of memory in new forms, a process often misinterpreted as forgetting. Indeed, memory and forgetting are co-constitutive processes; each is essential to the other's existence."[76]

With the establishment of the IRS TRC, we saw a shift from "memory-as-possibility" to "memory-as-necessity."[77] Prior to the establishment of the TRC, survivors often repressed memories of their experiences in the schools. In contrast, with the establishment of the TRC those same stories were sought from and even demanded of survivors. In addition to the open process of sharing testimony at TRC national events and community events, survivors were obligated to recount memories of trauma as a requirement for the Independent Assessment Process, which was established to handle claims for cases of sexual abuse, serious physical abuse, and "other wrongful acts committed at the Indian Residential Schools."[78] From the standpoint of the state, remembering the past through the TRC became a tool for reconceptualizing the imagined community that is the nation-state known as Canada. In this way the duty to remember became a way for the Indigenous citizen-subject to perform the project of national unification. But remembering a tragic event can become a form of justice that then overshadows the need for further action through policy changes or legislation. It is true that processes of historicization, like truth commissions, draw attention to the past, but there is always also the risk that they may do so in ways that disconnect that past from the present and the future.[79]

The IRS TRC aimed to reckon with national memory. In Prime Minister Harper's official apology in 2008 to Indigenous peoples for the IRS system, Harper signaled a national duty to remember: "The burden of this experience has been on your shoulders for far too long. The burden is properly ours as a government, and as a country." With these words, Harper's apology pointed toward both a duty to remember and a transfer of memory from the private to the public, from Indigenous to settler. In some ways it was a call to rewrite Canada's history by incorporating long-silenced memories. But this call for a national duty to remember remained oriented toward serving settlers' understanding of their nation's history. Indeed, the TRC had little if any relationship to Indigenous communities' conceptions of nationhood or struggle for sovereignty.[80] As Dale Turner (Tamagami) has argued, reconciliation should be (and should have been) framed as a process unfolding between nations, between multiple Indigenous nations and the colonial nation of Canada, rather than between communities or individuals. In other words, for Turner and many others, Indigenous sovereignty and the discourse of nation-to-nation dialogue are necessary components that have been missing and remain marginalized from the Canadian engagement with reconciliation.[81]

Although a significant critique of the TRC was that it was merely a forum for the nation-state to absolve itself from much larger issues of reparation, it is equally important to note that for many Indigenous people, the TRC's limitations were recognized and the commission was never intended to serve as a site for engaging in political processes of Indigenous self-determination.[82] In this way, as in others, the IRS TRC frequently stood in contrast with the larger politics of reconciliation, a social and political process that tends to be tied to moments of national transformation (particularly transitions to democratic rule, as was true in South America and Africa, for example). Because the IRS TRC did not coincide with a radical change in government or with a moment of profound political transition, the dynamics of power that defined the Canadian state remained essentially intact. It is true that the IRS TRC provoked more subtle transitions whereby, for instance, Indigenous people have been increasingly able to assert their own versions of the past and disrupt narratives that attempt to write them out of Canadian history. But historicization alone cannot rectify the injustices of colonial policies of assimilation. There must also be action in the form of restitution, not just reconciliation.[83]

Assimilationist Visions

They learn not only games and traditions such as the celebration of St. Valentine's Day but the mastery of words which will open to them the whole range of the ordinary Canadian curriculum.... Instead of the isolation and neglect of the past, a free and equal chance for children in urban centers.... For the oldest Canadians, a new future.
—VOICE-OVER, *A New Future*

This statement is from a short segment that aired on the CBC in 1955.[84] The segment is called *A New Future*, and it focuses on the Indian residential school in Moose Factory, Ontario, where students are shown smiling in classrooms, playing sports, and learning English. Looking at the segment now allows us to see how visual representations of life at the schools worked to construct a particular image of both Canadianness and indigeneity. The clip suggests a specific vision of assimilation, common at the time, framed and furthered by an educational system whose violence could be obscured and deflected through the guise of benevolence (see figure 1.5).

In *A New Future* a teacher writes a series of words on the blackboard. The words are just legible through the lens of the television camera: *conceal, purchase, desire, remain, attempt, wealthy, grateful,* and *sufficient*. Taken together, these words construct an image of Canada that suggests a climate of desire and consumption, of appropriate affect and action. In projecting an image of the ideal Canadian citizen-subject, the words also prescribe normative emotions, such as desire and gratitude, as well as appropriate actions, such as attempt and purchase. In this way each word reveals something of the assimilation process. Some read almost as commandments, as if they were part of the program of indoctrination upon which the IRS system was built. Indeed, it is valuable to reread some of these words now, against the grain of their intent, to name and interrogate some of the values that underpinned the IRS's program of assimilation.

Conceal. The Indian residential school system was one of concealment. Some students were moved to schools that were in remote locations far away from their homes even when there were other schools that were closer to their communities. Students were taught to keep their emotions hidden and were forced to suppress cultural practices, languages, and community relationships. Relations of kin were often severed. Brothers and sisters were forbidden from speaking to one another. Sexual abuse and physical abuse were among the deepest secrets at the schools, ones that many survivors continued to conceal from their families and loved ones after returning home.

FIGURE 1.5 Still image from *A New Future*. Image courtesy CBC Archives.

Desire. The Indian residential school was a system that regulated affect. It taught students to disavow their intimate kin relationships with family and community members and attempted to fashion new affective relations with church and nation. The citizen-subjects the schools fashioned were desiring, and these desires were directed in ways recognizable and valorized by both church and state.

Grateful. Representations of the system also emphasized the benevolent nature of the schools. It was framed as a system that was established to do good, but it taught students that they were inferior and should be thankful for the help of church and state.

Attempt and *Remain.* These words capture the double bind in which students found themselves. Students were taught to strive toward becoming model citizens, to attempt assimilation. Yet they were also taught that they should not expect too much. Boys were taught to be laborers; girls were shown how to sew and be homemakers. They were taught not to question authority and that they should always remain in their place.

Purchase, Wealthy. In large part the IRS sought to distance Indigenous people from cultural values of reciprocity and the relations that underpinned

Indigenous economies and subsistence. For instance, Section 3 of the Indian Act banned gatherings often called potlatch, gatherings that supported inter-community well-being and sustained cultural wealth.[85] Indigenous systems of gathering and exchange were here replaced with Western economic values of accumulation, commodity, and property.[86]

Through the values underlying the Indian residential school system, Indigenous children were taught what it meant to be citizens of Canada, to integrate into the workforce, to restructure their families and communities to model settler lifestyles, and to forget their claims to land and resources. And broadcasts like *A New Future* showed the rest of Canada a carefully constructed and whitewashed view of the "civilizing" process. The clip also reveals how the classroom became a site for ideological indoctrination. Although speaking about colonial Kenya, Ngugi wa Thiong'o's description of the colonial classroom proves useful here: "The night of the sword and the bullet was followed by the morning of the chalk and blackboard. The physical violence of the battlefield was followed by the psychological violence of the classroom."[87] Students were told that their cultures and languages were wrong, even evil, and that they should not look back but look forward to "a new future."

The broadcasting of this program on state-sponsored television reveals the extent to which visual culture played a role in perpetuating and justifying the violence of assimilation policies in Canada. This is not necessarily specific to the Canadian context; many historians and scholars have shown how scopic regimes have been integral to establishing relations of power in colonial societies. In *The Right to Look*, Nicholas Mirzoeff focuses on the central role that such regimes have played in securing the skewed relations of power that have gone hand in hand with events such as colonial expansion, the establishment of plantation slavery, and the implementation of the (imperial) military-industrial complex. Mirzoeff's work places relations of looking at the center of colonial societies. For him, visuality is both "a medium for the transmission and dissemination of authority, and a means for the mediation of those subject to that authority." If visuality is a tactic that is actively adopted and strategically deployed by colonial power, "countervisuality," Mirzoeff proposes in contrast, represents a challenge to that authority, a decolonial framework that rests upon the colonized or oppressed claiming the right to look: "The contest of visuality and countervisuality is not, then, a simple battle for the same field. One fought to maintain the 'colonial environment' as it was, the other to visualize a different reality, modern but decolonized."[88] In this way, countervisuality should be both a goal of and a tactic for reconciliation, a process that should always and actively be working to help "visualize a different reality" and then, even more importantly, helping to usher it in.

Reconciliation as a Way of Seeing

Shawn A-in-chut Atleo, hereditary chief from the Ahousaht First Nation and the former national chief of the Assembly of First Nations, has recounted the experience of sitting in the House of Commons and listening to Prime Minster Harper's official apology in 2008. His grandmother sat beside him, and as they listened to the apology, she turned to him and said, "Grandson, now they are finally beginning to see us." Atleo's grandmother had raised seventeen children, who all attended residential schools. He recalls listening to her words of optimism upon hearing the apology:

> At that moment, a peaceful calm and happiness washed over both of us—the knowledge that, at last, in the final years of her long and incredibly rich life, she had the opportunity to witness a modest measure of justice for her and for so many of her generation. Optimism was, in that moment, a possibility. Perhaps the next generation could live in an era of true reconciliation and experience the opportunity to fulfill their personal and collective potential as Indigenous peoples and as Canadians.[89]

Atleo's words invoke the ways that reconciliation can be understood as a call toward a shift in relations of looking, of seeing and of being seen. Past injustices that were kept "out of sight" can be brought into national consciousness, and long-held assumptions about visibility and invisibility can be called into question. Acknowledgment and awareness of past wrongs are framed in terms of making those wrongs public and *visible*. However, the emphasis of the Canadian TRC on recognition and awareness about the IRS system brings up vexing questions. As discussed earlier, Canada has positioned itself as the first country to enshrine multicultural ideologies into official state policy, ushering in an emphasis, more generally, on the politics of recognition. Such an approach has subsequently been criticized for reproducing "the very configurations of colonial power that Indigenous peoples' demands for recognition have historically sought to transcend."[90]

As something that is "granted" to Indigenous populations, recognition and its underlying assumptions rely on deeply embedded colonial relations of power. In framing reconciliation as a way of seeing, as being bound up with visual culture, my goal in the remainder of this chapter is to shift the conversation away from the limits of recognition, which are often constrained by the logic of Canadian multiculturalism, toward thinking about reconciliation as an opportunity for cultivating new ways of seeing.

Images and their uses and meanings change over time. They are tied not only to the moment of their production but also to the ways in which they circulate and are received.[91] It is important to note that the photographic image can be manipulated when it is taken (through lighting or staging, for instance), as it is being developed, and in the ways it is circulated and framed for consumption. In this way any engagement with images requires the viewer to see them as sites of complex negotiations. Still, the evidentiary role of photography has framed it as a tool that offers proof of past events. Even when one recognizes the constructed nature of photography, it is still difficult to deny that the camera captures some kind of truth. Marianne Hirsch elaborates on this difficulty: "As much as I remind myself that photographs are as essentially constructed as any other representational form, that every part of the image can be manipulated and even fabricated, especially with ever more sophisticated digital technologies, I return to Barthes's basic 'ça a été' ('this has been') and an unassailable belief in reference and a notion of truth in the picture."[92] Hirsch recognizes that any "notion of truth" that is found in the picture is mediated but that within the mediation, there are still traces or representations of the real that call for a more engaged, dynamic reading of photographic images. The image may indeed represent a moment that occurred, but the context of that moment (whether or how it was staged, for example) is more difficult to ascertain. In a sense, one must look beyond what is shown in order to understand more fully the relationship between what is seen and what remains unseen in any particular image.

Take, for instance, the image of Ojibwe Chief Maun-gua-daus (see figure 1.6). As one of the earliest surviving Canadian daguerreotypes (circa 1847), it reveals a great deal about its particular historical moment, in relation to both indigeneity and photography. The daguerreotype was invented by the French artist and inventor Louis Daguerre in 1839. Created with silver-plated copper, it had a reflective surface and hence became known as the "mirror with a memory."[93] The process was relatively expensive to execute, creating unique images that were difficult to replicate, on a surface that was very easy to damage, which meant that both the production and circulation of daguerreotypes was limited. In discussing the use of daguerreotypes in nineteenth-century Canada, Randolph Lewis tells readers that "at the very beginning of photographic history, Native people exercised a surprising amount of control over their own images." Although "all manner

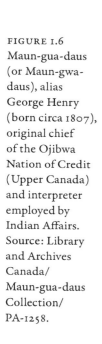

FIGURE 1.6
Maun-gua-daus
(or Maun-gwa-
daus), alias
George Henry
(born circa 1807),
original chief
of the Ojibwa
Nation of Credit
(Upper Canada)
and interpreter
employed by
Indian Affairs.
Source: Library
and Archives
Canada/
Maun-gua-daus
Collection/
PA-1258.

of mischief" and exploitation was certainly possible, in theory, given daguerreotypes' fragility and the difficulty of reproducing such images, early
photographers were more inclined to "respect the wishes for their Native
sitters and let them decide the fate of their own portraits."[94]

A shift occurred shortly after Maun-gua-daus's daguerreotype was produced, when glass-plate negatives were invented and reproducing images
became easier and less expensive. This resulted in a loss of control for Indigenous subjects, transforming the relationship between individuals and
communities with respect to photographic technologies. Lewis elaborates:
"Losing control of the physical object meant losing control of how it was
presented—and, more generally, that Native images were now ripe for commercial and ideological exploitation. Thus, in the middle of the nineteenth
century, the photographic representation of Native people had begun its

long descent into exploitation and misrepresentation."[95] But if reconciliation can be understood as a call to transform collective ways of seeing, part of the process demands that images of Indigenous people be reread and recontextualized in light of these insights; reconciliation means seeking to excavate and challenge these histories of exploitation and misrepresentation.

Writing about this very image, Jim Burant has noted that Maun-gua-daus "looks preoccupied and serious, and is wearing a costume that combines a European-style cloth coat with native beadwork and trimming, as well as one of the medals presented to him by King Louis-Philippe of France. There is a hint of play-acting in the pose, almost as if he was uncertain about who he was or where he would be going."[96] Though not a derogatory or demeaning reading of the photograph, Burant's description here nonetheless frames Maun-gua-daus as a troubled and somewhat lost figure. But this reading does not tell the whole story. Maun-gua-daus lived a life of many transitions. Born circa 1807 in Upper Canada, he was later baptized with the Christian name George Henry.[97] He learned English as a child and later worked as a translator for the Methodist Church. When he became disillusioned with the church, he reclaimed his name, Maun-gua-daus, which means "great hero" in Ojibwe. He assembled a group of Indigenous dancers and began to tour throughout North America and Europe. On these tours, Maun-gua-daus met royalty and layperson alike in the countries that had colonized Canada.[98] He eventually resettled in Canada with the Mississaugas of the New Credit First Nation (Ojibwe) in Ontario.

Given his dynamic and distinct trajectory, the suggestion that Maun-gua-daus was uncertain about who he was, though perhaps not false, appears reductive. Perhaps his demeanor and dress in this photo were part of a strategy, a strategy of resistance or survival. Artist and professor Hulleah J. Tsinhnahjinnie (Seminole-Muscogee-Navaho) has written powerfully about her relationship to early photographs of Indigenous subjects, reminding readers that if a picture is worth a thousand words, "the complexity of the subject being photographed never seems to be included in the thousand words." Describing various experiences with and encounters in the photographic archive, Tsinhnahjinnie evocatively details how she manages to see survival and continuity in photographs conventionally framed to represent the deterioration or disappearance of Indigenous life.[99] Her work points toward the complexity of these early images in compelling and useful ways.

It was during Maun-gua-daus's lifetime that the Indian residential schools were starting to gain influence. By dressing in the combination of cultures, maybe Maun-gua-daus sought to project an image of perseverance while still recognizing that his life had been transformed by the presence of European settlers. Reading Maun-gua-daus's image in tandem with his biography can potentially transform the way viewers *see* him; it is no longer the subject of the photograph who seems uncertain, but rather it is the viewing subject whose gaze is rendered uncertain by the dynamic story that the still image is trying to convey. As with my earlier discussion of the photographic representations of Chief Sitting Eagle and the Mountie, and the Oka Standoff, effecting a countervisuality of reconciliation means that images like the one of Maun-gua-daus can and should be read with the recognition that meanings shift and the gaze looks more than one way.

Although colonial photography has generally been understood as a tool for the project of forced assimilation, in some cases the images produced in the colonial context can also be read as moments of negotiation, where neither the photographer, nor the camera's lens, nor the subjects who were positioned in front of the camera were fully in control. Writing about the colonial image archive in Australia, Jane Lydon comments: "Although photographs reveal the power of the colonial gaze, they also express its moments of uncertainty, offering a less-mediated view of the past that exceeds their maker's intentions, capturing details and attitudes beyond their original purpose, and setting in motion the compelling play of past and present, Aboriginal and European, self and other."[100] Images and films that reveal the colonial process as it unfolded in the past remind contemporary viewers that colonialism has never been an "abstract process" and that relations of looking have played an important role in the establishment of colonial rule and the oppression of Indigenous people. But in revisiting the visual narratives of Maun-Gua-daus's portrait, the CBC's *A New Future*, and the illustrations used to recruit Canadians to the task of assimilating Indigenous peoples, this chapter has sought to rethink and renegotiate several iconic images. As Faye Ginsburg and Fred Myers write, "The re-narration of already existing images—working with the heightened but slippery indexicality of media such as film and photography—ruptures their attachment to regimes that effaced Aboriginal experience."[101] By opening these images up to new contexts, conversations, and interpretations, I have attempted to *un*settle some of the power of colonial vision while also suggesting a more complicated "relationship of exchange" between settler Canadians and Indigenous people.[102]

Indigenous people in Canada have also mobilized image-based media to "talk back" to dominant media structures, deploying their own forms of countervisuality, both historically and in the contemporary media landscape.

And in recent decades the development of the Aboriginal Peoples Television Network, the first national Aboriginal television network, and IsumaTV (an Inuit production and distribution company) has given Indigenous self-representation and community rebuilding an important platform.[103] As noted by Marian Bredin, "Aboriginal people's growing demand for access to the means of cultural production in Canada is part of a global movement toward decolonization and self-determination in which media played a key role.... Indigenous and Aboriginal media worked to counteract the mass media in settler societies like Canada's, resisting negative and often racist stereotypes and generating more accurate and meaningful representations of the cultural and social conditions in indigenous communities."[104] Some of the potential of Indigenous media production resides in its ability to reframe and disrupt the colonial narrative. As opposed to having media structured by and around colonial vision, communities have positioned their own beliefs, cultures, and languages as the privileged point of view. Paying attention to these media forms and images can also be an important part of the reconciliation process, for they can open Canadians up to the "existence of plural ways of seeing."[105]

Some of the images discussed in this chapter have become iconic representations of Canadian and Indigenous identities. Iconic images have the potential to trigger feelings of both identification and alienation, and they are tools of both remembrance and forgetting. As Robert Hariman and John Lucaites write, such images can "provoke powerful moments of identification while also casting deep shadows within public memory." Hariman and Lucaites go on to discuss how "democracy is a way of seeing," arguing that civic space is constituted, at least in part, by what we see.[106] It is my contention that the process of reconciliation also constitutes a way of seeing in which regimes of visibility can be disrupted, contested, and renegotiated. In reference to the iconic images of Indigenous people that circulate in the Canadian context, Shawn Atleo implores the viewer:

> I encourage everyone to truly observe these images and all images of indigenous peoples, from the beginning of Canada and long before. Through reconciliation and justice, we can look anew at the history of relations between settler governments and indigenous peoples. If we take this time and care, we will be enriched by the incredible history and enduring legacy of the indigenous world view, a world view that values the land and our place in it, that emphasizes the interconnection between all things, and that recognizes our responsibility to one another. This

is my hope and humble request—an invitation to all Canadians to see us, and ultimately to join us, in a celebration of the indigenous heritage and the future of Canada.[107]

The process of reconciliation in Canada has proved to be a complex negotiation not only of a violent and traumatic past but also of an unknown future. Discourses of reconciliation often focus on leaving the past behind and moving toward a new, unified future. The goal is consensus, an understanding about what happened in order to construct possibilities for what is to come. What makes visual representations so compelling in the context of reconciliation is their capacity to act as reminders of this past while also allowing for active engagement and resignification in the present.

Images of Contact

*Archival Photographs and the Work
of Reconciliation in Canada*

*It was on June 11, 2008, in front of millions of Canadians, that words of sorrow
and profound regret resonated in the heart of Parliament. . . . And I remember
quite vividly the images brought to mind by those words.*
—MICHAËLLE JEAN, governor general of Canada

On October 15, 2009, the governor general of Canada, Michaëlle Jean, participated in an IRS TRC event in Ottawa. As discussed in chapter 1, though established in 2008, the IRS TRC had already experienced the resignation of its first three commissioners. Having regrouped one year later with three new commissioners, the beleaguered commission was marking a fresh start with the Ottawa event. In her opening address, Jean spoke of Prime Minister Stephen Harper's official apology to survivors of the IRS system and of the images brought to mind by his words:

> I thought about the devastating archival photos that I saw for the first time in the Tr'ondëk Hwëch'in First Nation Cultural Centre, which welcomed me in June 2007, in Dawson City, Yukon.
>
> Those photos were heartbreaking, infinitely sad, showing Aboriginal children forced by the dozens onto the backs of trucks, eyes wide with alarm, terrified.
>
> You know what I am talking about.

Her last sentence reverberated through the grand conference room at Rideau Hall: *You know what I am talking about.* Here Jean addressed her audience in

Ottawa, those watching via live web streaming, and those who accessed the now-archived speech online. The implication was that Canadians know this history and know it through its visual representation, particularly through the proliferation and circulation of archival images from the schools. Although she mentioned a particular set of images, for the purposes of this chapter the specifics of her reference are of less concern. What does matter is Jean's acknowledgment of these images and their circulation in the Canadian context, as well as her claim that they inhabit collective memory in Canada. Jean even suggested that it was unnecessary to see the images, for her public could simply imagine them. "In order to see a photograph well," Roland Barthes once wrote, "it is best to look away or close your eyes."[1] In other words, images don't just circulate as objects but also as memories; as one looks away from a photograph, its contours and colors may fade, but the mind can recall its essence.

Far from static entities, photographs, like memories, are ephemeral, and their meanings can change with time. I take that inherent instability as my starting point in this chapter. In particular, I focus on how photographs from the IRS era have been used as evocative tools for representing both the "everyday" experiences of students at the schools and also something more "spectacular"—namely, a history of colonial oppression that is only now coming to light. I use the words *spectacular* and *spectacle*, following Guy Debord, to signal "a social relation among people, mediated by images."[2] The images produced by and in the IRS system have had very particular "social lives": they have made their way through personal scrapbooks, church pamphlets, and the state press, and they have often come to reside in church or state archives.[3] Originally, they may have spoken to the efficacy of a system designed to "kill the Indian in the child."[4] Now they can be seen to speak to the subtle and not-so-subtle violence of that system. In many ways the photographs from the IRS system can be read as a "self-portrait of power" through which a colonial, institutional gaze was produced and maintained.[5] But this is not the only way they can be read. The photographs reveal multiple layers of complex and mutable social relationships between students and staff, between colonized and colonizer, and between the students themselves.

Contrary to the images evoked by the governor general, where the children appear sullen or scared, the images discussed in this chapter show the *everydayness* of the schools; they reveal those kinds of daily activities that frame the IRS system in ways that seem more familiar, with children posing for team photos or participating in school plays (figures 2.1 and 2.2). Such photographs constitute a large portion of the IRS image archive, where one

FIGURE 2.1 Indigenous children in class at the Fort George Catholic Indian Residential School, Fort George, Quebec, 1939. Source: Archives Deschâtelets.

FIGURE 2.2 The cricket team from Battleford Indian Industrial School, Battleford, Saskatchewan, circa 1895. Source: Library and Archives Canada/David Ewens collection/A182265.

might also find photographs of children doing chores, for instance, or learning a trade. Young girls are sewing or cleaning. Boys are learning carpentry or doing yard work. In the residences, rows of beds line the dormitories. Young faces peer back at the camera, sometimes smiling, often not.

Such school photographs are pervasive in everyday life. Confined largely to private homes and photo albums, they are generally thought of as separate from political life. They are rarely seen as works of art or as images of persuasion. Yet these photographs also reveal the mechanisms of powerful institutions and the threads that bind the private and the political.[6] There are, of course, many ways to read such photographs. The students in their rows may represent a moment of solidarity, a period of innocence, or, in some cases, a history of assimilation. They may dramatize a particular moment in a nation's history, or they may signal an "individual child's struggle between singularity and ideological interpellation."[7] Gerald McMaster (Plains Cree) writes that the IRS photos often work to capture a moment of "colonial alchemy," a process whereby the "the savage [is turned] into a civilized human being."[8] But McMaster also sees traces of resistance within these images. For instance, in a photo of a school football team from the Battleford Indian Residential School, the young men are dressed in uniforms embroidered with the letters "IS." Though an acronym for "Industrial School," these letters are read by McMaster as a declarative statement of existence and, thus, as evidence of a particular kind of self-assertion.

This chapter traces the trajectories of several IRS images to understand how these images frame students as subjects of colonial alchemy and how they suggest a kind of resistance. By analyzing a selection of these photographs, I make several arguments about the nature of archives, the circulation of images, and the dialectical relationship between the subject and object of the photographer's gaze. I argue that although image archives should be recognized as having been produced through certain contexts and within specific constraints, they are also productive, cultural spaces in and of themselves, where narratives form, coalesce, *and* change. In a sense, one must "look past" any particular image, beyond what is shown, to understand more fully the relationship between what is visible and what remains hidden. "'Looking past,'" Christopher Pinney explains, "suggests a complexity of perspectival positions or a multiplicity of layers that endow photographs with an enormously greater complexity than that which they are usually credited."[9] Pinney writes persuasively about how the indexical quality of photographic imagery—its capacity to reveal traces of the reality that it represents—has often led people to (mistakenly) assume that the meaning of any given photograph is self-evident. He contests this idea, suggesting instead that we "understand photography's indexicality to be the guarantee not of closure and fixity, but rather of multiple surfaces and the possibility of 'looking past.'"[10] In other words, as I argued in my previous chapter, it is possible through thoughtful rereadings and resignifying practices to challenge how images have been assigned meaning.

Reflecting back upon Michaëlle Jean's assertion that the IRS images have left their mark on the collective memory of Canadians, it becomes possible to qualify these images as a type of colonial debris. The colonial debris of IRS images, as Jean's statement points toward, accrues in memory. As Plains Cree Métis scholar Emma LaRocque writes, "Before we can trouble paradigms, we must sift through colonial debris, much of which sits in the hearts and minds of the colonized."[11] In LaRoque's formulation, such debris does not merely have an external physical life in the world but also an internal affective life. It is here important to note that the "sifting" that has taken place in the hearts and minds of settler Canadians through the IRS TRC process and beyond is of a different order than the "sifting" done by Indigenous people. Debris can refer both to the dust that accumulates in the corner of a room or what remains after infrastructural demolition. Indeed, the extreme difference between these definitions parallels the different affective impacts of such colonial debris on the lives of Indigenous people and settler Canadians, differences that will be further examined in chapter 3, where I discuss the IRS TRC national gatherings.

IRS images may be considered colonial debris in a very physical sense; they are material traces that remain after the long event, some of the visual waste and ruin produced by the IRS. *Fragments of Truth* seeks to reckon with multiple visual and material forms of this debris, but taking the time to examine IRS archival photographs reveals how sifting through this debris can open up important questions about how "colonial meaning-making" takes shape in part through visual representations.[12]

As colonial debris, photographs from the IRS era represent various moments of "contact" between Indigenous and non-Indigenous peoples. Here, contact should not be understood as something that occurred only at the moment of "discovery" but rather as a phenomenon that has structured Indigenous and non-Indigenous interaction throughout time. Mary Louise Pratt has used the term *contact zone* to name "social spaces where disparate cultures meet, clash, and grapple with each other, often in highly asymmetrical relations of domination and subordination—like colonialism, slavery, or their aftermaths as they are lived out across the globe today."[13] Continuing the metaphor of colonial debris, we can understand these photographs as the material traces of the physical and material clashes of contact. Seeing archival photographs from the IRS era as examples of contact zones allows us to better comprehend how these instances of contact were also moments of negotiation, and to think about how such images can be mobilized now as the relations they represent continue to evolve and morph.

My goal in discussing these images is to explore the tensions between the visual subject and object, the relationship between visibility and invisibility, and some of the difficulties that arise when archival documents are called upon to unearth past injustices. On the one hand, photographs of Indigenous peoples and settlers in the Canadian archives were born from the "representational violence" that served "the interests of a colonial settler culture."[14] On the other hand, as I will discuss, the photographs may also help illustrate how Indigenous people and communities have challenged the colonial system and the logic that produced the images.

Before-and-After Images

Chapter 1 examines several iconic images of the settler-Indigenous relationship in Canada. In a similar vein this chapter asks why certain specific images, and types of images, have tended to circulate so frequently as part of the IRS TRC but also in wider media discussions in Canada about indigeneity and the legacy of the IRS schools.

Throughout the course of my research on the IRS system, two images appeared and reappeared. Generally coupled together, they picture a young boy frequently identified as Thomas Moore, who attended Regina Indian Residential School in Saskatchewan in the 1890s (figures 2.3 and 2.4). These images have become iconic representations of the IRS system. They first appeared in the foreword to an 1897 government annual report. Their placement at the beginning of the document served as a powerful visual marker of the goals of government policy. The captions below the photos read "Thomas Moore, as he appeared when admitted to the Regina Indian Industrial School," and "Thomas Moore, after tuition at the Regina Indian Industrial School." No other text accompanied the images.

Like earlier examined photos, these photos rely heavily on tropes of the "savage" and the "civilized." The "before" image shows the young boy with long hair and in traditional dress. In the "after" image, his hair is shorn, and he is dressed in a school uniform. On the left he stands in front of a nondescript background, a nameless landscape. On the right he stands against a

FIGURES 2.3 AND 2.4
Thomas Moore before-
and-after images. The
Department of Indian
Affairs *Annual Report*,
1897. Images courtesy
Provincial Archives of
Saskatchewan.

low structure, casually leaning his hand on his hip. His hair, once long and braided, is now cropped close to his head. In both images, his body stands square in the center, looking directly at the camera. In the before image, he holds a toy gun, perhaps alluding to a lawlessness, a hint of danger, or an untamable violence. In contrast, the after image belies a subtler violence, one that has been enacted through the very act of taming. In the after image, Moore's stance is less confrontational.[15] With a hand on his hip and one leg leisurely crossed over the other, his positioning suggests a sense of ease. But there is nothing casual about the colonial alchemy performed in this photograph.

The power of these images is linked in many ways to the structures that shaped their making. Through processes of modernization and the growth of the modern capitalist state, photographic documentation played an important role in the formation of modern subjects. The camera, far from providing a neutral lens for society, is embedded within certain structures of power, and it exerts control over the time and space of a subject, locking them into one particular pose or role. In other words, entangled within the mechanical nature of the camera is a whole other set of apparatuses, involving the social order of a culture and the state's need for documentation.[16]

Scholar Lonna Malmsheimer has discussed the use of before-and-after images at the Carlisle Indian Industrial School (1879–1918) in the United States, which served as a model for the IRS system in Canada. Malmsheimer draws attention to how observable differences in before-and-after photographs lead to inferences structured by a very particular "cultural grid." This cultural grid helped the viewer to move from "initial interpretive steps to full-blown ideological assumptions."[17] When seeing the images side by side, the viewer is meant to understand that a transformation has occurred: an Indian has been assimilated to conform to standards set by modern society. As such, the images were meant to serve as proof of the power and virtue of the IRS system.

Many moments of "contact" are represented in Moore's before-and-after dyad. The before image gives shape to an imagined idea of indigeneity, to a "precontact" rendering of an Indian child. It represents the ways in which Indigenous peoples have been constructed as a noble yet "uncivilized" group. In contrast, Moore's after image represents another moment of contact, seeming to offer "proof" of the inevitable disappearance of Indigenous cultures and attempting to demonstrate the "civilizing" power of church and state. As Marianne Hirsch and Leo Spitzer write, "The extensive use of before-and-after images in school photos … throughout the world highlights widely shared assumptions about photography's indexicality and the medium's evidentiary ability to display change—or lack of change—from one moment in time to another."[18] In his reading, historian John Milloy draws the viewer's attention to the plant in the after image as an example of this civilizing power: "Elevated above him, [the plant] is the symbol of civilized life, or agriculture. Like Thomas, the plant is cultivated nature no longer wild."[19] The casual stance in the after image also connotes a cultivation of sorts. Moore is portrayed as having grown comfortable with his new role as citizen-subject. Before-and-after images are a promise—they are meant to serve as evidence that a transformation has taken place, and they suggest more to follow.[20]

In recent years these images of Moore have continued to resurface, circulating in multiple and diverse contexts, including as cover illustrations for two contemporary books about the IRS system: John Milloy's *A National Crime: The Canadian Government and the Residential School System, 1879 to 1986* (figure 2.5), and Ward Churchill's *Kill the Indian, Save the Man: The Genocidal Impact of American Indian Residential Schools* (figure 2.6). Interestingly, in both of these cases the original photographs have been manipulated in one way or another. For the cover of *A National Crime* the two separate images of Moore have been melded together at their center, and half of the before image is sutured to half of the after image. The two images have become one. And for *Kill the Indian, Save the Man*, the images remain separate, but inserted between them is an image of an American flag. Although Moore was a student at the Regina Indian Industrial School in Canada, Churchill uses the images to speak to readers about the residential schools in the United States. Thus, this young boy, named Thomas Moore in most of literature, has come to represent not only the Canadian IRS system but the American one as well.

The before-and-after pictures of Moore have also appeared within several books, in newspaper articles, on various websites, and as teaching tools, including as part of the Legacy of Hope Foundation's online teaching module *Where Are the Children?* and the traveling exhibit that accompanied it. Originally the photos spoke to the efficacy of a system designed to "kill the Indian in the child," but in these more recent circulations the images are taken up in ways that allow them to speak to the violence of that system.[21] In *Where Are the Children?*, for instance, curator Jeff Thomas wanted to go beyond simply showing institutional images as part of the exhibit, so he attempted to give the former students depicted in the photos more of a voice. "What was life like for Thomas Moore? Imagine the world from his

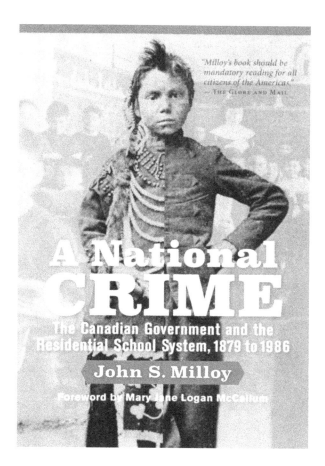

FIGURE 2.5 *A National Crime*, by John S. Milloy.

perspective," asks the text on the website. And with a click of the mouse, visitors can hear what Moore might have thought when he first saw the Regina Indian Industrial School:

My people have always lived here. My father and grandfather have hunted on this land for as long as I can remember. But now a new thunder shakes the ground, a train that has driven the great buffalo herds away, and white men have come to tell my family we have to move to a "reserve" far away from the land of our ancestors. Men called "Indian Agents" are everywhere. They tell us what to do and call us "savages"—even the elders. They will not let us have our ceremonies. Those who disobey are put in jail. My mother tells me that I will be going to school far away and that I will live there until next summer. She says that I must learn the language

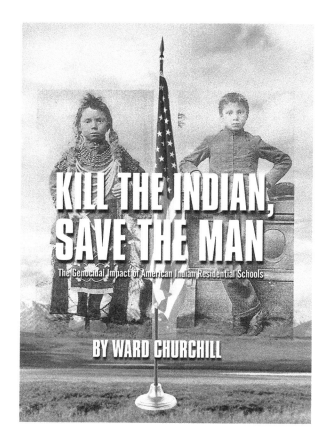

FIGURE 2.6 *Kill the Indian, Save the Man*, by Ward Churchill. Image courtesy City Lights Publishers.

and ways of the white man—so that I can understand them and help our people. I have many questions about the school, but my mother tells me only to be brave, to watch and listen, and to remember my people. I know that my mother is worried. She does not trust the Indian Agents.[22]

In this imagined text, Moore's story represents the amalgamation of many narratives from survivors who have told of Indian agents taking them away, of the destruction of their land and livelihoods, and of the feeling of insurmountable distance that separated them from their homes. In this way, Moore is made to stand in for the "average Indian" who attended the schools.

The two images of Moore are the most recognizable and reprinted example of a before-and-after dyad from the IRS system, but other images circulate as well. Animated by a similar logic, in these images the carefully orchestrated backdrops are gone, and the focus is often on two or more students. The "traditional" dress in the "before" image is replaced with more common clothing of the time: shirts and pants for boys, dresses or blouses and skirts for girls. The after images show students neatly arranged in rows, often posing with priests or staff from the schools. For instance, figure 2.7 is from the scrapbook of Reverend Arthur Henry Sovereign. In handwritten script above the respective images one can read the captions: "Before" and "After." The text beside the before image states, "On the reserve." Beside the after image, it says, "In School." The names of the children have not been included. The children in the first photograph (taken in 1916) appear stoic. An older woman stands behind them, peering at the camera, watching over the children. In the second image (figure 2.8, taken in 1918), the two children are smiling. Behind them, one can see the structured space of a dormitory.

Before-and-after images were also used by the church as an ideological tool to justify their work at the schools and to recruit new staff. Figure 2.9 is an example of an Anglican pamphlet that was likely distributed during religious services. The before-and-after images within these documents were used as evidence of the efficacy of the schools. Calls to action would be less effective without this visible proof. As the pamphlet implores the reader, "Help these children... to become... like these," with illustrations of hands pointing toward the two images. The pamphlet is faded now, but the larger photograph, positioned above the other, appears to show three children (two girls and a boy) standing with a priest. The children seem to be in good health, with no signs of malnutrition or abuse. It is difficult to discern whether the children in this top image are also pictured in the one below, but that seems to be beside the point. The children in the top photograph are meant to stand in for Indigenous children in general. The image positioned at the bottom of the pamphlet is meant to represent their potential: to become assimilated members of Canadian society, absorbed into the body politic.[23]

The children in the after image of the Anglican pamphlet stand arranged in several rows. Their hands are clasped in front of them or hang by their sides. The orderliness of the arrangement is juxtaposed against the untucked appearance of the children in the photo at the top of the page. No specific details are given about who the children are, about when the two images were taken, or about how much time had elapsed between the two photos. Inside the pamphlet the text reads "Nearly two thousand Indian and Eskimo boys and girls are placed in Residential Schools under Anglican direction. Many of them are in serious physical need when they arrive, far below normal weight and plainly showing the ill effects of malnutrition. They need much loving

FIGURES 2.7 AND 2.8 Before-and-after images on display at the Inuvik Truth and Reconciliation Commission national event. Images from Reverend Arthur Henry Sovereign's scrapbook. Original caption: "Students before and after, on the Reserve and in School, 1922–1931." Images courtesy the General Synod Archives, Anglican Church of Canada. M2006-08, 688–89.

ANGLICAN ADVANCE
FOR OUR NATIVE CANADIANS

**HELP THESE
CHILDREN**
☞

TO BECOME

ANGLICAN CHURCH OF CANADA
GENERAL SYNOD ARCHIVES

LIKE THESE
☞

FIGURE 2.9 An Anglican Church pamphlet, circa 1940. Image courtesy the General Synod Archives, Anglican Church of Canada. 6575-103, box 137 9-14.13.

care by earnest Christian men and women to enable them to build healthy bodies and develop in mind and spirit also."[24] The text reveals the paternal undertones of the assimilationist project, suggesting that Indigenous parents were incapable of taking care of their own children. The photos are used as visual proof of the "good work" done at the schools, conveying something that mere text would be unable to communicate.

Another Anglican Church pamphlet (figure 2.10) asks "What of the Indian's future?" The church then answers its own question: "The Canadian government is concerned that he be equipped physically and mentally to take his place beside other citizens of this Dominion, and on equal terms. To this end it has provided education, medical services, baby bonuses, old age pensions and other benefits, as for its other citizens."[25] This text is accompanied by an illustrated version of a before-and-after dyad, where an

The Indian looks to the Future
... and to his Church!

Events of the twentieth century and the northward movement of civilization have forced many Canadian Indians to make a rapid transition from their primitive mode of life to that of the complex mechanized civilization of today.

There are now Indians in all walks of life from the primitive trapper to the highly skilled technician and the learned professional man. But in the north country where the wild game is no longer procurable on the former scale, many Indians have had to leave their traplines and seek work among the white men. For life in these busy communities they have no preparation. Those qualities once considered part of the Indian character—manly strength, dignity and integrity—need to be acquired again.

What of the Indian's future? The Canadian Government is concerned that he be equipped physically and mentally to take his place beside other citizens of this Dominion, and on equal terms. To this end it has provided education, medical services, baby bonuses, old age pensions and other benefits, as for its other citizens. But the fullest life is also spiritual. It is therefore the Churches' obligation and privilege to provide the spiritual nurture and the opportunities for worship which will develop a firm foundation of faith for life at its best.

FIGURE 2.10 An illustrated before-and-after image from an Anglican Church pamphlet, circa 1949. Image courtesy the General Synod Archives, Anglican Church of Canada. 6575-104, box 137 9-14.13.

idealized, noble Indian is turned into a manual laborer. Like other versions of the savage/modern trope, this stylized version of the before-and-after image relies on several stereotypes, particularly that of the noble Indian. In the before image, the man is bare-chested and is holding a traditional tool of some sort, perhaps a bow or a tool for hunting. In the after image, he wears overalls and work gloves, and he wields a tool of a different sort. His feather and braids have been transformed into a hard hat. The two versions of the same man are framed by totem poles on either side. The totem pole, a symbol of Indigenous cultures, gestures toward the aspects of Native culture that were deemed acceptable.[26]

Such dyads represent the colonial alchemy attempted by the government and churches in Canada. They reveal both a vow of transformation and a commitment to a process of erasure, even when they evince sentimentality about the past. For instance, Moore's portraits were obviously taken in a studio and were clearly staged, although the extent of this staging is less clear. It is highly unlikely that the young boy named Moore arrived at the Regina IRS in the 1890s donning the outfit featured in the before image. Indeed, sources from the nineteenth century show that many Indigenous people were already dressing in Western-style clothing at this time. For example, writing for the *Christian Guardian* in 1837, the missionary George Henry described how the "Indians" he met were "well-dressed" and "becoming civilized": "Yes, Mr. Papermaker, if you had seen these Indians a few years ago, you would think they were the animals you called Ourang Outangs, for they appeared more like them than human beings; but since the Great Spirit has blessed them, they have good clothes; plates and dishes; window and bed curtains; knives and forks; chairs and tables."[27] Writing in 1899, poet Charles Mair claimed that the "Indians" he encountered were

> respectable-looking men, as well dressed and evidently quite as inde-
> pendent in their feelings as any like number of average pioneers in the
> West.... One was prepared, in this wild region of forest, to behold some
> savage types of men; indeed, I braced to renew the vanished scenes of
> old. But alas! One beheld, instead, men with well-washed unpainted
> faces, and combed and common hair; men in suits of ordinary store-
> clothes, and even some with "boiled" if not laundered shirts. One felt
> disappointed, even defrauded.[28]

And in 1906, Manitoba Methodist T. Ferrier wrote that "in all my travels this year I have not seen an Indian man dressed according to their old Indian customs."[29] These reflections from the nineteenth century and early twentieth century suggest that the before image of Moore was, among other things, a very carefully curated moment of contact.[30]

The kind of disappointment noted by Mair at the disappearance of traditional dress was not unique to the poet, and it frequently manifested as nostalgia for the "noble savage." In some cases this nostalgia prompted non-Indigenous Canadians to dress up and participate in the practice of "playing Indian."[31] Dressing up in traditional Indigenous garb was not uncommon at the turn of the century. In both Canada and United States, settlers donned headdresses and "war paint," sometimes in an effort to make political statements but also to act out colonial fantasies. Writing about the practice in the United States, Philip Deloria explains, "Playing Indian is a persistent tradition in American culture, stretching from the very instant of the national big bang into an ever-expanding present and future."[32] Deloria traces this history in the US from the Boston Tea Party to the present day, proposing that ideas about nationhood in the US tend to simultaneously position Native Americans at both the center and the margins of national identity, revealing a vexed and dialectical relationship between settler identity and indigeneity. These ideas resonate deeply with the Canadian context.

FIGURE 2.11 Hayter Reed, deputy superintendent general of Indian Affairs, and his stepson, Jack Lowery, dressed in Indian costumes for a historical ball on Parliament Hill. Image courtesy Library and Archives Canada/ Topley Studio fonds/a139841.

In the same year that the images of Moore first appeared in the *Department of Indian Affairs Annual Report*, Hayter Reed, deputy superintendent general of Indian Affairs, and his stepson, Jack Lowery, were photographed wearing Indian costumes for a historical ball on Parliament Hill (figure 2.11). Like the young boy named Moore, the father-and-son duo also stand against a staged backdrop. Fake grass and a large rock set the scene for their Plains Indian costumes. Reed's stepson looks straight at the camera and, like Moore, is unsmiling (a common convention of portraiture at the time). Reed is turned away from the camera, staring off into the distance. The image of Reed and his stepson illustrates that moments of "contact" could be arranged and represented even as Indigenous peoples were absent, producing a very particular form of cultural alienation that has its own unique logic and harms.

It is worth noting that, as deputy superintendent general of Indian Affairs, Reed was responsible for some of the most restrictive policies against Indigenous peoples. In 1885 he wrote "The Memorandum on the Future Management of Indians," which focused on restricting Native peoples' right and ability to move freely (with the pass system), ability to sell goods (with the permit system), and other restrictions. While working among Native populations in Saskatchewan, he accumulated a large collection of cultural dress and objects. In the photo, Reed is dressed as Iroquois chief Donnacona. But in his portrayal of the chief, he mixes items from different Native cultures "indiscriminately."[33] On the surface, the image may suggest an appreciation of sorts, however misguided, of Indigenous culture. But in reality, Reed was known for his harsh policies against Indigenous people, which ultimately gave rise to his nickname, "Iron Heart."[34]

All of these images demonstrate that visuality played a central role in imaginings of both indigeneity and Canadianness. Writing about the effects of before-and-after images, Rayna Green (Cherokee) has written that "as Native people, we're grateful for the romantic 'before' portraits of what we were like when the bad guys came and mucked it all up, and then we feel worse when we learn how badly they've tricked us, given us illusions, dreams of a past we can't get back. The Age of the Golden Tipi. Then we also hate these 'after' pictures where they've made us just like them."[35]

Before-and-after images must be understood as prescriptive. The after image prescribes a future—in this case, a modern Canadian subject—and the before image prescribes a past—in this case, a memory of and for Indigenous people, a memory that could be contained by colonial power and a memory that was already nostalgic for the "picturesque Red Man."[36] In this way, colonial regimes of representation worked both to erase Native cultures (by falsely representing them) and to project them into a state-mandated future, where members of various Indigenous nations were to become compliant subjects of the Canadian state.

Until the Records Disappear

Over the course of my research, the images of the young boy named Thomas Moore raised myriad questions for me. Some were about the system that produced the photographs: Who commissioned the images? Who stands outside the picture, or, phrased differently, who controls the gaze of the camera? Who decided how the portrait would be styled and composed, with the toy gun, the plant, and the casually posed stance? Other questions were about the young boy himself: Where was he from? What happened to him after he left the IRS system? Was Thomas Moore really his name? After all, it was common practice at the schools to strip Indigenous students of their given names and call them by a new name or, in some cases, just a number.

Throughout my research, I attempted to find out more about Moore. I sought out information about where he went after his time at Regina Indian Industrial School and, whenever possible, about his life prior to arriving there. In one email exchange I was told that although the government report from 1897 identified him as Thomas Moore, his school records list his full name as Thomas Moore Kusick.[37] That seemed like a promising lead at the time, as my research progressed, but it quickly became clear to me that very little was actually known about this figure or about what might have happened to him. It also became clear that if I was going to find more information, it would probably not come from the archives.[38] From what I could ascertain, the original images of Moore are nowhere to be found. Only reproductions are available, different versions based on the 1897 report. An exchange from 2010 with an archivist at the Saskatchewan Archives board is representative of the fragmented nature of the information available:

> Thank you for your enquiry. Yes, the two photos are probably some of our most popular images. No, we do not have the original photos. They were copied from the Canada *Sessional Papers*, No. 14, Volume XXXI, No. 11 (1897). This Department of Indian Affairs Report was for the year ending at June 30, 1896. The photos would have been taken before that date.
>
> The only information we have on Thomas Moore comes from the student register for the Regina Indian Industrial School, 1891 to 1908 (microfilm R-2.40, see entry No. 22). He was actually admitted to the school on August 26, 1891 when he was 8 years old. He was a full blooded Indian from the Saulteaux tribe. He was from the Muscowpetung Band which is about 35 miles northeast of Regina. His full name was Thomas Moore Kusick. His father was St. (?) Paul Desjarlais (deceased) and his mother's name was Hanna Moore Kusick. The boy was a Protestant and had previously attended Lakes End School. His state of education upon admission consisted of knowing the alphabet. His height was 3 feet, 11 inches and he weighed 54 ½ pounds. There is a note in the admission register that directs one to look for page 20 in the Discharge Register. However, we do not have this document and therefore we do not know when he completed his education.[39]

The school closed in 1910 and became the Regina City Jail and then a boys detention house. In 1948 it burned to the ground. In 2012 investigations into a cemetery that remained near the site of the school were undertaken by the TRC.[40]

The young boy's discharge register, referred to by the archivist, appears to have been lost. But in 2015 Ocean Man First Nation filmmaker Louise BigEagle also sought to uncover a deeper understanding of the living history behind these images. Through her research, BigEagle discovered that the boy's full name was Thomas Moore Keesick and that he was enrolled in the school with two siblings, Julia and Samuel, on August 26, 1891.[41] BigEagle tells viewers that Moore Keesick was given the institutional identification "Number 22" and was frequently referred to by number rather than his name. After four years at the Regina school, Moore Keesick was sent home to his community with an illness, which was believed to be tuberculosis. There he died shortly after he reached the age of twelve. His sister, Julia, also died as a child. BigEagle's description of Moore Keesick's short life at the residential school contrasts powerfully with the "after image" of the boy. The dyad offers an imagined outcome of assimilation, but the prescribed future of "Thomas Moore" in the "after" picture used by the government differs drastically from the reality of Thomas Moore Keesick's lived experience.[42]

The challenges involved in learning more about Moore Keesick's life and experience are not uncommon. Records from the various schools are often hard to find. Many of the schools didn't keep their records or lost them. Basic facts and numbers, such as how many students attended the schools and how much funding the system received, are still disputed. Although the general number of students who attended the schools is approximated at 150,000, the records were so poorly kept that this is difficult to confirm, creating much difficulty for former students who rely on that information in order for them to be acknowledged under the IRS TRC compensation package. Many former students, family members, journalists, and researchers have written about the problems they have encountered when pursuing documentation about former residential school students, and about the difficulties they have faced in finding the paperwork necessary to process claims for former students. The amount of documentation in the IRS archives is both overwhelming and insufficient. One is often left pursuing the documents "until the records disappear," as one journalist wrote in reference to Uta Fox's work on the Red Deer Industrial School in Alberta. Fox was a graduate student at the University of Calgary when her research on Red Deer Industrial School—which ran from 1893 to 1919—led her to the discovery that the school's records simply ceased to exist after 1916.[43]

There is nothing clear-cut about such disappearances. They might be explained by carelessness or by deliberate obfuscation. Often, the accessible archival records chart out the mundane details of everyday administration:

deliveries, salaries, and supplies needed.[44] In contrast, details that pertain to the biographies or whereabouts of IRS students are rarely available. The lack of information about Moore Keesick and other students serves as a reminder that the gaps found in archives are not simply absences, but active erasures, evidence of a silencing of the past.[45]

"There is no political power without control of the archive," writes Jacques Derrida.[46] Archives can be seen as a foundation, the establishment of authority. In *Archive Fever*, Derrida discusses the connection between the archive and beginnings. He notes that the word *archive* is a derivative of *arkhe*, which communicates a sense of both commencement and commandment, of beginnings and authority. In Canada, as elsewhere, the national archives were built as part of a system of governance. In 1871 Henry H. Miles wrote about the need for more centralized and accessible archives in Canada. He described them as "records of facts and events which are of a more important and public character."[47] But archives do more than house such records; they also work to define what is "important" and what should be considered of "public character." Built in 1872, the Canadian national archives have been referred to as a "memory institution," and they are often taken to be the basis of a national collective memory.[48] As archivist Jean-Pierre Wallot has written,

> The National Archives of Canada collects, organizes, preserves and makes accessible a large variety of documents of national importance in all types of media. These efforts are aimed at transmitting from generation to generation the collective memory of Canadians, the value of which grows with each passing day. Without this memory, which translates into a common destiny the organic layers of the past, no awareness of our identity and destiny would be possible. The nation would drift like a ship without a compass, with the crew focusing on its immediate interests ignorant of each other's rights and of past experiences that could have shaped a dynamic community and guided it on its way.[49]

According to Wallot, the national archive is a key component in creating "a common destiny," demonstrating the link between the past and the future in issues of national identity.

Almost a century and a half after the archives' founding, many people still consider them a national treasure, one that comprises "the basis for memory, continuity, and social order" and "the very foundation of civil order."[50] But, as noted by Isabel McBryde, the past is possessed by those in power.[51] The governing body that dictates what gets documented, reproduced, and disseminated can control its own image; it has the power to shape collective memory and in turn shape the image of a collective future. In this way, sovereignty is "the power that archives."[52] The national archives can be thought of as the seat of that power, a fact that has prompted many Indigenous peoples—who are well documented in the archives but without much of their own input—to feel as if they are "captives" of the institution.[53]

The images of Thomas Moore Keesick are not simply evidence of the destructive impulse of the residential school system (although they have been read that way by many scholars and in the popular press); they also create an opening for a discussion about the limits of archival knowledge and about the role of visual culture in constructing ideas of indigeneity and national citizen-subjects. In many ways, Moore Keesick's photos were the motivation for this research. The young boy looked at me as I sat at my desk, as I pored over research and spoke to artists, archivists, and former students involved in the reconciliation process. I felt that the only way I could look back at him was to try to find out more about the system that shaped and transformed his reality so profoundly, that constructed these images of his "reality."

In trying to understand this exchange of looks, I was brought back to Ariella Azoulay's work on the role that she believes photography should play in the Israel/Palestine conflict. An Israeli scholar, Azoulay uses photographs to "rethink the civic space of the gaze and our interrelations within it." For her the photographic image is not only a trace of the historical context in which it was taken; it also gestures toward a duty that we have in the present, to continue engaging with the subjects in the photo. This "complex fabric of relations" began to make itself manifest to me through Moore Keesick's image.[54] But where Azoulay asked "Why is he looking at me?" I wanted to know "Why am I looking at him?" By phrasing the question in this way, the labor of interpretation fell on me, the viewer, and I was more urgently implicated in the relations of looking that were established between us.

By framing reconciliation as a way of seeing, I want to shift the question once more, now asking, "Why have I been looking *to* Thomas Moore Keesick?" And this is my tentative response: I have looked to Moore Keesick because his images speak to me about much more than absences in the archives or Canada's history of assimilation. The ubiquity of these images, coupled with the lack of information about this young boy, is a beckoning or, even more, a call to account for my role in the intergenerational legacy of the schools. Moore Keesick's images beckon to different pathways of knowledge, to profound shifts in how we understand the construction of historical and visual narratives. Azoulay discusses the importance of what she calls the act of "watching" photographs. She explains:

> One needs to stop looking at the photograph and instead start watching it. The verb "to watch" is usually used for regarding phenomena or moving pictures. It entails dimensions of time and movement that need to be reinscribed in the interpretation of the still photographic image. When and where the subject of the photograph is a person who has suffered some form of injury, a viewing of the photograph that reconstructs the photographic situation and allows a reading of the injury inflicted on others becomes a civic skill, not an exercise in aesthetic appreciation.[55]

Developing new ways of seeing can become "a civic skill," and "watching" Moore Keesick in these photos should therefore require an acknowledgment of and engagement with the injuries inflicted upon him, as well as the thousands of Indigenous children who attended the schools. In this way, engaging with the IRS visual archive should allow for the excavation of new ways of reading and understanding the politics and histories both implied and denied in the images themselves.

Moore Keesick's images continue to be watched, and they continue to draw attention to the contact zones of both colonialism and reconciliation. In 2010–2011, his image was on display at the Royal Ontario Museum in Toronto as part of Jane Ash Poitras's (Cree) *Potato Peeling 101 to Ethnobotany 101* (figures 2.12 and 2.13). A large mixed-media piece, the work focused on how Indigenous knowledge has been both incorporated into and effaced by Western culture. The images of Moore Keesick, along with other archival photographs, were used to represent the complicated intersections of Indigenous knowledge and Western education. In the piece, Poitras used archival imagery to represent the violence of the IRS system, but she also reframed the selected photographs "within her own larger frame," a "decolonial framework."[56] Images from the colonial classroom were thus mobilized to critique Western institutions and to interrogate Western concepts of education and civilization in relation to the colonial context.

Using a blackboard as the backdrop for the piece, Poitras sought to reclaim the "familiar image of schoolrooms" and transform it "into a representational strategy of her own teaching."[57] A small desk sat in the middle of the room, facing the blackboards. The desk was too small for an adult, making it clear that the intended subject for the lesson was a child. It was as if visitors were invited to imagine themselves as young people being confronted with a representation of culture and history that was difficult to decipher. Poitras

FIGURE 2.12 Jane Ash Poitras's *Potato Peeling 101 to Ethnobotany 101* at the Royal Ontario Museum. Photo by Naomi Angel.

FIGURE 2.13 Close-up of Thomas Moore's images in Jane Ash Poitras's work at the Royal Ontario Museum. Photo by Naomi Angel.

has described this work as a "decolonizing visual text," where colonial visions were deconstructed and put together again from a different perspective.[58] Her work is just one example of how Indigenous artists have worked to reframe colonial imagery, including photos from the IRS image archive.[59] Through her work the significance of Moore Keesick's images was transformed yet again, and rather than being seen as evidence of his victimhood at the hands of the IRS system, the images were mobilized and reframed as part of a powerful critique of empire.

The Archive and Its Afterlives

Like Poitras, many Indigenous artists have taken up archival images in order to renegotiate their meanings. Former students of the residential school system have also turned their attention to the images from the schools, suggesting that these photographs have an afterlife outside of the archives. In her discussion of cultural memory in Chile, Macarena Gómez-Barris discusses the use of two related terms: *aftermath* and *afterlife*. She uses *aftermath* to describe the "political economic legacies" of state-sanctioned violence and *afterlife* to signal "the persistent symbolic and material effects" of this violence.[60] The aftermath and the afterlife of violence help to set the stage for an ongoing entanglement between the past and the present. It is my contention that the archive also has an aftermath and an afterlife, and that the political nature and the symbolic nature of archives make them a productive space for examining the social relationships they represent. Thomas Moore Keesick's images are one example of this phenomenon, but I turn now toward the afterlife of an altogether different kind of photograph. I have chosen this image not because it stands as extraordinary but rather because of its ordinariness, because it both leaves me searching for speech yet calls for a cascade of words. I have chosen it because it reveals traces of the familiar and the uncanny, and because it speaks to the dialectical relationship between the everyday and the spectacular.

The image (figure 2.14) was taken at Fort Simpson Indian Residential School in 1922 and is now housed at the National Archives in Ottawa. Although photographs and documents from the schools are scattered across the country in smaller archives (church, municipal, and school archives) and personal collections, the National Archives houses the largest collection of materials related to the Indian residential school system. In the photograph, two girls and five boys stand in a row, spelling out "Goodbye." In top hats and dresses, the children look prepared for an event. Perhaps they are

FIGURE 2.14 First Nation children holding letters that spell "Goodbye" at Fort Simpson Indian Residential School. Original title: "Indian children holding letters that spell 'Goodbye' at Fort Simpson Indian Residential School." Source: Library and Archives Canada/Department of Indian Affairs and Northern Development fonds/a102575.

putting on a play or attending a graduation ceremony at the school. Over the course of my research, I came to call this picture "the long goodbye." The boy second from the left is turned away from the camera. The letter "o" hangs low in his hands as he moves toward the door of the building. This movement disrupts the "goodbye," prolonging and delaying a farewell, drawing out its conclusion. By capturing a seemingly innocuous moment of children dressed for a celebration of sorts, the photograph reminds us of the everydayness of the oppression inflicted by the IRS system.

If, as Roland Barthes writes, "Photography is subversive not when it frightens, repels or even stigmatizes, but when it is pensive, when it thinks," this image allows for that thoughtful moment. It asks us to look closer, and when we look away, it stays with us. For Barthes, photographs attain meaning through the studium and the punctum. The studium is the cultural meaning of a photograph. It is "of the order of liking, not of loving; it mobilizes a half desire, a demi-volition; it is the same sort of vague slippery, irresponsible interest one takes in the people, the entertainments, the books, the clothes one finds 'all right.'" The studium involves the intent of the author. However, the punctum is an accident. It disturbs. It is a wound, and it bruises.[61] It is often a detail, perhaps not noticed at first. As I look at this photo, I first assume that it is the boy with the letter "o" that is the punctum, that thing that wounds, that leaves its mark on me, the viewer of the image. But with another look, my eye is drawn to the boy who stands third from the right, the only boy without a top hat, the only boy who looks directly at the camera. He holds the "b" in "goodbye." His direct gaze back at the camera, unsmiling, seems to span the time between the moment of the photograph's taking and the moment of its viewing.

Elizabeth Edwards characterizes the photographic image as an "ongoing entanglement," part of a larger project that engages "multiple histories and thus multiple trajectories."[62] The photographic image, in other words, signifies without end. "The long goodbye," for instance, may be read in relation to the myth of the "vanishing Indian." This is a theory that was widely believed by colonists at the turn of the century, when settlers assumed that the Indians would die off, be bred out, or for whatever reason not survive late into the twentieth century. The myth was so deeply ingrained in the dominant culture that Indigenous communities felt its reverberations too. As actress/activist Tantoo Cardinal (Cree-Métis) has said, "I remember feeling that to be Indian was to be a part of the past. There was no future for us."[63]

Indoctrination into this belief ran deep at the schools. Students could neither recognize themselves in the mythical Hollywood Indians portrayed on screen nor see a way out of the systemic forms of violence and devastation that were taking place in their communities. "The long goodbye" captures a moment in Canadian history when the myth of the "vanishing Indian" was not simply a Hollywood fantasy; policies of forced assimilation predicted its success. In Avery Gordon's work on haunting in the sociological imagination, she explores the role of apparitions and shadowy manifestations from the past in the construction of the present: "Haunting recognition is a special way of knowing what has happened or is happening."[64] The myth of the vanishing Indian is powerful not when the Indian *vanishes* but because the figure is always and forever *vanishing*. Images like "the long goodbye" capture this haunting recognition. The image is a visual representation of both the myth of the vanishing Indian and of its disruption, for both the child who turns away and the child who gazes back at the camera work to unsettle the assimilationist narrative. In this way, the photo can certainly be seen to document the system's push toward assimilation, but it also represents Indigenous resistance and persistence.[65]

Like "the long goodbye," many images from the IRS archive capture moments that could also be found in personal photo albums: pictures of classrooms, school plays, and sports teams. In fact, photo albums are part of the IRS archive, and they took up a significant amount of space at TRC national events, where tables were set up for survivors to look through church and National Archive scrapbooks. Often very thoughtfully prepared, the worn pages of these albums frequently contained carefully placed photos and handwritten captions, pointing toward some of the intimate relationships engendered through this colonial system.

"Matters of the intimate are critical sites for the consolidation of colonial power," Ann Stoler writes.[66] By managing relationships between parent and child, brother and sister, as well as extended family and community relations, residential schools became sites for the regulation and surveillance of the intimate, for the exertion and "consolidation" of colonial power. It is important to remember that images like "the long goodbye" are not simply photographs that capture a singular moment in time; they also help to form a picture of the system as a whole. As Hirsch and Spitzer note, the school photographer's camera is a form of technology, one that helps to socialize and integrate children into a dominant worldview. Hirsch and Spitzer continue: "By staging the school's, and the society's, institutional gaze, class photos both record and practice the creation of consent."[67] The institutional gaze that pervades the IRS image archive extends itself through these photographs as they make their way through state archives, but the afterlife of these images does not end with the archive.

Reconciling the Archive

In the context of reconciliation, images from the IRS system have started to circulate in novel ways, and new pathways of looking have begun to form. From June 28 to July 1, 2011, the IRS TRC hosted a national gathering in Inuvik, Northwest Territories. At the event, former students were given the opportunity to share their stories through many means, including artwork, dance, song, and the giving of testimony. It is estimated that a thousand survivors attended the event, traveling by boat, car, and plane to the small town of Inuvik (population 3,500). The days of the national gathering were very long. In the summer months in Inuvik, the sun does not set. In the evenings, under the brightly shining sun, the activities moved outside. In comparison to the intense emotions of the days of testimony, the evenings focused on song, dance, and entertainment that often went late into the night. The national gatherings will be discussed in more depth in chapter 3,

FIGURE 2.15 Survivors look through archival images at the Catholic church area in Inuvik. Photo by Naomi Angel.

but for the purposes of this chapter I would like to explore the role that archival images played at these events.

At the Inuvik national gathering, several state and church archives sent binders full of photographs taken at the schools. As former students of the schools looked through the binders in an effort to identify themselves, friends, or loved ones, the institutional gaze of the colonial state was negotiated and challenged (figure 2.15). The images, while still representing colonial vision, were also able to speak to more personal and intimate relationships. When a former student recognized a family member or friend, the archivist made a copy of the photograph. The original remains with the archive, but its copies now move through new, more personal pathways. Having journeyed through personal collections to the shelves of archives and back again, these images carry both residues of the past and the promise of new meanings along with them. Representative not only of years of oppression in the schools, they can also signal the resilience and strength of Indigenous people in spearheading the reconciliation process. No longer a trace of a forgotten, unnamed past, the images and the subjects in them can be firmly rooted in a present.

"The long goodbye" was one of the hundreds of images contained within the large black binders brought to Inuvik by the Catholic Church. Unfortunately, no former students have identified any of the children in the image. The lack of knowledge surrounding their identities marks a profound absence. "Modern memory is, above all, archival," writes Pierre Nora. "It relies entirely on the materiality of the trace, the immediacy of the recording, the visibility of the image."[68] Perhaps. But one must also recognize that the archive can tell us only so much because "the production of traces is always also the creation of silences."[69] Although the IRS TRC called for an end to such silences, "the long goodbye" reminds us that silence is also a part of this history. Far from representing a static image, the photo illustrates that the archive must be read as an ongoing negotiation of past, present, and future. According to Derrida, "The archive: if we want to know what that will have meant, we will only know in times to come."[70]

In some ways "the long goodbye" may be the photographic equivalent of Sigmund Freud's concept of "screen memories." According to Freud, screen memories are seemingly innocent recollections of childhood. Often vividly remembered vignettes of everyday activities, they mask a more traumatic memory that remains repressed below the surface. In these memories, "what is important is suppressed and what is indifferent retained." The screen memory acts as a substitute to protect the individual from the traumatic past: "A wealth of meaning lies behind their apparent innocence."[71] On the individual level, screen memories allow people to continue on with their lives after experiencing an emotional wound. "The long goodbye" may act as such a memory stand-in, masking the brutality of the schools with an image of the everyday. Indeed, Lorenzo Veracini writes about the importance of settler "screen memories" that mask the violence of settler invasion with narratives of settler belonging and national cohesion.[72] But it is also important to note that screen memories can be subverted. In writing about Indigenous media, Faye Ginsburg inverts the term and introduces the concept of *memory screens*: "Here I invert the sense in which Freud used this term to describe how people protect themselves from their traumatic past through layers of obfuscating memory. By contrast, Indigenous people are using screen media not to mask but to recuperate their own collective stories and histories—some of them traumatic—that have been erased in the national narratives of the dominant culture and are in danger of being forgotten within local worlds as well."[73] In contrast to Freud's concept of a screen memory, which suppresses the recollection of the past, memory screens are a restoration of that past.

FIGURE 2.16 Photographs from old school yearbooks (from the Mossie Moorby Collection at the Anglican Archives). Photo by Naomi Angel.

Ginsburg illustrates that many kinds of screen media—including those mediated through the lens of a camera, such as photography—can be used by Indigenous subjects to tell or show histories through their own eyes. And through this process, erasures and absences can be resurrected and reversed.

At the national gatherings and elsewhere, former students have taken up this task with regard to the IRS image archive.[74] In Inuvik, for instance, the Anglican archives had set up photographs from the schools on large black partitions (figure 2.16). Former students noticed that some of the names on these partitions were misspelled or incorrect, so they began to use Post-It Notes to fill in the missing information. In some cases the notes indicated the fate of certain students. One note told of a student who had drowned not long after leaving school; another added that Edna Pigalak had gone on to become the commissioner of Nunavut.

The practice of leaving Post-It Notes gestures toward an ongoing engagement with these school photos. It also evokes something of a temporal relationship with the images, a sort of "post-ness." The terms *postcolonialism*, *postmodernism*, and *postmemory* all reference a temporal and theoretical sense of an "after." These Post-Its propel these images into an ever-evolving afterlife. As impermanent markers, they also gesture toward the mutability and transient nature of the knowledge involved in reading the images.[75]

The Digital Archive

As archives begin to digitize their holdings, their authority, commands, and constraints shift. Digitizing can help survivors, community members, researchers, and others access documents from across geographical borders, but the process also restructures and delimits how the archive is organized. In her work on photographs of Indigenous and non-Indigenous families from Canada taken during the early 1900s, Julia Emberley explores the novel techniques of framing that have emerged along with digital archives, questioning how such technologies "reframe or limit" how those images will be read. In recent years, many archives have started to digitize their collections. Emberley found that when archival images went online, they were not only digitized; they were also reframed and embedded within different logics.[76]

Indeed, in some cases even the image itself changes during the process of digitization. For instance, in 1983 a series of photographs from the Saint Paul Indian Residential School were given to the North Vancouver archives. Several of these images have since been uploaded to the institution's online database, making electronic versions easily accessible. A keyword search for the IRS in North Vancouver brings up a number of images, one of which shows the school basketball team. At first, the image appears somewhat unremarkable in that it resembles many team photos. The boys are dressed in shorts, tank tops, and sneakers. A boy kneels in front with a basketball that reads "Saint Paul's 1940." Their shirts read "INDIANS." The bold writing can be read as both a strange form of branding or a statement of misrecognition. The word *Indians* is likely the name of the basketball team. But it can be read differently as well. The IRS system, a powerful tool of assimilation, not only tried to get rid of the "Indian problem"; it also helped to create ideas of "Indianness." In other words, the system not only assimilated; it defined as well.

The online version of the image shows eleven boys in the picture (see figures 2.17 and 2.18). But a visit to the archives reveals that the actual image has been torn. In the last row a careful tear has been made to the image. The hole created by the tear is large enough to imagine that a person once stood there. The online version shows that the tear has been replaced, covered up. The brick wall background has filled in the absence. This masked absence invites speculation. Perhaps the coach of the team, a teacher, or another player stood there. Perhaps it was torn to remove a painful memory. Or perhaps the person missing was taken from the image to be placed in a wallet or frame, cherished. Or, of course, perhaps the tear is simply that, a tear.

FIGURE 2.17 St. Paul's basketball team (digitized image).

FIGURE 2.18 St. Paul's basketball team (original image), 1948. North Vancouver Museum & Archives, #4795.

When I mentioned the discrepancy in the online and offline versions of the two images, the archivist expressed shock. "Whoever scanned that image must have filled in the tear. But we always remind our staff not to change anything about the images when they are scanned." I read the tear not only as a representation of the many "yawning gulfs in the archives" but also as a reminder that reading fragments can lead to more fragments.[77] "Photographs are fragments of stories," writes Hirsch, "never stories themselves."[78] The digitization of archival images participates in the creation and telling of these stories but also in their fragmentation.

Digitization plays a role in "redefining the key features of the photographic object," and it has implications for both technological and cultural understandings of both photography and the archive.[79] Joan Schwartz has written about the power that archivists have in selecting and describing images for digitization: "Both inspiration and information are lost when interaction with the artifact itself is achieved through a digital surrogate."[80] In her work, Schwartz draws attention to the materiality of the image and to the interactions that this materiality can engender. As in the case of the St. Paul basketball photograph, a digital surrogate can misrepresent the original, but in doing so it may also draw attention to how the very idea of "an original" is problematic—for the original is also and already a fragment.

Not long after seeing these twin images, I spoke to a representative of the Squamish Nation in North Vancouver who had donated the original image. He/she asked not to be named and asked instead to be referred to as an "Educator" at Squamish Nation. This photo, along with several others, had been donated to the archives in the mid-1980s. The Educator explained that the Squamish Nation began the process of setting up its own archival system several years ago, where its own practices regarding display will be incorporated. For example, there are certain rules about the public display of traditional ceremonies as well as restrictions regarding the viewing of images of people who have passed away. Some recordings done by anthropologists did not respect traditional protocols regarding what could be recorded and what could not. The new Squamish Nation archive will incorporate these rules as the archive is built.

In the absence of the Squamish Nation's own archive, the municipal archives provided a space for the preservation of photographs and documents. Although relationships between Indigenous peoples and government archives can be contentious, the Squamish Nation now has a positive relationship with the North Vancouver Municipal Archives. In 2011 they worked together on a display of documents and artifacts that signaled the first collaboration of its kind. The elders from their community went to the archive and looked at portraits, basketwork, fabric, and other materials, providing important information about their uses and meanings. It was the first time they had been asked by the archives to do this kind of work.

The Educator I spoke with had also attended St. Paul Indian Residential School and had mixed feelings about their experience there. It was not an easy time, but it was also the reason the Educator had met many students who would go on to become friends and allies in future political struggles. Because students were often assigned to schools far from home, the schools brought together people who would not have otherwise met. Without downplaying the immense harm that occurred in the system, the Educator noted that this bringing together of people was one aspect of the schools that brought some comfort in later years. When I asked whether they would be giving their testimony to the commission as part of the IRS proceedings, they answered, "No, probably not." In discussing the torn image, the Educator noted that the grandson of one of the students in the photograph was active in the community. I had the opportunity to speak with him.

Norm Guerrero is the grandson of Alfred Fred Baker, one of the students in the image. Norm did not know whether the tear in the image was intentional and was unsure whether someone was missing from the image. However, he did provide some information about his grandfather. Alfred Fred Baker went by Fred or Freddy and was born October 17, 1933, in Squamish, British Columbia. He was the youngest of eleven. Fred attended St. Paul's Indian Residential until grade 8. He was the first to win the Tom Longboat award, named after the famous Onondaga distance runner. He excelled in basketball, lacrosse, and gymnastics. He was the first Buckskin Boy (a boxing club) from the Totem athletic club. Baker had fourteen children and passed away on May 1, 2006.

Before he died, Baker had done all the paperwork for a settlement under the Indian Residential School Agreement. The family received it after his death. Norm Guerrero said that when his grandfather spoke of his school experience, he shared a few of the negative things about the nuns, the punishments inflicted, and the rotten food, but he also focused on the positive things, primarily his active life in sports. The image of Baker and his teammates certainly points toward an absence (in the form of the tear), but it can also be seen to represent the ways that students managed to carve out spaces of camaraderie and comfort for themselves.

In some ways the images of the St. Paul basketball team can also be read as a before-and-after dyad. The images signal the changing archive, the image before digitization and after. Like Thomas Moore Keesick's before-and-after images, the St. Paul basketball photos are evocative of some of the profound silences within the IRS image archives. But if the St. Paul photo was deliberately torn, perhaps the image also gestures toward a deliberate withholding, thereby suggesting that certain types of intimate knowledge never make their way into the archive at all.

This chapter has focused on several images that represent different moments of colonial contact between Indigenous and non-Indigenous communities across the lands now known as Canada. In looking at these photographs, I have explored the work of erasure that occurs through the archive and the notion of the archive as a projected future. For the archive is not simply a structure where photographs and documents reside; it also produces an image of national identity—it is how the state imagines itself into coherence, the essence of a collective memory and a projected future. But archives are always incomplete. Archives speculate. They suggest histories, but they do not write them.

I began this chapter with Governor General Jean's speech and her recollection of archival images from Dawson City, Yukon. In evoking these particular images, Jean also conjured a larger body of archival images. These images haunt the Canadian imaginary and undermine the narrative of Canada as a nation of tolerance. Similar photographs from across the country help to tell the history of the IRS system and to recuperate the stories of those who endured its violence and indignities. I have used the images discussed in this chapter as a starting point to discuss how visual representations of the schools can act as reminders of this past while also allowing for resignification and reframing in the present. In this resignification I have argued that the subjects in these images, though often unidentified and/or unknown, experience a sort of return. In representing the quotidian aspects of the Indian residential school system, such archival images act as reminders that the everyday and the spectacular go hand in hand. The context of reconciliation in Canada has become fertile ground for a recontextualization and the restaging of the archive, where Indigenous subjects have been able and continue to assert agency and interpretive privilege in reclaiming IRS images. When one works with these photographs, the interrelations and imbrications between images and the imagination make themselves manifest. Jean's words here continue to reverberate: *You know what I am talking about.*

Nations Gather

Public Testimony and the Politics of Affect

The government of Canada sincerely apologizes and asks the forgiveness of the aboriginal peoples of this country for failing them so profoundly. We are sorry.
—CANADIAN PRIME MINISTER STEPHEN HARPER in the house of commons, June 11, 2008

For some reason I missed my mother then. I was numb and had an uncontrollable urge to cry, but the residential school had taught me to keep my cry underground.
—JOSE AMAUJAQ KUSUGAK, Indian residential school survivor, in response to Harper's apology, 2009

These statements highlight two of the many registers in which the rhetoric of reconciliation has occurred. The first excerpt is from the apology of Canadian prime minister Stephen Harper to Indigenous communities for the implementation of the IRS system. The second is a response from a former student, Jose Amaujaq Kusugak (Inuk). Prime Minister Harper mobilizes the language of the state, of forgiveness and moving forward, of making history through healing and apologies. Kusugak engages the language of affect and intimacy, of remembrance and looking back, of family ties broken and lasting wounds.[1] Both statements can be read as gestures: one is a gesture of apology, and the other gestures toward the work required after an apology is given. As gestures go, they encapsulate moments that point toward larger actions and processes yet to take place.

In the previous chapters I focused primarily on photographic media, looking at how images circulate in the context of reconciliation and looking at the work of Indigenous media makers and former students who have been recuperating and renarrating these images. This chapter focuses on other forms of public negotiation with the IRS legacy, both the gestural and what unfolds from it. In particular, I explore the forms of engagement that arose at two of the seven IRS TRC national gatherings, both of which I took part in. The first event was held in Winnipeg from June 16 to 19, 2010, and the second was held in Inuvik from June 28 to July 1, 2011.[2] Because many of the testimonies from former students were taken in private throughout the commission's mandate, the national gatherings were the most public aspect of the commission's work. The TRC estimates that "there were as many as 155,000 visits to the seven national events; over 9,000 residential school Survivors registered to attend them (while many others attended but did not register)."[3]

The national gatherings were in many ways grandly staged performances, where "embodied culture" played an important role in producing meaning and negotiating memories of the IRS system.[4] The events in Winnipeg and Inuvik included statement taking, traditional ceremonies, plays, film screenings, concerts, and performances. In discussing these events, my goal is twofold: I want to contribute to a dialogue about the forms of "truth" that are elicited through truth commissions, and I want to interrogate the politics of affect that developed at the gatherings.

Although this chapter focuses on the IRS TRC, and the national gatherings in particular, I have also drawn upon examples from the South African Truth and Reconciliation Commission (SA TRC) as a point of comparison. Rosemary Nagy has argued against the too-easy conflation of the *origins* of the Canadian TRC with inspiration from the South African predecessor, but she suggests that drawing comparisons between the two TRCs offers valuable insights into the localized specificity of the IRS TRC.[5] Much of this chapter explores such specificities of the testimonial genre in the Canadian context, discussing how it has, at times, conformed to or challenged the parameters set up by the commission's mandate as outlined by Schedule N of the Indian Residential School Settlement Agreement.

This chapter also considers political affective space, where affect is engaged as a "form of thinking" and represents a "different kind of intelligence about the world."[6] The word *affect* is meant to mark the slippery terrain between emotion and cognition. A significant amount of recent scholarship has drawn attention to the role played by affect within the context of the TRC national events.[7] Expanding upon these engagements with reconciliation and affect, my own focus is on moments when, in Lauren Berlant's words, "the inwardness of the intimate is met by a corresponding publicness," where the intimate nation and reconciliation meet.[8] Survivors often used the space of public testimony given at the national gatherings as a site to speak not only to the commission but also to their family members and other former students.[9] I use the term *intimate nation* to signal how national gatherings gestured toward an imagined national community while also negotiating more intimate kin relationships by those in attendance.

The IRS system regulated emotion in many ways. In their attempt to "civilize" native children, the schools sought to create skilled laborers and rational citizens. Emotional responses to the separation from their families, reactions of grief, or feelings of frustration in not being able to speak their languages were all meant to be suppressed. In sharing their experiences in the public forums at the national gatherings, survivors challenged the regulation of emotion enforced by the schools, claiming their own emotional responses as valid expressions of political agency. I argue that the affect that inflected the testimonies and environment at the gatherings represented a reclaiming of power and agency by former students from the colonial regulations that governed the Indian residential school system. Far from positioning survivors as perpetually wounded victims or infantile citizens, the varied affective responses of survivors and intergenerational survivors created community and connection in unexpected ways.

A Fragmented Truth

In order to highlight some of the complexities of the research process—of amalgamating and producing a coherent narrative from diverse and divergent theories, histories, and voices—this chapter differs from previous chapters in its incorporation of my field notes. By so doing, I have sought to draw attention to some of the challenges of working within emotionally charged sites, where distinctions between the private and the public, between affect and reason, and between the personal and the academic get blurred. My hope is that these field notes will help readers recognize that the politics of affect discussed in this chapter cannot be separated from the emotions that I experienced while at these events as a researcher, participant, and witness. Such reflexivity constitutes part of a long-standing epistemological project that helps to deconstruct the research process, allowing for interpretations that go beyond the recounting of observations and delve more deeply into an exploration of the relationships formed through research encounters.[10] Throughout this chapter I follow the style of field-note integration used by Kirsten Emiko McAllister in her book *Terrain of Memory: A Japanese Canadian Memory Project*. McAllister writes about the difficulties she experienced while conducting her research: "As I attempted to write this manuscript, I strove awkwardly to create a narrative that showed readers the difficulty of shedding one's disciplinary training, without reducing my project to a self-indulgent self-exploration. Even more challenging was the task of creating a language to present what the elders shared with me, to find ways of writing that did not reduce their accounts into evidence for my own arguments."[11] McAllister's approach helps to convey the conflicts that arise between research subject and object, disrupting any facile notions about researcher objectivity and allowing personal experiences and emotional valences to be integrated into the research and writing process.

I have also drawn extensively on the work of Antjie Krog, author of *Country of My Skull: Guilt, Sorrow, and the Limits of Forgiveness in the New South Africa*. As a journalist and a white South African of Afrikaans descent, Krog has written eloquently about the complexities of covering the SA TRC. Exploring her own struggle, both professionally and personally, in listening to the testimonies given at the SA TRC, Krog tells of how the events followed her home, to her family and her personal relationships. *Country of My Skull* is generally described as nonfiction, but Krog's work has sparked some debate regarding the distinction between fact and fiction, and critics have raised questions about the veracity of her writing.[12] Almost as a preemptive response to expected criticism, Krog writes:

> I am busy with the truth … my truth. Of course, it's quilted together from hundreds of stories that we've experienced or heard about in the past two years. Seen from my perspective, shaped by my state of mind at the time and now also by the audience I'm telling the story to. In every story, there is hearsay, there is a grouping together of things that didn't necessarily happen together, there are assumptions, there are exaggerations to bring home the enormities of situations, there is downplaying to confirm innocence. And all this together makes up the whole country's truth. So also the lies.[13]

In part, I reference Krog's work to raise the question "What does it mean to write about 'truth'?" I want to recognize the constructed nature of what I have presented here. In explaining her use of the literary "I" in her texts, Krog explains:

I do not know "he," or "she," or "they" well enough to tell their story convincingly. As the whole point of writing is to interact with the "you," I am left with "I." . . . [It] seems to be the most honest word I can say. The only word I really know and can give an account of. It allows me access to fact. . . . Many times I read works where the hiding of the "I" produces such cluttering, such loud echoing that one wants to say: for God's sake, come out, be yourself, so that we can talk, and stop hiding behind elaborate manifestations of yourself.[14]

In employing the first person in this chapter, I contribute to an existing yet always evolving conversation. Using the "I" in field-note form is an attempt to make clear the person who is speaking and to recognize that ideas of distanced objectivity are problematic.[15] What I present in the pages to follow is a fragmented truth: a partial recollection of the two TRC national gatherings that I attended.[16]

In discussing the idea of a fragmented truth, I am also leaning on the work of several Indigenous authors who have problematized the notion of a single truth. "Although each of us has our own truth, which is part of the greater truth of the collective," explains Jo-Ann Episkenew (Métis), "those truths are constantly shifting as our experiences and our contexts change."[17] Understanding shifting truths and sharing them are important aspects of Indigenous epistemologies. In some cases the retelling of certain narratives or stories can be seen as an act of empowerment, a form of speaking back to the dominant narrative that left Indigenous voices out. As Susan Dion (Lenape/Potawatami) notes, "In the moment of (re)telling, we are both witness and testifier, bearing witness to the stories of our ancestors and giving testimony as Survivors of the policy of forced assimilation."[18] Indigenous peoples can act as both witness and testifier in sharing their experiences of colonial policies in Canada. As witnesses, they have lived through these policies, surviving violent conflict and injustice. As givers of testimony, they rupture silences about colonial policies of assimilation and oppression, giving voice to long-denied or stifled experiences. Many individuals were able to inhabit this dual role through their participation in the IRS TRC and the national gatherings. In sharing their experiences, individuals and communities were able to "(re)tell" or "restory" narratives about the IRS system, about Canada framed as a "benevolent" and "tolerant" nation, and about a wide array of phenomena that had long been silenced.[19]

Academic writing has also played and can continue to play a part in this "restorying" practice. As Lee Maracle (Stó:lō) explains, "It takes a lot of work to delete the emotional and passionate self from story, to dehumanize story into theory." But as she reminds us, "Academic theories / are but the leaky summations / of human stories."[20] As a sort of corrective, Maracle proposes "theory through story."[21] Theory can be universalizing, a movement toward the overarching themes and explanations for phenomena. Story has the ability to remain personal while still engaging these universalizing or general themes. "Theory through story" recognizes that although these two registers differ, they can work together in representing a more robust picture of particular dynamics and actors at play. In my own writing I have tried to keep Maracle's emphasis on "theory through story" in mind.

In addition to the use of first-person narrative and field notes, this chapter also incorporates some of the photographs that I took, when appropriate, at national gatherings. In many cases, taking photographs or using any form of recording device was not permitted—for example, at traditional ceremonies. As with my field notes, the photographs I chose to include present only a fragmented portrait of the gatherings I attended. In selecting and placing images throughout this chapter, I often wondered about the claims to "truth" that each image makes. For truth commissions are not only about what can be spoken or heard; they are also about what can be seen.

Photographs are often called upon as proof, as evidence of something that happened. In this way, especially in the context of reconciliation, photography and other visual technologies (film or painting, for example) must also be seen to make claims to truth and objectivity. The image tends to take on a role as corroborator: a witness. But photographs are always framed; there is always something chosen for display while other phenomena are left out.[22] When I decided to incorporate my own photographs into this text, I understood that claims to truth were being made. This chapter explores, in part, the nature of those claims.[23]

Field Notes: June 17, 2010
Today I heard cries of anguish, a deep wailing. The women's sharing circle was held in the Manitoba Theatre for Young People. Because space in the room was limited, priority was given, understandably, to those women sharing their experiences. I stood outside the room with many others, facing the speakers that had been set up in the lobby of the Theatre. There were a few chairs and people sat wherever they could find space on the ground. Health support workers walked around the room handing out tissues. Many tears were expected.

Now, many months later, I try to remember specifics from their stories, and I can't. But I remember the profoundly affective register: the sound of the crying, the wailing. It is not something I can easily forget. I turn to my recordings of the event so I can listen to the testimonies. The recordings form an incomplete archive, a fragmented representation of the survivors' experiences. I listen to them, rewind, make notes, transcribe, take breaks, and return again to the stories shared. Many people spoke in their Indigenous languages. In the following text I have marked these sections, often just brief moments, with the words *Indigenous language*. If the language is known, I have included that information. The commission transcribed and translated some of these testimonies, which have been included in its six-volume report; hundreds of hours of recorded testimony not yet transcribed are housed at the National Centre for Truth and Reconciliation at the University of Manitoba.[24]

The issue of translating Indigenous testimony is one that needs to be carefully considered. At the TRC events, the issue of language (and of language reinvigoration) was ever present. Many former students spoke of the profound loss they felt in being forbidden from speaking their languages at the schools. If language is one of "the many elements that allow us to make sense of things, of ourselves," then the destruction of language contributes to a profound loss of self.[25] The inability of former students to communicate with their families and communities in their mother tongues has left lasting scars. "It was impossible. I found it impossible to exist," explains Cree artist Alexander Javier. "And then I couldn't speak it, I couldn't speak my truth. They [the nuns at the school] spoke French or English and none of my language."[26] Some survivors gave their testimony to the commission in Indigenous languages. At some events, simultaneous translation was offered. In Inuvik, for example, translation was available for nine languages (Chipewyan, Dogrib, Gwich'in, Inuktitut, Inuvialuktun, North Slavey, South Slavey, English, and French). At other events, no translation was offered.

In regards to testimony, translation is a particularly charged issue. "Translation is not an innocent, transparent activity," write Susan Bassnett and Harish Trivedi. "[It] is highly charged with significance at every stage; it rarely, if ever, involves a relationship of equality between texts, authors or systems."[27] And as Emily Apter writes, the act of translation can play a significant role in "subject re-formation and political change."[28] In other words, both the act of giving testimony and the act of translation can be acts of transformation, transition, and change. Such acts are not uncomplicated. In the case of Indigenous testimony, in particular, the first question is frequently not *how* to translate but rather whether it should be done at all.

Under a system that attempted the decimation of Indigenous languages, should the testimony of former students be translated into the language of the colonizer? Even a "thick translation"—where the broader context of colonization and oppression are incorporated into the translation—may not sufficiently circumvent the ethical issues involved in translating testimony.[29] Translation may have the potential to create greater awareness among the Canadian public, but it can also enact a form of violence upon the individual. Some Native communities may encourage translation; others may withhold it, to keep some knowledge privileged for their own members. In the pages that follow, words spoken in Indigenous languages are left out, untranslated, representing some of the gaps and barriers of listening to testimony.

TESTIMONY, JUNE 17, 2010: WOMEN'S SHARING CIRCLE

We have many tears to shed before we even get to the word *reconciliation*. ... And that's why I say ... let us go easy, let us go slow. Because if we don't feel that middle part, I'm afraid, my brothers and sisters, we're sitting here for nothing. And for my grandchildren, your grandchildren, your great-grandchildren, my great-grandchildren, they will continue to hurt. If we don't do a good job, we're given this time, if we don't do a good job my brothers and sisters, let us do it right. [*Indigenous language.*] ... And listen to us. Listen to us, the ones that suffered in the residential schools. Listen to us when we say this is what we were like. Listen to us. [*Indigenous language.*] Listen to us. Listen to us. Thank you.

This woman's name does not come through clearly on my recording. She speaks several times in an Indigenous language that is unknown to me. She asks the commission and others present to listen to her, to her community, and to other survivors. She repeats: "Listen to us. Listen to us." And even though I try to hear her, it is still only in fragments. Testimonies are not monologues; they cannot take place in solitude. At the national gathering, survivors emphasized the labors of listening. In his work on Holocaust testimony, Dori Laub writes that "bearing witness to a trauma is, in fact, a process that includes the listener. For the testimonial process to take place, there needs to be a bonding, the intimate and total presence of an other—in the position of one who hears. The witnesses are talking *to somebody*: to somebody they have been waiting for a long time."[30] Traumatic testimony occupies a liminal space "between the sayable and the unsayable," as Giorgio Agamben has written, and it is expressed not only in words but also through affective forms of communication: tones, cracks in the voice, pauses, silences. For both Laub and Agamben, there is much work to be done by those who listen.

In Winnipeg, listening became an ethical act, entailing responsibilities and active engagement.[31] Cautioning against forms of listening that strengthen rather than deconstruct the settler-Indigenous relationship, Paulette Regan has shown how even empathetic responses may still be "colonial in nature." To confront forms of colonial listening, Regan maintains that both settler and survivor must commit to a broader project of decolonization. For the settler, she suggests that this involves "unsettling the settler within."[32] For the settler-listener, it is not enough to grieve or feel empathy, for settlers must also recognize their own complicity in the theft of lands from and the violence directed at Indigenous communities all across Canada.

Truth Commissions as Structures of Feeling

Truth commissions mobilize ideas of justice, reconciliation, and healing while also setting the stage for an acting out of affective relations: between family members, between former students, between survivors and the state, to name only three examples. When Raymond Williams wrote about "structures of feeling," he referred to an emerging or established cultural ethos, those defining moments, structures, or movements that, often in hindsight, define an epoch.[33] Williams used the word *feelings* to signal a general cultural ethic or durational experience; ideas of justice can be seen to bleed into these structures. Since the 1970s, there have been more than two dozen truth commissions established around the world. Ideals and mechanisms of transitional justice, of which truth commissions are a part, are part of a particular post–World War II ethos that centered around ideas of restorative justice. Indeed, I argue here that the proliferation of TRCs can be seen to mark a particular structure of feeling.[34]

In part, this structure of feeling is tied to what some scholars have termed a "memory boom" or "memorial mania," where looking to the past plays a crucial role in the negotiation of national and collective identities.[35] Some of the literature on truth commissions has arisen from within this body of work, incorporating ideas about the labors of memory, transitional justice, and reflections on the notions of forgiveness and reconciliation.[36] Dealing publicly with traumatic events is complicated, and there are both dangers and possibilities for political agencies that coalesce around cultures of trauma.[37] Still, the events at the national gatherings that I attended seemed to demonstrate that affective spaces can be politicized in ways that create connection and community while also demonstrating political agency.

Significant qualifiers must be used when engaging the discourse of trauma in an Indigenous context. Nancy Van Styvendale proposes the idea of a "trans/historicity" of Indigenous trauma, challenging a concept of trauma that is rooted in a singular event. Instead, she proposes that Indigenous communities have faced a continued form of trauma that "takes place and is repeated in multiple epochs and, in this sense, exceeds its historicity, conventionally understood as a singular location in the past."[38] In other words, the IRS TRC, which focused on one aspect of the traumas inflicted on communities, was not designed to address the trans/historical nature of Indigenous trauma. Also, standard techniques of coping with and healing from trauma have frequently emphasized a "Western view of the self as agentic, rationalistic, monological, and univocal," which does not reflect the diverse traditional Indigenous ideas of the self as rooted in intimate connections to both land and kin relationships.[39] This is not to say that these versions of the self do not evolve or overlap; it is simply to highlight that there can be no easy application of trauma theory in this context.[40] Seeing the past through a lens of trauma can also obscure some of the cultural complexities involved in disentangling a contested history.[41] And it can contribute to the sentiment that the injustices committed against Indigenous peoples are firmly and solely rooted in the past.

Before attending the TRC's national gatherings, I had been critical about the emphasis on a confessional or testimonial mode of engaging the IRS system and its legacies. My concern was that individuals would share their experiences, opening up their personal pasts for national consumption, and that they would perhaps not feel the "healing" or support that they needed in return. I was also worried that the TRC would confirm a therapeutic imperative and position former students as perpetually vulnerable victims, but I found that this was not the case. Testimonies often spoke of strength and resilience through adversity. Former students took up the collective identity of "survivor," and the term *victim* was rarely used. Even those former students who had passed away were called survivors. Anishinaabe scholar Gerald Vizenor has written about the concept of "survivance," which draws attention to how the very act and expression of survival can be seen as a form of resistance.[42] At the TRC events I attended, alongside the tears and grief, there was also a celebration of evolving Indigenous traditions and ongoing perseverance.

Truth and Testimony

Proponents of TRCs argue that the commissions are able to produce an understanding of the past that was previously impossible to achieve. However subjective, disjointed, or even difficult to understand some testimonies may be, they are privileged for the insights they offer into the atrocities and injustices of the past. But it is important to note that these testimonies (and the forums for witnessing that they demand) produce their own forms of meaning about trauma, healing, and what it means to witness. Certain narratives are elicited more frequently than others, for instance, and the dominant culture still manages how the testimonies circulate and the role that they will play in the reconstruction of national identities.[43] In many cases, the subject who testifies comes to stand in for a larger community, and the testimony offered becomes part of an official discourse, separated and disconnected from its origin.[44] So it is important to recognize that even as truth commissions appear to empower oppressed groups, they can also work to define and constrain their possible narratives. As an example of such a constraint, truth and reconciliation commissions generally rely on the taking of testimonies.[45]

The testimonial genre brings with it many concerns. For instance, some have criticized how it tends to overemphasize the role of language in the process of healing. By promoting a "talking cure," critics argue, testimony can overlook other forms of healing, including traditional rituals and embodied practices.[46] It can also run the risk, as Elizabeth Jelin points out, of turning personal stories of suffering into "a banal and overexposed spectacle of horror."[47] In many ways, TRCs must be understood as part of what Allen Feldman has called "the current cultural predilection for confessional trauma narratives," and this predilection can obscure the political agency and calls to action that such narratives often seek to create.[48]

Of further concern with the IRS TRC in Canada was the fact that testimonies were set up around the principle that people would *voluntarily* participate in the process. Indeed, the mandate of the TRC, as defined by Schedule N, specifically prohibited the commission from "naming names," and the commission had no powers of subpoena through which participation might be compelled. This resulted in a lack of testimonies given by perpetrators of violence.[49] Indeed, following legal proceedings and a settlement, it was mandated that perpetrators could not be named unless the individual had given their consent or had been recognized for wrongdoing in a court of law. If an unverified name was spoken during a testimony, the commission was obligated to "anonymize" the statement. Specifically, the IRS TRC mandate stated that the commission "shall not name names in their events, activities, public statements, report or recommendations, or make use of personal information or of statements made which identify a person, without the express consent of that individual, unless that information and/or the identity of the person so identified has already been established through legal proceedings, by admission, or by public disclosure by that individual. Other information that could be used to identify individuals shall be anonymized to the extent possible."[50]

Despite this mandate, and despite verbal reminders given by the commissioners following testimony where specific names of perpetrators were given, survivors often continued to assert their prerogative to disclose the names of individuals who inflicted physical, emotional, or psychological harm on them. For many former students, the naming of names was part of their truth; such an act can be an important step toward justice and, in certain cases, part of a process of healing. Indeed, "the writing and righting of names" has been identified by many as an important focus for Indigenous history.[51] For students who had their names anglicized or changed upon arriving at the schools, the rewriting of names can help them reclaim their Indigenous identities. But the naming of individuals who committed crimes against students is an equally important aspect of this reclamation. Although the performative act of naming names against the IRS TRC's request may have provided some former students with a sense of closure, its efficacy as a gesture was compromised by the fact that staff members who committed abuse were not held accountable for the harms they caused.

Even with these numerous criticisms, the IRS TRC collected almost seven thousand statements during its tenure, and the National Centre for Truth and Reconciliation is mandated to continue gathering and housing statements in perpetuity. For some survivors, telling their story was an important step in the healing process. For others, a desire to engage in dialogue propelled them to give their testimony. When testimony was given in public settings at the national gatherings, sometimes there were several addressees put in dialogue with one another, gesturing to the fact that multiple conversations could be initiated through the act of giving testimony. For example, the commissioners often responded to testimonies with comments or condolences.[52] Sometimes former students would reference a specific public testimony that they had heard in order to draw attention to the similarities and/or discrepancies between experiences at the schools.

In this way, dialogue around the IRS system took (and continues to take) place on multiple levels.

The role of witnessing testimony at the TRC was a foundational part of the events, and indeed an explicit "call to witness" was often expressed by commissioners at the very beginning of sessions. But what did it mean to stand as a witness to testimony at these events? The IRS TRC mandate explicitly stated that it would give credence to "Aboriginal concepts of witnessing" and provide a "culturally appropriate setting" for survivors to share their stories. However, the mandate did not clarify what that entailed, and the diverse First Nations, Inuit, and Métis communities and individuals taking part in the IRS TRC have significantly different, and sometimes diverging, ideas of what constitutes witnessing. David Gaertner has argued that homogenizing all these diverse ways of being under the moniker of "Aboriginal" masks the divergence and difference among these views.[53] At a talk at the International Center for Transitional Justice (ICTJ) in New York, I had the opportunity to ask the commission what was meant by an "Aboriginal concept of witnessing." Justice Murray Sinclair relayed that the commission itself had been obliged to inquire about the meaning of this phrase, further explaining that because the mandate had been passed on to them from the previous commissioners (who, as discussed in chapter 1, had all resigned), he and his fellow commissioners were also uncertain about how to interpret this clause.[54] After consulting with elders from different communities, the new commissioners took the phrase to mean that witnessing calls for an active engagement, for a presence that goes beyond simply watching. Certain communities expect that in traditional ceremonies, including weddings and namings, a witness must carry the event with them, must remind those present and tell those not present what happened there, and must recognize their own role in the event.[55]

In some TRCs, as in South Africa, testimony has been offered in juridical-style hearings. In Winnipeg, by contrast, public testimony was given in sharing circles, and an eagle feather or talking stick was passed from person to person as they shared their experiences (see figures 3.1 and 3.2). The audience (ranging from dozens to hundreds of people) fanned out around the circle and listened through large loudspeakers set up around the commissioner's tent or, when it began to rain, in the auditorium or lobby of the Manitoba Theatre for Young People. People spoke of being taken from their families and separated from siblings. Even when siblings attended the same schools, students discussed how they were kept apart from family members by

FIGURE 3.1 Oodena Circle after the lighting of the Sacred Fire, Winnipeg, June 16, 2010. Photo by Naomi Angel.

FIGURE 3.2 Participants and observers around Oodena Circle during the Winnipeg national gathering, June 16, 2010. Photo by Naomi Angel.

imposed divisions according to age and sex. Some survivors spoke of life after the schools, detailing the reverberations and legacies of the abuse in the system. Cree scholar Gregory Younging has written about these legacies and their relationship to theories of memory: "Indigenous peoples often refer to our 'blood memory,' meaning that the experience of those that have gone before us is embedded in our physical and psychological being."[56] The aftermath of the Indian residential school experience still pervades these communities, touching generations that, even without firsthand experience of the schools, remain deeply affected. During the Women's Sharing Circle on June 17, 2010, Barbara Eaton from Kamloops, BC, spoke: "I am a Survivor, along with my grandmother, my uncle, my brother. I at times have felt alone, since the passing of my grandmother, my mom, and my uncle. I went to the residential school when I was five years old. I didn't really remember the day that I went there until 2008 when I went to the house of healing and began talking about my life in residential school." For Eaton, the memories from the school didn't surface until she started to speak about her past. She spoke of feeling ashamed and silenced, and of the horror of her school experience.

Those who taught or worked at the schools were also in attendance in Winnipeg. In the sharing circle held on the first day, a pilot recounted his experience of taking a young girl away from her Inuit family and home to bring her south to school. He told of her inconsolable sadness and unstoppable tears. He had thought he was doing what was right, but he has now come to realize his own role in a system that tore families apart. A teacher told of her own experiences and the difficult conditions at the Indian residential school where she taught. She read the names of her students in their honor.

The testimonies given in the public sharing circles were recorded by the TRC and by others in attendance. All of the testimonies offered for public disclosure now circulate as research, as historical data, and as recollections of lives lived. The TRC was mandated to develop a national research center—now known as the National Centre for Truth and Reconciliation—that was tasked with gathering and maintaining the collected findings of the TRC and housing its *Final Report*. According to the wishes of those who shared them, these testimonies have now been made available there as part of the center's archival repository. The TRC's *Final Report* also recommended that new curricula be devised at all levels of education—from primary to postsecondary—which would include sections on the IRS system. Some of the IRS TRC testimonies may be (indeed may have already been) incorporated into textbooks and educational documentaries.

Field Notes: June 17, 2010

In the Morning: Academic Conference. Papers are read. Q. and A. Everything is orderly.

In the Afternoon: Hurricane Warning. Not so orderly.

This afternoon, I volunteered at the statement-gathering tent. I stood near the entrance to the Inn at the Forks and directed people, told them where to sign up, and where to go for their allotted time. A woman sits nearby and we start to chat. She is from the Long Plain First Nation in Portage la Prairie, about an hour and a half away from here. "See, we are stirring things up here. There's so much emotion," she says. "Heavy rains come when that happens." The hurricane warning shuts down some of the events. Tents are pulled down. People move inside to hear the testimonies in the sharing circle.

The national gathering included testimony outside the sharing circles as well. For example, during a special evening devoted to "Writing Truth, Imagining Reconciliation," Basil Johnston (Ojibwe), author of *Indian School Days*, spoke about his experiences at the Spanish Indian Residential School (located in northern Ontario). He also spoke of how he was asked, after his book was released, why he didn't focus more on the difficult times at Spanish. Although the book mentions some abuse, confusion, and difficulties at the school, it focuses on the more universal tropes of childhood: pranks, camaraderie, rebellion, and flirtations. He explained that he wanted to tell one part of the story, and he specifically wanted to focus on the resilient aspects.[57] He wrote *Indian School Days* for his friends and other survivors of the IRS system. At the gathering in Winnipeg, he took the opportunity to shed light on parts of the story that he did not mention in the book, speaking frankly about the sexual abuse he suffered at the schools. He went on to talk about his life after Spanish, about moving to Toronto, about meeting his wife, and about their life together. He drew attention to the fact that the experiences shared at the national gatherings should not come to represent the totality of the survivor's life.[58]

Survivors at this first national event, in focusing on other aspects of their life when giving testimony, did so, in part, to reclaim power over the construction of their own life narratives. Ronald Niezen has argued that throughout the life of the TRC and its seven national events, the framework for facilitating, supporting, and framing testimony inadvertently encouraged speakers to focus on the most traumatic and painful aspects of their memories. However, other scholars have shown, and the *Final Report* has corroborated, that speakers frequently "chose to deny expectations," subverting

FIGURE 3.3 Gus Higheagle riding into Oodena Circle, June 18, 2010. Photo by Naomi Angel.

the structuring of the events and instrumentalizing their command of the cameras, the microphone, and the public forum to their own ends.[59]

Although the national gatherings were structured through the realities of colonial policies (past and present), survivors were able to inject the discourse with reflections about their lives that did not place colonial relations at their center. For example, on the third day of the Winnipeg event, there was a ceremony honoring the Unity Riders, a group of men and women who rode on horseback from Virden, Manitoba, and arrived in Winnipeg seven days later (figure 3.3). Their journey was made to honor residential school survivors and to show unity among the First Nations in the prairie provinces. Gus Higheagle, one of the riders, addressed the audience in his Dakota language, explaining that to do so was a way to prove to himself that he could speak his own language, despite all the efforts that had been made to extinguish it. He then called his daughter to the circle to sing a melody to commemorate the ride.[60]

The Unity Riders reveal the extent to which the alliances and connections forged at national gatherings were often among Indigenous peoples and not necessarily between Indigenous and non-Indigenous Canadians. The song performed by Higheagle and his daughter symbolized family bonds and ties to the land—both those that have been damaged and those that are being rebuilt. It also demonstrated the central role of language reinvigoration in the reconciliation process. After the song, Higheagle explained that "I wanted my daughter to be a part of this because our young people can speak our language, and it's very important because that's what we are fighting for: to keep our language as a nation. I thank you." Through wide-ranging means of expression, survivors of the schools often upset the dyadic expectations of the commission, speaking to multiple audiences in diverse ways. In many cases, non-Indigenous Canadians were not envisioned by survivors as the primary audience for these testimonies. Rather, Indigenous family members and communities were the primary audience, with non-Indigenous Canadians playing an indirect or secondary role as listeners.

Like many aspects of the events in Winnipeg, the ceremony welcoming the Unity Riders included disruptions and contradictions. As some of the riders were presented with blankets in commemoration of their ride, a residential school survivor in the audience shouted his disappointment at being unable to give his testimony that day. The number of people wanting to share in combination with the hurricane warning had made it difficult for some to give their testimonies. The man walked into the crowd and started to yell. He was visibly upset. "They won't take my statement," he shouted. The audience remained quiet. "They had to shut down the tent, and there is a line of people wanting to tell their experiences. I can only be here for one day, and I won't be able to tell my story." The man stormed off, and the audience turned back to the circle. Not far away, on the outskirts of the event, protesters held up signs drawing attention to the need for more resources to find out what happened to students who went missing at the schools.[61] The ceremony, only briefly interrupted, began again. Elder Albert Taylor introduced the riders, and Commissioner Wilton Littlechild, a survivor of the schools, spoke:

> When I was a little boy, my only friend was a horse. So when they took young people like me away from our families, they also took us away from our horse, an important spirit in our culture. There is a song. It's a song for the horse and the horse dance. It's a song and a sun dance with the horse spirit.
>
> When I was taken away to school, it was on a buggy like that [pointing to a wagon nearby]. I don't know how old I was, that's how young I was. But I never rode back from the school … until today.

FIGURE 3.4 Commissioner Wilton Littlechild on horseback, exiting Oodena Circle, June 18, 2010. Photo by Naomi Angel.

In other settings, Chief Littlechild has spoken of the difficulties of listening to the thousands of testimonies collected thus far. Before having a successful career in sports, politics, and law, Littlechild attended residential school for fourteen years. He is still negotiating his own relationship to both truth and reconciliation. At the time of the Winnipeg national event, Littlechild had yet to give his official testimony to the commission, in spite of his role as commissioner. When asked whether he would, he responded by saying, "Yes, definitely, but not yet. I need to tell my family the whole story first."[62] Littlechild's comments reveal how sharing one's story on the intimate level can often precede or even replace the desire to tell it on a national level (figure 3.4).

Lost Together

After full days of public testimony, the evenings at the Winnipeg gathering included concerts and entertainment. On June 16, about twenty thousand people gathered for a free outdoor concert (figure 3.5). Starting while the sky was still light, the audience filtered into the grassy area in front of the stage. A list of predominantly Indigenous artists, including Susan

FIGURE 3.5 The crowd at the opening-night concert, June 16, 2010. Photo by Naomi Angel.

Aglukark and Inez, performed throughout the evening. A large TRC banner hung across the stage; between songs, artists tried to draw attention to the commission's work.

As I go over my notes and photos, the above image stands out. I try to read the faces of those in the forefront of the photograph. There are those that look toward the stage; a woman holds up her own camera, and some look directly into my lens. I try to imagine why these people have attended the concert. Some are wearing the orange badges given out by the commission to staff, volunteers, and survivors. Some have brought out their own chairs, ready to enjoy the night of performance and music. At the back of the photo, you can see the outlines of people standing atop the parking lot, straining to see the stage. Later in the evening, several children climb onto a temporary stand to watch the show. My camera captures their arms moving to the music. As darkness falls, the lights from the stage reflect off their bodies, creating traces of trailing light (figure 3.6).

At the end of the evening, Buffy St. Marie and Blue Rodeo take the stage and perform "Lost Together." They sing the chorus:

FIGURE 3.6 Audience members watching the stage, June 16, 2010. Photo by Naomi Angel.

> And if we're lost
> Then we are lost together
> Yeah, if we're lost
> Then we are lost together

In that moment, the audience sings along, swaying together. Buffy St. Marie, a Cree singer/songwriter and veteran activist who has had a long and successful international career, and Blue Rodeo, a Canadian popular folk and country band, sing together as the crowd cheers. Elijah Harper (Cree), the politician who helped block the Meech Lake accord, joins the artists on the stage. He holds up his eagle feather.[63] Twenty thousand people are in attendance. The crowd goes wild for Harper and his eagle feather. The song and its lyrics, "we are lost together," create the sensation, at least temporarily, of togetherness. But they also belie the fact that the groups being called together (Indigenous and settler Canadians) have played very different roles in the residential school history and that togetherness is not something easily achieved, nor is it necessarily a goal for everyone involved in the reconciliation process.[64]

The opening-night concert highlights the complicated dynamics of cultural consumption at the national gatherings. In relation to cultural representations of the Other, bell hooks has written that "the over-riding fear is that cultural, ethnic, and racial differences will be continually commodified and offered up as new dishes to enhance the white palate—that the Other will be eaten, consumed, and forgotten."[65] Before attending the gatherings in Winnipeg and Inuvik, my concerns echoed hooks's critique. I thought that perhaps Indigenous communities were being called upon to share their stories of oppression for the consumption of the Other, in this case, to satiate the white settler's palate. hooks writes about the consumption of the Other, soon to be forgotten. But my skepticism arose from the concern that in the case of the IRS TRC, the dangers of being forgotten could in fact be eclipsed by the dangers of being remembered.

For the TRC, survivors of the IRS system were called upon to give their testimonies and perform. The presumption was that testimony would lead to individual and collective healing. I went into the gatherings assuming that the duty to remember could also be harmful. I thought that the idea that the TRC could bring closure, forgiveness, or political action of some kind was an assumption that needed to be challenged. I found that this assumption *was* challenged, not only by the academics and observers in attendance but also by the survivors and the commission itself. Even while recognizing the limitations of participation, survivors still wanted to share. The gatherings were not solely about expectations of healing and moving forward; sometimes a desire for dialogue propelled survivors to give their testimony. The public at these events was mixed and, in some gatherings, predominantly Indigenous, challenging the assumption that reconciliation was something being staged for a settler or national audience. This opening-night concert demonstrated to me that white settler consumption was not the only kind of politically meaningful consumption taking place: survivor, family member, bystander, perpetrator, and settler were negotiating different levels of and ideas about reconciliation as the event unfolded.

An important contingent of public participation also came from the churches. The role of the churches in the reconciliation process is representative of the uneasy and shifting roles that certain groups played at the national gatherings. I had come to Winnipeg expecting religious leaders to be painted as perpetrators of abuse and violence. What I found instead was a far more complicated relationship between "perpetrator" and "victim," and between what I had taken as a secular process (the TRC) and its religious underpinnings. The churches played an instrumental role in running the

Indian residential school system and have also played an important role in reconciliation, as signatories to the broader Indian Residential Schools Settlement Agreement (IRSSA)—to date, the largest class-action lawsuit in Canadian history and the legal decision that launched the TRC participants in the Independent Assessment Process compensation program—and as ongoing participants in the movement toward IRS educational reform and redress. But throughout my time in Winnipeg, it became clear that this role was, and perhaps remains, ill-defined. I noticed some visible discomfort from some people in the audience when church representatives addressed the crowds. This discomfort and even resistance was reiterated at subsequent events, where clergy who attempted to represent their own banal or even positive experiences of the schools were condemned by those searching for the "truth."[66] At the same time, I also heard former students express their connections to Christian faiths. For example, Peter Yellowquill, a survivor present at the Winnipeg gathering, remarked: "The churches committed spiritual genocide. But I am still a Christian man. It's complicated."[67] For some former students, religion has been part of their journey toward healing from the past. For others, religion or those who represented religion at their schools were perpetrators of abuse and violence. Throughout the event, the roles that various religious leaders played were indeed complicated. At times, they offered apologies; at others, there were still denials.

Field Notes, June 16, 2010
At dawn, about 40–50 people gathered around the fire pit. This morning's sunrise ceremony took place around the fire pit in Oodena Celebration Circle. "Oodena" is Ojibwe for "heart of the city" and the small circle is located where two rivers meet. As the ceremony began, I wondered, "Am I allowed to record this?" It quickly became clear that I wasn't, so my camera and audio recorder remained in my backpack. The sacred fire was lit and traditional prayers were said. As the ceremony came to its conclusion, the chair of the commission, Justice Murray Sinclair, closed with the Lord's Prayer. It was strange. I looked to my right where several priests and ministers were standing. They smiled over the proceedings, seeming pleased that the Lord's Prayer was incorporated into the ceremony.

Before he began the prayer, Justice Sinclair (Ojibwe) introduced it by saying, "I will close with another traditional prayer." *Traditional* is a word often used in relation to Indigenous ceremony. By using this word, Sinclair drew attention to the ways in which Christian and Indigenous traditions have come together.[68]

The role of religion is one of the many points of contention in the literature on truth commissions. For example, in the case of the South African Truth and Reconciliation Commission, religious discourse played an important role in contextualizing the TRC as a tool to enable forgiveness. These links among ideas of forgiveness, moral absolution, and reconciliation were formed in part through the rhetoric put forward by the SA TRC's charismatic chair, Archbishop Desmond Tutu. Tutu's concept of reconciliation was heavily influenced by his own Anglican theology, incorporating ideas of "miracles" and forgiveness that had deeply religious overtones.

Critics of the SA TRC often refer to back to these underpinnings as part of their critique of the commission's work. But as noted by Jonathan VanAntwerpen, these Christian ideas of reconciliation were not often critiqued from within South Africa. Rather, the critiques began to surface after the fact, by international scholars, once the SA TRC started to become a model for transitional justice around the world.[69] The secularization of truth commissions, in other words, was necessary only when the SA TRC was taken up as a model for reconciliation elsewhere. In the Canadian case a clear tension between the IRS TRC as a healing or confessional mechanism and the TRC as a pseudo-juridical body for civic action was ever present. And the churches' roles in officiated reconciliation were frequently complicated by their role as perpetrators of abuse and signatories to the massive civil lawsuit that institutionalized the TRC.

On that first day of the Winnipeg event (and indeed at all the national events), representatives from the churches addressed the crowd. The United, Presbyterian, and Anglican churches offered apologies. Each of these churches had already made official apologies. The practice of apologizing has become standard at these types of events. The repetitive act of apologizing could signal various things: the need for continuing recognition of the wrongs committed, a continued emphasis on repentance, and a lack of focus on more-practical steps toward righting the relations of the past. The Catholic Church was the only church present that refused to offer an official apology.[70] In Winnipeg the representative of the Catholic Church, Archbishop Gerard Pettipas, chose to focus on some of the contributions the church has made to Indigenous communities. By sidestepping the issues of abuse at the schools, Pettipas and the Catholic Church continued to allow for denial, thereby silencing the voices of former students.[71]

Minister of Indian and Northern Affairs (INAC) Chuck Strahl also spoke on the first day at Winnipeg.[72] In his brief speech, Strahl promised to remove the portions of the Indian Act (sections 114 to 122) that allowed the

Indian residential school system to be established. Although the sections he mentions have not been enforced for years, their removal, Strahl noted, would signal the government's commitment to reconciliation: "This is a long overdue gesture of reconciliation. I want to eliminate forever the portions of the Indian Act that caused such suffering among Aboriginal families. This gesture reinforces our government's unwavering commitment to establish a new relationship with Aboriginal people."[73] As he made this announcement, behind me in the crowd someone said, "It's about time." That same day, Strahl participated in a sharing circle.

Field Notes, June 16, 2010

I am standing around the edge of a large circle. There are about 8–12 people sitting on chairs in the center of the tent, and we are fanned out around them. They have been chosen to share their thoughts and experiences about the Indian residential school experience. Chuck Strahl is one of the speakers. When he is given the opportunity, he explains that he didn't know how bad the schools were. He explains that he is a grandfather now and can imagine his grandchildren being taken away. He claims that he didn't realize how bad the schools were. While expressing this thought, he becomes overcome with emotion. Two survivors lay their hands on his shoulder to offer their support. It is a powerful moment.

The next day, media coverage of the event focused on Chuck Strahl's emotional breakdown. Images of survivors comforting Strahl were splashed across television screens and newspapers. This reinforced the narrative of the unknowing, well-intentioned settler who now sought to share in the grief over the past. Like the responses to Harper's official apology, some survivors were moved by this moment while others felt it was staged or disingenuous. The intermingling of settler and Indigenous grief might suggest that both parties were equally harmed by the Indian residential school experience.

By engaging and often supporting discourses of forgiveness, truth commissions can emphasize experiences like Strahl's, which risks putting too much emphasis on settler grief, thereby eclipsing the voices of survivors. Although the image of survivors comforting Strahl provides a powerful tableau—one that is easily understood as a moment of reconciliation—it strikes me that, in looking back at that moment, I cannot remember many of the details shared by the survivors in that particular sharing circle. The stories blend together. I remember that the experiences were difficult and sad, that there was abuse, that families were torn apart. But my mind will not recall the details. Was there a brother who didn't return home? Was there a mother who fought to keep her kids? It is shocking to me that I do not remember. Yet it highlights one of the risks of the truth commission's work. The varied and distinct stories of individuals can tend to become one single narrative. And although on some level this may create a general awareness of abuse and oppression, the impact of individual stories is slowly diminished.

It is jarring to me that, over time, the main piece of testimony I recall from that circle is from Strahl. This seems to highlight how affective experience can (dis)color the rich nuance of memory. The impact of trauma on one's ability to remember is often discussed in this way, but we do not necessarily give equal attention to the ways in which "positive" affect may also produce the same effect, eliding the details of memory. Intrigued by these discrepancies and disturbed by my own ellipses, at the prompt of my friend and colleague Dylan Robinson I returned to an online video of the same moment, now housed in the National Centre for Truth and Reconciliation. For Robinson and me, the goal was to consider how our memories of the TRC events compared to archival videos and media representations of those moments.

I watch the Strahl clip embedded in a longer video about the overall gathering. From what I recall, when I saw the media coverage of the moment, Strahl's breakdown was the main focus, which I found frustrating. But in this video the Strahl moment is simply one among many. In my memory, Strahl broke down after discussing his own family, his own grandchildren. But here he is shown having difficulty even before he starts talking about his own family. As I watch the video, it strikes me that it is after Strahl looks at the survivor beside him that he stumbles and needs to collect himself. It is this same look, I think, that prompts her to reach out her hand to him. Before watching the clip, I didn't recall this exchange, but now it seems significant. A moment of recognition, of face-to-face eye contact—that is what allowed for connection and then for the gesture of touch.

Field Notes, June 19, 2010

Powwow [figure 3.7]. There seemed to be two circles emanating out from the center. Having missed the earlier announcements that day, I walked toward the inner circle, to get closer so I could see. A woman asked me, "Are you a survivor?" "No," I responded. "This circle is for survivors." I felt embarrassed, a trespasser. "It's so hot today," she continued. "Yes," I said and nodded, wondering if it was more rude to stay or to slip away. She turned away, and I took that as my cue to walk away from the inner circle and back to the outer. The settler was the trespasser, the one outside the intimate circle.

On the final day of the event, Governor General Michaëlle Jean arrived in Winnipeg to participate in the reconciliation process. As the liaison between

FIGURE 3.7 Powwow on June 19, 2010, at the Winnipeg national gathering. Photo by Naomi Angel.

the government of Canada and the queen of England, the governor general signaled executive approval of the events of the day. Jean arrived with her security in tow, bringing a sense of formality to the scene. Throughout the day, Jean participated in the offering of the sacred fire ceremony, the youth sharing circle, and the powwow. Although there were many moments over the course of the four days that attracted media attention, Jean's presence at the gathering drew much of it. But even this coverage was fleeting. The G20 summit was scheduled for the following week in Toronto, and protests had begun in advance of the event. The news focused heavily on images of police in riot gear, tear gas, a flaming police car, and clashes between protesters and police. Discussion of the protests in Toronto quickly overshadowed the events in Winnipeg, with instances of police brutality against protesters and bystanders making evident the violence that the state can enact upon its citizens. In Winnipeg, the state was involved in a very different process, atoning for the violence of the past. But in a hierarchy of visibility, images of violence trumped images of reconciliation. On the last day of the event, in the Manitoba Theatre for Young People, Jean addressed the audience. "This is our duty now," she said of the reconciliation process, of Canada's duty to remember. "It is time for a rebirth."

FIGURE 3.8 Closing ceremony, prior to the fireworks display, in Winnipeg, June 19, 2010. Photo by Naomi Angel.

The closing ceremony for the Winnipeg national gathering was held at Oodena Circle and involved fireworks, fanfare, and the promise of more work to be done (figure 3.8). The fireworks were likely intended to entertain the children and families who were in attendance, but they also created a strange sense of spectacle and finality. They seemed both too joyful and too sad to signal the end of the event.

To Know Is to Weep

Field Notes: June 27, 2011

We were served bannock on the plane, a taste of the north, and the atmosphere on the trip was surprisingly jovial. "Are you going up for the reunion?" I heard people ask each other. "Yup." It was strange to hear people speaking of the TRC's national gathering in Inuvik as a reunion, but I suppose it was a reunion of sorts. It seemed that for many people, they were more interested in connecting with other former students than with the work of the commission.

"Are you going to give your testimony at the event?" I asked one woman on the plane. "I don't think so," was her response. She told me about her long day of travel. She had traveled from Chesterfield Inlet, Nunavut, which was as far north

FIGURE 3.9 At the welcoming ceremony in Inuvik. The former Indian residential school stands in the background while the Canadian flag flies in the wind, July 27, 2011. Photo by Naomi Angel.

as Inuvik, but further west and there was no direct way to travel from straight across, so she flew south only to turn around and fly north again. "Do you know where you're staying?" I asked. "Not yet. I think there's some accommodation being set up for us. I hope we get to camp. The weather's been nice so it'd be great to set up camp somewhere." But the bus dropped her and some others at what looked like a cluster of mobile homes, perhaps lodgings for seasonal laborers. "A bus will be by later to take you to town," she was told. And we continued on our way.

The town of Inuvik, population 3,500, welcomed more than 2,500 people who traveled by boat, car, and plane to the national gathering. Given its remote northern location, the event was much smaller than Winnipeg's, which had about twenty thousand people in attendance. During the welcoming ceremony in Inuvik, Chair Murray Sinclair addressed the audience (see figure 3.9): "The purpose of this event, simply stated, is to gather, record, and preserve the experiences of residential school survivors and others at the schools; to deepen our understanding of the impact of the residential school system and its continued effect on individuals, families, communities and our country as a whole[;] and to encourage and engage in a dialogue to set a better path for the future so that we can achieve a state of reconciliation."

Unlike the Winnipeg event, the second national gathering took place at a former residential school. Although the two student residences, Grollier Hall (run by the Catholic Church) and Stringer Hall (run by the Anglican Church), had been demolished years ago, the school itself, Sir Alexander MacKenzie (the school is known as "SAM" to locals), is still standing. It is currently used as the high school for the town. The location of Stringer Hall is now covered by the school's curling rink. Grollier Hall has been paved and, at the time of the event, had gray military tents erected where it once stood. (The Canadian Department of National Defense set up these tents to provide overflow housing in case it was needed for the TRC event.)

The first day of the event started with morning prayers. These were offered by Indigenous elders and were said in a mix of English, French, and several Indigenous languages, including Inuktitut and Inuvialuktun, North Slavey, South Slavey, Dogrib, Gwich'in, and Chipewyan. As in Winnipeg, these prayers involved a blend of Indigenous traditional prayers and blessings from the Christian faith. After the morning prayers, the ceremony for the lighting of the qullig, a traditional Inuit lamp, was conducted, and several drummers from the region performed (figure 3.10). Members of the community and the commission were welcomed, and then the day of testimony giving began. Each of the three subsequent days began in the same way. People were given the option of giving their testimony in private or in public. Those who wanted to share their experiences publicly did so in the high school gymnasium. Former students would be giving their testimony in the very same school they attended.

Throughout the gathering, many survivors incorporated their Indigenous languages into their presentations, and some noted that this in itself was healing. Some survivors spoke their testimonies directly to their own families, as opposed to speaking to the commission or those people in the audience. Some people broke down as they shared their experiences of being taken from their parents and separated from their extended families and communities. Some spoke explicitly of the verbal, physical, and sexual abuse that they endured at the schools. Others discussed their lives once they left school, detailing some of the system's long-term effects. Many former students offered apologies to their own children, explaining that because they were taken from their parents, they had not learned how to be parents themselves. Former student Ernie Bernhardt called for his three daughters to stand so he could publicly apologize. "I'm sorry I put you in harm's way," he said. He spoke of wishing he had been a better father to his children. Testimonies like Bernhardt's disrupted the relationship set up

FIGURE 3.10 Inuvik drummers at the welcome ceremony, July 27, 2011. Photo by Naomi Angel.

by the commission and the assumption that the colonial relationship was the most significant one being reconciled. Some survivors, like Bernhardt, chose to speak to their families, some of whom were present. Others spoke of family members who were not present. They held up old photographs. One woman held up the old Canadian two-dollar bill (see figure 3.11): "My ancestor is on this bill." She drew attention to how his image had circulated all these years, in people's everyday lives, in people's pockets. "You respected this bill more than him," she explained.

Often the testimony went beyond the school experience. Paul Voudrach spoke of the abuse he suffered in Grollier Hall and how it affected his life and family members:

> I thought I would be brave to face the demons that haunted me for 49 years, but I see today and since Monday that it still affects me. That the things that happened through the 49 years that I kept hidden in me. I left home and I didn't know why or where I was going, but I went in a plane with my sister and brother...and then they separated us. I don't know why they separated us. Their clothes were taken and mine were taken as well. My parents gave me some clothes and they were taken. My

FIGURE 3.11 A survivor holds up an old two-dollar bill. Photo by Naomi Angel.

winter clothes were taken too.... My mom came to visit me one time
and I couldn't even see her. I was taken from my bed with my mouth
covered, and... I don't remember going into his room. I developed a
scab between my crotch from below my belly button to my inner thighs.
I don't know how long it was like that. I was too scared to go see the
sister, the nun, or the nurse. I don't know how it healed. But I carried
that secret with me for 49 years. My first wife passed away in 2007, and
she never even knew about this.

I contemplated suicide in 1989. But it is by the grace of god that I
sit here today. It's by the grace of god that he stopped me from going to
those rifles on the porch. I stopped and I thought, what are my children
going to say, to see their dad dead on the porch.

I no longer live by the number 142. I'm Paul Voudrach, and I have
the right to live. And I have the right to be happy because I know I
deserve it. And my children, if they can hear me, they have the right
to come to me and say, "Dad, we didn't like what you did," and I can
say I know and I'm sorry. And I thank this gathering here for listening to my story. It hasn't been an easy road, but we're not alone in it.
Thank you.[74]

Voudrach's testimony was a moving tribute to the resilience of survivors, but it was also a powerful example of how his residential school experiences followed him into adulthood. When he said that he no longer lived by the number 142—referencing the number assigned to him at school—he publicly reclaimed his name. By ending his testimony with these words, "we're not alone in it," Voudrach gestured toward community and the intimate ties that bind families and former students together. At times during his testimony, Voudrach's voice shook with emotion. At the national gatherings, grief was the emotion that was most expected. But Voudrach showed how other emotions were also critical. Anger and frustration rippled to the surface as he spoke, as did pride and love.

At times during the gathering, humor and laughter also found their place. As Richard Neyersoo, chief of Gwichin Tribal Council, said in the Inuvik opening ceremonies, "We are here to cry together, but also to laugh and dance together." In participating in the national gatherings, the survivors of the IRS system challenged the affective regulation imposed upon them at the schools. Some also resisted the dominant discourses of healing and traumatic memory circulating at the event. For instance, Petah Inukpuk spoke about the knowledge his great-grandfather had of the land and the traditions of his people, disrupting the therapeutic discourse common at the event (figure 3.12). This was an important gesture for Inukpuk. Talking to Michael Swan, a journalist for the *Catholic Register*, Inukpuk has explained that the Inuit were different before the residential schools tried to break their families, traditions, and forms of knowledge. In regards to the national gathering and its participants, Inukpuk shared some of his thoughts about pain and remembrance: "These people are in pain, but it's not our nature to feel pain.... Our people are becoming like white people, lingering on their pain too long."[75] Drawing attention to how showcasing forms of grief and healing can also be colonial and privileged in nature, Inukpuk's speech reveals some of the many different structures of feeling that ran through the event and reveals the potential of testimony to disrupt expected narratives of grief.

Writing about an Inuit "ethical injunction to remember," anthropologist Lisa Stevenson has emphasized that Inuit knowledge is about experience. Given as much, she claims that the ethical should be understood not as rules or codes of living but as "a series of skills one learns by practice."[76] According to Stevenson, memory is one such technology in Inuit communities. Building upon her field research in Nunavut, she distinguishes between three different forms of memory as they intersect in Inuit communities. Nostalgic memory longs for a past, often a precolonial past. Traumatic memory is that

FIGURE 3.12 Petah Inukpuk holds up an image of his great-grandfather, Quaguag, while giving testimony in Inuvik. Photo by Naomi Angel.

which has been imposed upon a person or community; it is inescapable in the sense that it is a burden forced upon the survivor "from the outside, as something at once personal and foreign, at once recognized and unwanted."[77] In contrast, ethical memory requires practice and transformation. In Inuit communities, ethical memory requires not simply the *knowledge* of traditional practices, such as seal hunting, but also their *practice*. In other words, the ethical injunction to remember demands action. In Petah Inukpuk's testimony at the national gathering, he spoke about his great-grandfather's knowledge of the land—not out of nostalgia, or mourning, but as a way to draw attention once again to the ethical practice of remembering. In his interview with Swan, Inukpuk explains that his ancestor's knowledge needs to be revived. Swan, focusing on the overflow of grief at the national gathering, wrote: "To know this truth is to weep." For Swan, and for many observers, memories of the IRS system were mediated through grief, through traumatic memory. However, Inukpuk sought to point toward an ethical injunction to remember.

Spaces of trauma can also be spaces of empowerment. Although writing about a different context, Ann Cvetkovich's work about "an archive of feelings" in queer art practices is useful here: "The fear of encountering trauma can be debilitating, lending itself to the assumption that political movements cannot incorporate affect or conflict, or that the negotiation of affective life within public cultures is not important work."[78] In Inuvik the fear of encountering trauma was eclipsed by the strength inspired by survivors who shared their pasts. The negotiation of affective life at the national gathering was a reclamation of power and a demonstration of agency by students who were once forbidden from expressing their own emotional responses to an oppressive system. By sharing their experiences, former students reclaimed their own affective responses to the losses they incurred at the schools; they asserted their own affective sovereignty.[79]

History is constructed, narratives are compiled, and collected memories become collective memory. These processes are not uncomplicated. Even in including partial transcriptions of testimony in this book, I have filtered survivors' words through my own lens. What I have produced is not a comprehensive narrative; it is a rumination on the dynamics of reconciliation as I saw them unfold in Winnipeg and Inuvik. I have attempted, following Lee Maracle, to focus on "theory through story," allowing for the testimonies of survivors and the work of Indigenous scholars to come through the narrative constructed. But what I have described is just one possible interpretation of these events, and it is necessarily fragmented.[80]

This chapter points toward how memory can be recast, performed, and transmitted through various means, including testimony, but also through tradition and protest. It gestures to the multiple ways that the work of the TRC can be framed: as an archival project, for example, as a performance, or maybe as a site of struggle. For instance, Gus Higheagle's song at Winnipeg and the lighting of the sacred fire can also be seen as testaments to survival. They are reminders that both language and action are important.

The TRC national gatherings were spaces of layered affective experience and contrasting emotions where Indigenous participants managed to assert their own agency and speak against a coherent program of "reconciliation" and any facile presumptions about "truth." Although there was certainly a prescriptive form for the events as laid out by Schedule N, this form was inhabited by survivors and intergenerational survivors in ways that allowed for the work that needed to be done, respondent (like much Indigenous protocol) to specific individuals, to time, and to the feeling of coming together in gatherings. Given as much, TRC events must be understood as much more than opportunities for settler Canadians to learn and understand more about the IRS and its devastating legacies; these were gatherings that reaffirmed intergenerational kinship between Indigenous peoples and across the communities and nations to which they belong.

Reconciliation as a Ghostly Encounter

Discourses of Haunting and Indian Residential Schools

It was an evil place. It was a beautiful place.
—TERRY GLAVIN, *Amongst God's Own*, 2002

On a clear day in May 2011, I find myself walking through the Fraser River Heritage Park in Mission, British Columbia. The grass is green and well-manicured. The Fraser River is not far away, and its blue water is visible from the hills of the park. A small gazebo casts shade onto a narrow patch of grass, and a family has spread out a picnic blanket and some food. A few people sit on the benches provided. The scene is idyllic. Not too far away, in the corner of the park, there is a small cemetery. Scattered throughout the park are several cement slabs, large gray plots of land with moss growing through their cracks. I wonder how many people know that St. Mary's Indian Residential School once stood here.

This chapter returns to the framework of "colonial debris" through a consideration of the residential schools themselves, of their physical structures, of their continuing presence, and of Indigenous initiatives to build new futures from the rubble of the IRS system. It is a chapter about remnants, material traces, and ephemeral experiences of things long past, focusing on the narratives that continue to spring from the schools. Because many of the schools have been abandoned or demolished, this is also a chapter about hauntings, about cemeteries and bones, about burials and excavations. And because some of the schools have been taken back by Indigenous communities, this is a story about reclamation and occupation, about resilience and resurgence.

In chapter 3, I focused on the work done through and at the IRS TRC's national gatherings, looking at how survivors were able to claim the space and act of public testimony in order to assert their own forms of affective sovereignty. Although the schools sought to control and limit the students' emotions, survivors have reclaimed their right to express themselves—often in very public ways—at these gatherings. The national events provided an opportunity for memory work to be done on a grand scale. But to understand the history and legacies of the IRS system, one also has to look outside the confines of the IRS TRC and its activities. This chapter moves away from the orchestrated events of the TRC and explores how local communities have embarked on their own processes of reconciliation. I argue that the sites of former schools can be seen as another kind of archive. Whether they have been demolished or have been taken back by Indigenous communities, these spaces constitute a sort of living archive where questions about forms of reconciliation are also very much at stake.

As we have seen throughout *Fragments of Truth*, colonial documents, archival images, and memory in the form of testimony are all phenomena that can be seen to represent the IRS legacy in different ways. But the schools themselves are perhaps the largest physical remnants of this legacy. In this chapter I focus on the stories told by these structures. To help reveal and excavate these narratives, I refer to literature written by Indigenous authors about these schools, cinematic representations of the schools, media coverage of their selective demolition, and a wide array of stories about the ceremonies and events that have taken (and continue to take) place in and around these structures. I have also referenced my own field notes, taken while I visited several sites of former Indian residential schools.

Imagining as Haunting

The concept of haunting has become an emergent theme for many scholars interested in exploring colonial and postcolonial societies.[1] In processes of reconciliation, hauntings can tell us about whose stories have been left out, about silences, and about gaps in the historical construction of the past.[2] José Colmeiro has argued that haunting narratives "make visible the disappearances and absences silenced in normative historical accounts, and replicate the process of confronting a difficult past that still needs to be dealt with in the present."[3] Such narratives also gesture toward the often unseen hierarchies of power that pervade postcolonial societies.[4] The language of haunting helps reveal and challenge these hierarchies. Still, academic discourses of haunting have generally focused on Western concepts of ghosts and specters, whereas Indigenous cultures often have their own diverse epistemologies of the spirit world. By turning to the physical structures of the Indian residential schools, as well as the stories that have been told about them, this chapter seeks to open a dialogue with epistemologies of haunting in newly productive ways.

Stories about the nation have always been, in part, constructed through ghostly presences. In his seminal work on nationhood, *Imagined Communities*, Benedict Anderson begins with a discussion of the tombs and cenotaphs of "unknown soldiers." As markers of anonymous men who died in service of their countries, these tombs, Anderson claims, are "saturated with ghostly *national* imaginings," helping to develop an imagined kinship among citizen strangers.[5] Building on Anderson's insights, Justin Edwards takes this one step further, arguing that "the nation is not just a socio-political fact, but also a ghost story."[6] In the Canadian context, many authors have written of the specters of colonialism and the "great white North" as a haunted landscape.[7] In general, these ghosts are evoked in a metaphorical or theoretical way to discuss the complex manner by which the past makes itself manifest in the present. As Avery Gordon has written, haunting "alters the experience of being in time, the way we separate the past, the present, and the future. These specters or ghosts appear when the trouble they represent and symptomize is no longer being contained or repressed or blocked from view."[8] But there are also thinkers such as Eve Tuck (Unangax̂) and C. Ree, who discuss the haunting produced by the colonial encounter in a more literal way: "Haunting is the cost of subjugation. It is the price paid for violence, for genocide."[9] Tuck and Ree explain that, along with the restitution of Indigenous lands and sovereignty, decolonization means "attending to ghosts, and arresting widespread denial of the violence done to them."[10] In a collaboration with the Super Futures Haunt Qollective, Morrill and Tuck argue that "settler colonial societies are haunted by the ghost of gone peoples."[11] For these thinkers, haunting can be understood as a practice of power, a strategy of resistance on the part of Indigenous peoples.

When I started the research for this chapter, I believed that these discourses of haunting would be useful to me as I engaged with the histories and physical traces of the IRS structures. But as my research progressed, I found that many former students discussed ghosts and hauntings in ways I had not anticipated. Indeed, some former students spoke openly about encountering ghosts at the schools, and there was even some media coverage focusing on paranormal activity at former school sites.[12] At first, I bracketed these ghostly encounters as anomalies. I was uncertain what to make of these spectral presences, and my instinct as a researcher was to dismiss these tales in favor of a more theoretical haunting. Still, the ghost stories stayed with me.

In 2010 I attended the Truth, Reconciliation and the Residential Schools conference at Nipissing University in North Bay, Ontario, a small city located about five hours north of Toronto. I presented a paper that focused on reconciliation in South Africa. In particular, I focused on a book that was coauthored by Antjie Krog (Afrikaner author and journalist), Nosisi Mpolweni (Xhosa lecturer and linguist), and Kopano Ratele (psychologist). The book—*There Was This Goat: Investigating the Truth Commission Testimony of Notrose Nobomvu Konile*—discusses one particular testimony, given by Mrs. Konile to the South Africa TRC in 1996. Konile's testimony was a complex layering of cultural symbols that recounted memories from her dreams as well as her reality. Those responsible for taking, transcribing, and translating Konile's testimony did not understand the relationship between dream life and waking life in Xhosa culture. In recounting some of these complexities, the authors of *There Was This Goat* write:

> These "strange" testimonies underline the importance of refraining from "un-strange-ing" the strange—to allow it to be strange—but within its original logical and coherent context. Accommodation of "strangeness" would keep the spaces of tolerance open for many people emerging from contexts of conflict and estrangement. It could also provide an opportunity for the ideas, techniques and issues from non-Western communities to become part of intercultural exchange and genuine scientific innovation.[13]

At the end of my presentation, an older Indigenous man approached me. "It's similar in Canada," he said. "We look to our dream lives and visions for guidance. And to our ancestors too. Some people don't understand that." His brief comment suggested that ancestral communions can play an important role in contemporary Indigenous lives. His emphasis on a lack of understanding seems apt for getting at the discomfort that frequently arises when engaging discourses of spectrality. As I began to hear of hauntings at the schools, his remarks often came to mind.

In many Indigenous perceptions of the landscape now called Canada, spirits and ghosts are not just metaphors; they also play a role in debates about concrete, physical things. For example, disputes over land and resources often take sacred burial sites into consideration. The presence of bones and spirits, in other words, plays a very real role in contemporary negotiations of relationships between Indigenous and non-Indigenous Canadians.[14] But for me, encounters with ghosts gestured to a way of interacting and experiencing the world that was outside of my immediate experience and that felt uncomfortable. Instead of editing these experiences out, I found myself drawn to exploring the potentially unsettling concept of reconciliation as a ghostly encounter. According to Paulette Regan, "Rather than adopting the stance of the colonizer-perpetrator who listens to survivor testimonies with the empathy of a spectator, thereby simply re-inscribing colonial relations, we must attend to our unsettling responses to testimonies as important clues to our own decolonization."[15] If reconciliation involves a shift in ways of seeing, as I have argued, I began to wonder if ghostly presences might gesture toward such a shift. Or, phrased differently, I began to ask myself: What does it mean to see ghosts?

In the case of the Indian residential schools, discussions of ghosts seem to happen on several levels: as a discursive device to describe the sensation of a lingering, traumatic past; as apparitions in Indigenous literature that represent complex relations to family ancestors and the Creator; and as a way to describe paranormal or ghostly activity reported at the schools. Tracing out a theoretical framework of haunting, as both an analytical tool and a metaphor for colonial and postcolonial conflicts, certainly seemed to offer a productive (if imperfect) way to think about Canada's colonial past and "postcolonial" present, but it felt equally important to grapple with how and when talk of ghosts ventured beyond the theoretical and into the lived experiences of IRS survivors.

As one among many examples, we might turn to the history of Nova Scotia's Shubenacadie School, which burned to the ground in 1986. The school was said to be located on a Mi'kmaq burial ground, and students, both while attending the school and for years afterward, have often spoken of the ghosts they remember encountering there. Many of these ghosts were benevolent. Bernie Knockwood recounts hearing the faint voices of small children in the stairway in the middle of the night: "The third time it happened I sat there and prayed for the little boy and said, 'I hope your grandmother finds you. Be happy.' And he never came back. Maybe that was the part they were trying to quash in us—the ties with our ancestors."[16] For Knockwood the ghost was neither an ominous specter threatening danger nor a sad figure representing a traumatic history but rather a reminder that the schools were trying to sever his connections to the past and to the traditions of his culture. As I heard more of these ghostly narratives, I found myself wondering whether one can engage theoretical narratives of spectrality without also engaging testimonies and recollections that speak about spirits. Can a metaphorical discussion of haunting also accommodate the experiences of Indigenous peoples with their ancestors?

First, a note about the problematic nature of these questions. As a settler, speaking to a readership that I presume will also largely consist of non-Indigenous people, I recognize that to speak of ghosts is to venture onto difficult terrain, and it may spark debate about rational, secular thought versus "primitive" or spiritual ways of knowing. I don't think that I can bridge this divide, but I do hope to create a conversation where one is not dismissed in favor of the other. I turn to W. J. T. Mitchell's work to help address this difficulty. In *What Do Pictures Want?* Mitchell spends some time preemptively responding to critics who might object to his exploration of the subjectivity of images:

> To save time, I want to begin with the assumption that we are capable of suspending our disbelief in the very premises of the question, what do pictures want? I'm well aware that this is a bizarre, perhaps even objectionable question. I'm aware that it involves a subjectivizing of images, a dubious personification of inanimate objects; that it flirts with a regressive, superstitious attitude toward images, one that if taken seriously would return us to practices like totemism, fetishism, idolatry, and animism. These are practices that most modern, enlightened people regard with suspicion as primitive, psychotic, or childish in their traditional forms.[17]

Although I do not explicitly focus on the same issues, this chapter also deals with what might be called "dubious" subject matter. Following Mitchell, I would note that it is important to suspend disbelief in our discussion of ghosts, refraining from dismissing this talk as "primitive, psychotic, or childish." Instead, we might consider how spectrality can be seen to inform certain Indigenous epistemologies, frequently as a way of understanding one's connection with and responsibilities to one's ancestors and future kin. In particular, I want to ask what it means that the discourses surrounding residential schools can be bound to those of ghosts. To some readers, this may be an "objectionable question." However, it is important here to acknowledge that reconciliation always involves "objectionable questions," for the ongoing process of reconciliation involves returning to suppressed histories of so-called objectionable practices and epistemologies, including questions about human and nonhuman relations, not only of the spirit world but also of the living, animate world. Mitchell might categorize such a practice as "a dubious personification of inanimate objects," but in order to speak to reconciliation, it is necessary to intrepidly explore such supposedly "gray areas," even when they engender confusion or disbelief.

Memory and Place

Stories about hauntings are evocative in part because they are tied to notions of place while also invoking a sense of placelessness. They mobilize both a feeling of home and the specter of homelessness. Narratives of ghosts often allude to a sense of unmooring and evoke a feeling between connection and disconnection. In settler polities such as Canada, hauntings also draw attention to the demarcation between the governed and the ungovernable. Colonial policies attempt to govern every aspect of Indigenous lives.[18] However, a ghostly presence cannot be controlled; it cannot be governed away or into submission.

Following Brian Osborne, it can be argued that hauntings illustrate how "landscapes become psychic terrains."[19] All landscapes are living. They breathe and change with time, and they have stories to tell. The Indian residential schools and the land they were built upon speak of both cultural destruction and reinvigoration. Land is central to Indigenous concepts of self, to political, cultural, and spiritual identities. As Taiaiake Alfred writes, "The land, and all it has to teach, to give, and all it demands, is what it means to be Indigenous."[20] By drawing attention to the different ways that land is thought about and through, Indigenous scholars have helped to foreground how land can be understood as a powerful site for memory. It has been claimed that for many Indigenous communities, "places in their landscape are also sacred, as places of power, of journeys related to spirit beings, of entities that must be appeased."[21] In other words, landscapes and the structures built upon them are material traces where meaning gets produced and negotiated.[22] "Land," Alfred writes, "is not territory, except in a colonial way of looking at the landscape."[23]

In the case of Indian residential schools, the structures themselves can reveal how colonialism was, following Sarah de Leeuw's turn of phrase, "a spatialized set of endeavours." Writing about Indian residential schools in British Columbia, de Leeuw notes that "far then from functioning as mere containers through which colonial narratives were delivered, residential school buildings and grounds were colonial geographies in which First Nations students were enveloped. The buildings ensured First Nations students, from the moment they set eyes upon the places of their 'education,' were spatially disoriented in a place designed to exclude and expunge indigeneity."[24]

As de Leeuw's work highlights, some Indigenous students were able to resist these colonial efforts by renegotiating, challenging, even attacking the school structures themselves. Broken windows and school fires were not uncommon. Physically breaking down the schools became one way to express resistance toward the colonial system. So, just as the construction of the schools represented a spatialized set of colonial endeavors, the process of decolonization may also be initiated through these very same structures. Looking at the schools through the lens of reconciliation helps to reveal how the decolonization process is felt and experienced, in part, through place.

Place can work to lock memories in or to revive them. Pierre Nora's work on sites of memory has been influential in theorizing the role of spatiality (in addition to temporality) in memory studies. He traces the desire for preserving memory through specific sites of memorialization. For Nora, the past, present, and future are involved in a complicated and changing relationship: "We are no longer on very good terms with the past. We can only recover it by reconstructing it in monumental detail with the aid of documents and archives; in other words, what we today call 'memory'—a form of memory that is itself a reconstruction—is simply what was called 'history' in the past." According to Nora, whose work reveals nostalgia for an organic and embodied memory of the past, the modern preoccupation with memorials and museums is a kind of artificial construct of memory that reminds us of what we have forgotten. Nora argues that these "lieux de mémoire" exist because we have lost the "milieux de memoire," where memory exists as an active and real aspect of everyday life. As Nora argues, lieux de memoire can act to confine memories, locking them into particular forms and narratives, and disallowing for alternatives. However, milieux de memoire require active and constant negotiation. Ghostly encounters can be seen as part of milieux de memoire because they integrate experiences of the past into everyday life.[25]

Reconciliation and Haunting

Ghost stories are discursive formations, and, as such, they have a tradition and a scope like any other. But stories that revolve around hauntings can be particularly difficult to decode, for they are often layered and textured in a way that separates them from any known reality. Mohawk scholar Audra Simpson has written about how captivity narratives (where settlers are captured by Indians) worked as a form of "rhetorical (and political) possibility" in American literature. She argues that such stories "gave settler anxiety a textual locus for reflection and articulation."[26] Much the same can be said about narratives of hauntings, especially those where Indigenous peoples haunt the settler imaginary. But with stories of ghostly encounters at residential schools, spirit interaction is not necessarily about the settler imaginary; indeed, in some cases it is the settler who haunts the Indigenous imaginary.

In Loretta Todd's (Métis/Cree) documentary *The Learning Path*, we can start to get a sense of some of these multidirectional hauntings.[27] One of the five-part National Film Board series *As Long as the River Flows*, the documentary focuses on the stories of several Indigenous women and their experiences with education. The film opens with black-and-white archival footage. Indigenous children are in school uniforms, playing sports, running in a field. The next shot shows young boys standing behind a wire fence. They look beyond the camera, unsmiling. The film transitions from archival imagery to a shot of an empty school hallway, shot in black and white. Lockers line the corridors. A woman's voice is laid over the image; she tells of the racial taunts and teasing she endured while attending school. The film goes on to recount the stories of Olive Dickason, Dr. Anne Anderson, and Eva Cardinal, among others; each woman tells of her own experience in the Canadian educational system. They share stories of past abuses at residential schools, as well as the narratives of their eventual empowerment through education.

The Learning Path shifts seamlessly from archival footage to scenes of reenactment, blurring conventional distinctions between fiction and documentary. At one point, a young girl and an older woman, perhaps her grandmother, walk along a snowy and deserted road. They talk in Cree and smile as a car drives toward them. A man in the car gets out; while their backs are turned to him, the man says, "I have to take the child." These are the only English words spoken in the scene. As the car drives away, the grandmother waves, speaks in her native tongue, covers her face, and begins to cry. In another scene, a nun walks through a long school corridor. Shot in black and white, the nun seems to float through the hallway, an otherworldly silhouette. Todd has spoken about the figure of the nun as both "horrible and beautiful at the same time."[28] And she has discussed the evolution of this scene, recollecting memories from the schools:

> At night we would hear [the nuns] walking down the corridors, the heavy wool of their habits brushing against the corridor, and even though it

held terror, it was still our childhood sound. How could I convey that? I tried to create the sense of these beings in our lives who are both terrifying and comforting. That's when I decided to go to an abandoned residential school. I put the daughter of a woman who was working on the film in an old nun's outfit. I shot those scenes in black and white. I wanted the light to burn out the image and have the nun figure drift through the hallways and rooms. We never see the face in the film, because we never saw their faces in real life. They were just faceless. They drift through this place as ghosts, as haunting, terrible ghosts.[29]

The aesthetics of haunting allow Todd to approach the representation of the IRS system in a way that aligns with her memory of the lived experience. Todd has no interest in serving as an "interpreter of reality" who explains everything in detail. "All we ever do is explain," she once remarked.[30] Depicting the nun as an eerie, uncanny figure, the film leaves the viewer feeling unsettled, as if having experienced a ghostly encounter.

To Dance with Ghosts

In 1890 the Ghost Dance movement was sweeping across the American West and parts of the Canadian prairies. The ceremony predicted the fall of settler societies and the return of buffalo and lush landscapes. But the movement was violently put down, notably with the Wounded Knee massacre in 1890. James (Sákéj) Youngblood Henderson (Chickasaw) has described how Eurocentric writers have misunderstood the Ghost Dance: "The normative visions and the dances were not part of a messianic movement but a sustained vision of how to resist colonization."[31] In other words, the Ghost Dance was not simply a religious or sacred ceremony but a political one as well, one in which resistance played a key role. It was not only a sacred ceremony but also part of a political protocol that was, as Grace Li Xiu Woo writes, "designed to release the spirits contained in the old rites and ceremonies and restore traditional consciousness."[32] In many Indigenous cultures, ghosts are not to be feared; they are seen as benevolent, as figures of healing and resistance.[33] The Ghost Dance in particular was "essentially an assertion of Indianness in opposition to forced acculturation."[34]

The Ghost Dance has also taken on new forms. For instance, Cree poet Louise Halfe describes her writing as a Ghost Dance, a way to conjure spirits of the past who can return to the present and make things right. "The prairie is full of bones," she writes. "The bones stand and sing and I feel the weight of them as they guide my fingers on this page."[35] Warren Cariou has described Halfe's collection of poetry *Blue Marrow* in these terms: "These bones are not simply reminders of past crimes, chilling spectacles of violence. Instead, they also act as guides, moving the author's hand on the bone-pen that writes the poem in blue marrow—that is, ink. Halfe even goes so far as to reverse the direction of the haunting, describing her imprecations to the spirits by saying, 'É—pécimakik / I haunt them.'"[36]

By "reversing the direction of the haunting," Halfe provokes many questions about the various pathways for and potential conversations with ghosts. The writing in *Blue Marrow* constitutes a form of resistance. A ghostly apparition may represent something troubling about the past, but it may also represent strength or support in the present. According to Susan Gingell and Azalea Borrieses, Halfe's ghosts are particularly potent because they help "provoke an examination of the wrongs of the past and attempt to drive home the need to redress in the present."[37] The legacy of the IRS system, and the need to address that legacy, can be felt throughout Halfe's work. A survivor of the Blue Quills Indian Residential School, Halfe has written powerfully about the impacts of sexual abuse at the schools.

NITOTEM

He was tired of having his ears pulled,
squeezed and slapped
by Sister Superior. They bled and
swelled, scabbed and scaled like the brick wall.
Often he didn't hear the Sister shouting
and clapping her orders at him
or the rest of the little boys.
The others, when they could,
would nudge him so he could lip-read Sister's words.

He was embarrassed to undress in front of all the boys
and especially Sister.
At home he always looked out the window
when someone was undressing. Here everyone looked
and laughed at your private parts.
Soon they too were no longer private.

He suffered in silence
in the dark. A hand muffled his mouth
while the other snaked his wiener. He had no

other name, knew no other word. Soon it was no
longer just the hand but the push, just a gentle
push at first, pushing, pushing. Inside the
blanket he sweated and felt the wings
of pleasure, inside his chest the breath burst
pain, pleasure, shame. Shame.

On the reserve he had already raped two
women, the numbers didn't matter.
Sister Superior was being punished. It was
Father who said it was woman's fault
and that he would go to hell.

He walked, shoulder slightly stooped
and never looked directly at anyone.
When spoken to he mumbled into his chest.
His black hair covered his eyes. He no longer
tried to lip-read, no longer studied the
brick wall.[38]

Halfe's writing is many things. It is a powerful interpretation of ancestral
and familial stories. It is a representation of the intimate relationships between settlers and Indigenous peoples. It is both dark and light. She writes
of intermarriage, of ceremonies that bind people together, and of long
lines of lineage that cross boundaries of time and bloodlines. It was with
Halfe's poetry in mind that I made the trip to her former school, Blue Quills
Indian Residential School.

Blue Quills

Field Notes, May 25, 2011

*I arrived in Edmonton yesterday and drove 3 hours to St. Paul, Alberta.
The landscape was beautiful. Not the flat lands of the prairies I had been expecting, but low hills, fields of crops, hay bales, grass yellowed in spots to create
patterns that spoke to the wild weather sometimes experienced in these parts.
After arriving in St. Paul and checking into the hotel, I drove a couple miles
west and arrived at the Blue Quills First Nations College. The imposing brick
building stood directly ahead of me. To the left, there was a large white tipi.
Behind the school, along a short dirt road, stood a cluster of tipis [figure 4.1].
Cars and trucks were parked along the way and I could hear kids playing and
adults chatting. A group of women were skinning a moose hide nearby.*

FIGURE 4.1 Tipis behind Blue Quills First Nation College, May 26, 2011. Photo by Naomi Angel.

This was the annual Blue Quills cultural camp. Coinciding with the national Day of Reconciliation on May 25, the camp was a weeklong event held at the school. The schedule was filled with arts and crafts (rattle making, decorative drums, painting, clay works), sharing circles, wagon rides, sweat lodges, and traditional ceremonies (the Horse Dance ceremony and Chicken Dance ceremony). In attendance at the camp were many former students who attended the school when it was still Blue Quills Indian Residential School. In the 1970s the school was taken back by nearby communities, and it became the first Indigenous-run college in Canada. It is now Blue Quills First Nations College.[39]

Over the course of my trip, I heard the story of Blue Quills many times. People were rightfully proud of the school's history. In the 1960s the future of Blue Quills was uncertain. The St. Paul School Board was reporting a "94 percent dropout rate of Indian students from provincial schools."[40] In 1970 the First Nations of Saddle Lake and Athabasca district staged a sit-in at the school. They refused to move until they had control of the school. After several days the movement began to splinter:

> There was friction and controversy about the take-over growing from within the assembly that stemmed from people's fears of failure. In a

heart moving address delivered at the sit-in when protestors were being harassed by internal dissenters, Mr. Cardinal [one of the organizers] captured the attention of all present when he asked these jarring questions. "In the past 40 years, since the department had control over our schooling, how many of us completed grade 12? If you have, stand up." No one stood up. He went on to enquire, "How many of us completed grade 8? Let's stand up!" One person sheepishly rose from his chair. "How many of us completed grade 6?" A handful of people stood up. Then he said, "Look around. We can't do any worse by taking over this school! We need graduates who will return to our reserves to teach our people so that we can become strong as nations." His speech made such a resonating impact which caused the people in the room to unite and stand together to assert their responsibility to determine the educational destinies of their own children and grandchildren.[41]

The sit-in lasted twenty-one days. After negotiating with minister of Indian Affairs (and future prime minister) Jean Chrétien, Blue Quills became the first school administered by Indigenous people for Indigenous people. The school emphasizes educating students "in such a manner that their Cree identity or 'onehiawiwiniyiw' emerges free from a colonial mentality."[42]

On my first day at Blue Quills, former student Eric Large took me on a tour of the school. He pointed out the old dormitories where he slept, the nurse's supply closet, old classrooms. We walked through what was once the girls' dormitory. "I don't know much about this part of the building," he said. "We were never allowed here. They always kept us apart. We didn't take classes together, eat together, or play together. Even brothers and sisters were separated." The practice of keeping siblings or family members of different genders separated was common. "Place," according to Sarah de Leeuw, "particularly place as gendered and segregated, functioned within residential school to separate families and erode familial ties, furthering the colonial goals of assimilating and transforming Aboriginal peoples."[43] Former student Alice Blondin-Perrin has also written of the effects of this policy:

> It took me years to understand the dynamics of family structures and relationships. At my young age, I could only wave to my brother Joe if I saw him once in a while at the movies. I could not understand why I could not speak to him. They would not give a reason, and no one dared ask. Once I waved to him, and being shy, he did not wave back to me. The moment struck in my memory. If I had been caught, even that meek gesture of waving to my brother would have meant trouble and humiliation.[44]

FIGURE 4.2 Eric Large looking up at Blue Quills First Nation College, May 26, 2011. Photo by Naomi Angel.

As we walked through the third floor of the four-story building, Large pointed to a door, now locked. "This is where the traveling dentist worked from. I gave a tour of this building before, and the smell of the dental fluoride came flooding back to me. I asked the others on the tour if they could smell it. It was so strong. I guess that's my body remembering." Here, Large gestured toward the many modes of remembering, for the body, too, is a technology of memory.[45] As we toured the school, Large spoke of his past experiences at Blue Quills, but he also introduced me to several individuals working at and attending the college in that very moment, at the time of our encounter. Large guided me through his memories of each floor, each room. As I looked at rows of desks or walls of shelves, he painted a picture of what the school used to look like (figure 4.2). "This wall is new," he would say, or "This area used to be closed off." The school had become a palimpsest, layered and textured by memory.

Specters and Spectators

On my last day at Blue Quills, Charles Wood, a former student, told me that the school used to organize special evenings for film screenings once a month. He recalled watching cowboy-and-Indian films as a child on the big screen. "When the cowboys shot those Indians, us kids all cheered," he explained. "We didn't understand that we were those Indians."

In *Black Skin, White Masks*, Frantz Fanon describes something similar when he writes about his experience of sitting in a darkened theater relating to the characters he sees on screen. In the case of colonialist adventure films such as the Tarzan series, for instance, who can and does the Black spectator relate to: the gallant explorer or the primitive savage? "In the Antilles," Fanon explains, "the young Negro identifies himself de facto with Tarzan against the Negroes."[46] And in speaking of the images encountered in comic strips, Fanon further laments that "the Wolf, the Devil, the Evil Spirit, the Bad Man, the Savage are always symbolized by Negroes or Indians." For Fanon, the spectator's inevitable identification with "the victor" implies a splitting and a refusal of the self for the Black subject. Concerning the politics of (mis)recognition, Charles Taylor writes that "the thesis is that our identity is partly shaped by recognition of others, and so a person or group of people can suffer real damage, real distortion, if the people or society around them mirror back to them a confining or demeaning or contemptible picture of themselves. Nonrecognition or misrecognition can inflict harm, can be a form of oppression, imprisoning someone in a false, distorted, and reduced mode of being."[47]

The Indian residential school system contributed to a general environment of nonrecognition and misrecognition, and a student's sense of self became distorted through the school system. For many, this distortion was further amplified by movies and other forms of popular culture. As Fanon discusses, often the "Indian" in popular representations was portrayed as "Other," so for some IRS students, Indigenous identity was understood as something to be performed through difference. Even school photos reveal how, standing beside children dressed as witches and wizards, Indigenous identities could be reduced to costume and performance (figure 4.3). The idea of "playing Indian," then, becomes relevant for both Indigenous and non-Indigenous people.[48] Here, again, one sees indigeneity taking shape through the realm of the visual, both in terms of popular representations and in terms of how those representations circulate and operate in the everyday lives of those who consume them.

The visual field, of course, is never straightforward. Over the course of my short stay at Blue Quills, I acted as both participant and spectator in several events and ceremonies. At some points I was allowed to take photographs; at others I was not. For example, I was encouraged to take photos

FIGURE 4.3 Halloween at Shingwauk Indian Residential School, 1954. Source: Library and Archives Canada R-9409-IBC 200173769. A Sault Daily Star photo.

during Eric Large's tour. Outside the school, however, the issue was more complicated. Toward the back of the school, where several tipis were set up for the Blue Quills cultural camp, event organizers had scheduled various informational sessions, including one on traditional medicines. I sat in on the session, learning about different herbal remedies. Later that evening I also participated in the Chicken Dance ceremony. For both of these events, my camera sat at my side, unused. By asking questions and following the lead of others, I was beginning to understand the rules of spectatorship at Blue Quills, the primary rule of which was "Watch, but do no harm."

Field Notes, May 25, 2011

I saw kerchiefs hung from trees today. In the back of the school grounds, about a dozen yards from the school. I asked Eric about them, and wondered whether I could take a picture. "No pictures," he said. "No pictures of that." They were offerings to spirits, to ancestors. "No pictures." It was a reminder that not everything was meant for the consumption of a camera. It was also a reminder that there were barriers to what I was allowed to access, that I could not understand everything happening here.

A Prairie School

Like Blue Quills, there are many residential schools that have been taken back by Indigenous communities. Turned into new schools, museums, and office spaces, these structures have become integral and vital to communities being rebuilt from within. My first visit to a former Indian residential school happened in 2010, just after the first IRS TRC national gathering in Winnipeg. Just about an hour's drive from the fanfare of the events in Winnipeg stands the Rufus Prince Building, formerly the Portage la Prairie Indian Residential School. Once the national gathering had concluded, I drove over and spent a day in Portage la Prairie.

The school itself was built in 1916, and it is the oldest standing former residential school in Manitoba. In 2005 it was officially designated a provincial heritage site and renamed the Rufus Prince Building, after a former student who founded the Dakota Ojibway Tribal Council and the Dakota Ojibway Police Force (the first Indigenous law enforcement agency in Canada). When I arrived in 2010, the building was being used as development and tribal offices for the Long Plain First Nation. In 2003, after much organizing and fund-raising, it was chosen to house the Indian Residential School Museum of Canada. Originally slated to open in 2008, the museum was meant to tell the history and legacy of the IRS system from an Indigenous perspective. After the museum lost its funding, the project was put on hold.[49] Memories sat in waiting at the former Portage la Prairie school, in archival limbo. At the time of my visit, a good portion of the documents, artwork, and photographs designated for the museum were still housed in the school's basement.[50]

I was given a tour of the grounds from Barb Esau and Robert Peters, both former IRS students. Esau had attended a nearby residential school, Sandy Bay. Peters had attended the Portage la Prairie school, in the very building where he now found himself working. The remnants of the past are still visible at the school, but the space has in many ways been reclaimed.

INTERVIEW EXCERPT WITH BARB ESAU

NAOMI Do you know the age range of students who attended here?
BARB The youngest one that was ever here was my cousin Patsy, and she was a little over two years old. Because my uncle was sent off to World War II and her mother had died giving birth to her brother. So they brought her here [*pointing to one of the former classrooms*]. This room belongs to Spirit Wind. Spirit Wind is working on all the

day-school students, working on the claims. They weren't part of the settlement agreement.

N   There must be something powerful about working on that kind of project in this location.

B   Right, in a residential school. I remember when I started working here, I really didn't like this building.

N   Because you know there are such difficult stories here?

B   Yeah, my mom and dad have told me stories about students passing away here. People just kind of disappearing all of a sudden.

While on a tour of the grounds, we stepped into the shed located just behind the school. The walls of the shed had been marked by students who had scrawled their names and doodles onto the wood surface. The writing was of the sort one often sees in school buildings, where in moments of camaraderie or solitude young people leave their mark as a sign of youthful rebellion. A few were simply names: "Walter Cameron." "Harold Isaac." Others commented on the school experience: "Indian Starving School." Others were simply dates that marked the time students spent there. And some were a variation of the common statement "I was here," followed by the date: "1954." There was something particularly powerful about these declarative statements of existence. Written from within a system that had tried to assimilate the Indigenous population, these etchings had lasted for over half a century. When I posted the photo shown in figure 4.4 to my research blog (tracingmemory.com), one commenter left these remarks:

> Hi, I was just browsing this site because my dad went to this school when I noticed on the last picture, it looks like it [sic] written in white lettering "Louis Harper June 29, 1955." Louis was my father and was taken at a very young age, after graduating he went on to join the Queens Own Rifles of Canada, which meant that he never really got to see my grandparents throughout his childhood.... This is an amazing find and brings me to want to go see this in person for myself.

Through his act of writing on the wall at Portage la Prairie School, Harper's youthful transgression reached out through time and space, like an apparition, to touch his son: a father's presence still felt.

Field Notes, June 22, 2010
   At one point during the tour, Barbara Esau pointed up to the ceiling where there was a small hatch. It was probably about 2 feet square and one side had a small latch. "I heard that they put kids up there for punishment," she explained.

FIGURE 4.4 The writing on the wall: the writing of former students from Portage la Prairie Indian Residential School, June 22, 2010. Photo by Naomi Angel.

"My mom, and my cousin Patsy were up there." We stood and looked up at the hatch. Neither one of us wanted to investigate it further.

During my visit, the Long Plain First Nation was using the Portage la Prairie School as the home of its administrative offices. The classrooms were used for training sessions in computer skills and adult education classes. Outside the school, a large statue had been erected: an eagle sits overlooking the school, perched atop a tall, steel tree (figure 4.5). Erected in 2007, the 27.5-meter statue was built to honor IRS survivors. But the statue itself provoked some controversy, as some community members complained that the money used to pay for the piece ($175,000) could have been put to more productive use for social or health programs within the community.

Field Notes, June 22, 2010

At the end of my tour of Portage la Prairie, I asked Robert if he would be giving his testimony to the truth commission. He answered, "No, I don't really talk about that time." Before I left, he handed me a folded sheet of paper. It was a picture of him as a student at this school, a photocopy of an old newspaper article. Fourteen students were dressed in their hockey gear, lined up for a photo opportunity. "Are you in this picture?" I asked. "Yup. That's me. It's in

FIGURE 4.5 Outside the Rufus Prince Building (formerly the Portage la Prairie Indian Residential School), June 22, 2010. Photo by Naomi Angel.

'57," Robert replied. "We were the city champs." Robert had written the names of the students on the photocopy.

Robert's image, faded now, represented a moment of pride. Although he did not want to talk about that time in his life, he still held on to the image.

A few weeks after this visit, I wrote another blog post about my experience at the school. Shortly thereafter, a reader commented on the post: "My mother taught at Portage la Prairie," she explained. "She has passed on now, but I still have some of her old photographs.... Would you like them?" I got in touch with Ruth Roulette and Barb Esau at Long Plain to make sure it was OK to receive the photos and to ask whether they wanted to see them first. After they granted their permission, I pledged to send them on to the community afterward.

Field Notes, November 2010

The photos from X arrived today. [51] Clearly well taken care of, some of them are still in the scrap book pages that housed them long ago. Smiling faces of children look back at the person taking the photos, and they look at me too.

In an email exchange, I asked X, "Where do you think these pictures should end up—with the Long Plain First Nation or the IRS TRC archives or elsewhere?" She responded, "I am not sure where these photos should end up so I will leave that decision up to you. As far as my family is concerned, I am the only one so I don't need them. As it happened a long time ago, I don't know any of these people. It was before my time."

I held on to the photos for a long time, perhaps too long. I looked at them over and over, willing them to tell me more than they could. The images captured the smiling faces of students and staff (see figures 4.6 and 4.7). They didn't appear too weathered or worn. Most of them are dated from the middle of the last century, 1945–1950s. There were thirty-three loose images and two pages from a scrapbook. In discussing these images, X wrote, "Mom kept all these photos in her 'special' photo album which had a lot of old photos from her earlier days. Yes, she did cherish these photos very much. She enjoyed the interaction with the students very much." With regard to the IRS TRC, X explained in an email:

> I have not followed the progress of the IR [*sic*] commission, just what I had heard on the news. I would like to know more of their work. I have also heard both positive and negative comments about the schools. Personally, I think some of the things that went on in these schools was awful. Mom did mention how many of the kids were told to forget about their lives on the reserves. She was totally against that. She just felt that she was there to help the kids to maybe have a better life someday.
>
> Mom didn't talk so much about her past but I know she did enjoy teaching the kids very much. They were all her "special" students. Even the ones that got into trouble—she loved them all! I would be very interested to know if there is anyone out there who might recognize anyone in the photos and might remember my mom.

I sent the photos on to the Long Plain First Nation in the hope that they would find their way back to the people in them.

FIGURE 4.6 Students of Portage la Prairie Indian Residential School, circa 1950s. Anonymous, photo given to Naomi Angel.

Demolitions

The last Indian residential school was still in operation as recently as 1996. This school, White Calf Collegiate in Lebret, Saskatchewan, was torn down in 1999. On that Tuesday morning in March, a small group of former students gathered to watch the wrecking ball reduce the school to dust. "It's a very emotional day," reflected former student Michael Starr. "Some of the history is gone ... in a lot of ways the people who have been hurt by the residential schools have had some of that pain taken away by knocking it down." For many the destruction of the school was a symbolic end to some of the suffering they endured there. Starr then added, "At the same time there were a lot of good memories in the school."[52] Words like these reveal some of the

FIGURE 4.7 Photos of students at Portage la Prairie Indian Residential School, circa 1950s. Anonymous, photo given to Naomi Angel.

difficulty with constructing a single narrative about the schools, gesturing toward the multiplicity of possible narratives engendered by these histories.

Rumors and stories surrounding the demolition of schools abound. Grollier Hall, a Catholic residence in Inuvik, was also demolished in 1999. The students of Grollier Hall were among the first to organize legal proceedings in response to the sexual abuse committed at the schools. Several former students have committed suicide since leaving the school, and many have speculated that the abuse, and the silence that surrounded it, were central factors leading to these suicides. Four former dorm supervisors have since been convicted on charges of abuse. As with the demolition of White Calf Collegiate, some students gathered to watch the school being torn down. Spirits are said to have risen from the rubble.[53]

Some demolitions become sites for ceremonies of healing. Peake Hall, the former dormitory for the Port Alberni Indian Residential School in British Columbia, was torn down in 2009, and former students were invited to take part in dismantling the building. Two fires were kept burning all day, using wood and siding taken from the school. River water, sage, and cedar were on hand to be used in cleansing ceremonies.[54] In some cases, such ceremonies and rituals are not enough to cleanse the site. Pelican Lake Residential School in Ontario closed in 1973, and a First Nations high school now stands in its place. Rumors of ghostly and paranormal activity have often been reported there. As journalist Jody Porter writes,

> School officials say the students feel haunted by the past. "There's a lot of paranormal activity that goes on there, they sense it, they hear it, they see things," said Frank Beardy, a former director of the education authority that runs the school. "Some of the elders didn't want the school built there because of that. There are things that have to be dealt with," he added. "We've had a number of cleansing ceremonies... but it still happens."[55]

Like many Canadians, I had heard stories about missing children and cemeteries with unmarked graves at the school sites. There were many children who ran away from the schools, never to be heard from again, and there were children who died from sickness, abuse, and negligence. In some cases, their families were not notified. In other cases, families were contacted, but the child had already been buried, often many miles from their family homes. The issue of missing children with regard to the IRS system garnered so much attention that the commission created the Missing Children Project and the National Residential School Student Death Register to focus specifically on this issue and find out as much as possible about how and where these children disappeared. The register represents the first national effort to record the names of the students who died at school.[56] Although many of the chief coroners and appropriate record-holding bodies cooperated with the TRC's work, its *Final Report* recommends further cooperation from the federal government regarding historical records and further efforts to contact the families of missing children.

In the Canadian popular press, stories of cemeteries and rumors about school misconduct in notifying families about the deaths of children have circulated widely. For example, in 1974, Charlie Hunter, attending St. Anne's Indian Residential School (Fort Albany, Ontario), drowned while trying to save another student who had fallen into a lake. His body was buried near the school without his family's consent. After decades of struggle to bring him home to Peawanuck, a small community of 250 people, Hunter's remains were finally returned in 2011. His family welcomed him back with a funeral and a eulogy in Cree. The relocation was made possible, in part, when the story appeared in the *Toronto Star*. Readers raised $20,000 in order to help the cause.[57]

Other communities are less interested in relocating the remains of former students. They are more concerned with identifying the bodies. In some cases, the search has been going on for decades. Red Deer Indian Residential School has been closed for almost a century, and the building itself collapsed long ago. At the time of my writing, the school's cemetery was virtually invisible. As chronicled by journalist Suzy Thompson, "Grave markers have deteriorated and, until recently, the underbrush was so overgrown it was impossible to detect depressions in the ground where people were buried, but a 2008 archeological survey conducted for a housing developer hoping to build a 55-lot subdivision beside the graveyard estimates between 35 and 70 people are buried there."[58]

When graveyards are found to have the bodies of former students, it can galvanize a community. Since June 2012, eleven Indigenous communities near the Red Deer site and the United Church have held an annual commemoration ceremony, followed by a feast: "The variety of backgrounds means the ceremony demands sophisticated co-ordination in order to honour each group's customs. Each First Nation group follows a tradition of marking a death four times. The annual funeral event, from 2010 to 2014, consists of a small graveside ceremony, followed by a feast in Fort Normandeau park across the Kinnickinnick Creek."[59] The graveyards, newly relocated, allowed for new lines of communication between and within communities.[60]

Traces

In some cases, students return to their former schools to make peace. St. Mary's Indian Residential School in British Columbia was demolished in 1965. The students enrolled there at the time were moved to a new government-run St. Mary's not far away. Large concrete slabs, the remnants of the first school—the oldest permanent Indian residential school in British Columbia—can now be found in the Fraser River Heritage Park (discussed briefly at the beginning of this chapter). Former student Wayne Florence recounts his visit to the site of St. Mary's:

> I went through counseling and they told me to go back to the place it started and face it. So that helped quite a bit. I went back there, me and

FIGURE 4.8 Cement foundation marking a structure that was once part of St. Mary's Indian Residential School, May 2011. Photo by Naomi Angel.

> my wife went. The memories were devastating. I went to the old site. You see the buildings in your mind, nothing changes in your mind. Where the washroom was, there was [a] great big concrete slab and I walked down and that was frightening. The shower rooms. Like ancient days. The big concrete slab. Locked in there forever.[61]

Florence remarks that the memories were devastating. Memories tied to a specific location demonstrate the ways in which place can become a receptacle for memory. Treading on this territory can cause them to be released once again.

Field Notes, May 2011

It was a beautiful late spring day when I visited the park. I had printed out the map of the former school from the park's website before my trip and had it with me as I walked. Without the map, it's unlikely I would have noticed the low concrete foundations embedded in the landscape of the park [figures 4.8 and 4.9]. The map included buildings that were still standing, some that were gone but still marked in some way, and those whose traces had since vanished.

There were a few other people in the park that day, most walking their dogs, a few sitting on benches overlooking the water. I was the only one taking

FIGURE 4.9 Cement foundation marking a structure that was once part of St. Mary's Indian Residential School, May 2011. Photo by Naomi Angel.

notice of the cement structures, walking from one to another and puzzling over the map (figure 4.10).

I found it strange that the cement foundations weren't marked in some way, so I went to the visitor center to see if I could find more information. There I met Don Brown, a manager at the Heritage Park, who informed me that indeed the foundations were marked. He mentioned that some time ago, they had painted numbers on the structures to coincide with those on the map. But time and weather had worn those away. Then they marked them with small metal plaques. Unfortunately, Don explained, some of those had been stolen, likely to be melted down for the metal. We walked back out to the structures together to see if we could find them and, after checking out a couple, found one marking the old gym (figure 4.11).

Former students have written about feeling haunted when visiting the site. In researching and writing a book about St. Mary's, Terry Glavin has visited the park with several former students. He recounts his visit with Pierre Cyril:

> Pierre pointed to an overgrown rock wall. This is where the boy's dormitory was, he said. Over there, that was where the orchard was. That's

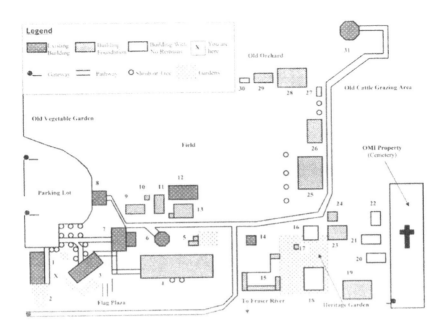

FIGURE 4.10 Map of the former site of St. Mary's Indian Residential School. Source: Heritage of Mission website.

FIGURE 4.11 A metal plaque marking the site of St. Mary's former gym, May 2011. Photo by Naomi Angel.

FIGURE 4.12 Original St. Mary's bell in wood tower at Fraser River Heritage Park, May 2011. Photo by Naomi Angel.

where the girls lived. There was a classroom here. This is where the gymnasium used to be. There are people who come here now, Pierre said, and they don't know anything about what was here once, but they leave because they feel something wrong. They can hear babies crying.

"That's how strong it is," Pierre said. "It's the hurt that's still in this place, and I know because my heart was broken here."[62]

In addition to the structural remnants from St. Mary's Indian Residential School, the site gestures toward the history of the IRS system in other ways as well. In one corner of the park stands a large bell tower. It is the original cast iron bell from St. Mary's. Located high upon a wood frame, the bell was dedicated to the park by former students in 2000 (figure 4.12).

Not far from the bell is a small cemetery. The plaque outside its gate reads "O.M.I. Cemetery. Dedicated to the Memory of the Pioneers" (figure 4.13). O.M.I. stands for Oblates of Mary Immaculate. According to the park's website, the cemetery, which was the burial site for both staff and students from St. Mary's, is still in operation. Originally, there was no partition demarcating the cemetery from the rest of the park, but because of vandalism a metal fence has been erected.

After I visited St. Mary's, I drove the short distance to the former Coqualeetza Indian Residential School in Chilliwack.[63] Like Portage la

FIGURE 4.13 O.M.I. Cemetery plaque in Fraser River Heritage Park, the site of the former St. Mary's Indian Residential School, May 2011. Photo by Naomi Angel.

Prairie and Blue Quills, the Coqualeetza school has been taken back by the community. Over the last century the Coqualeetza site has been used as a Methodist Indian residential school, a tuberculosis hospital, and an army barracks. In the 1970s the Stó:lō Nation occupied the former school to reclaim it as their own. A report in the *Chilliwack Progress* describes the occupation: "Acting under orders, with the sound of tribal drums ringing in their ears, members of the Canadian Armed Forced [*sic*] heaved against the front door to the former nurses residence at Coqualeetza. By 7:45 pm Monday 23 people were carried or led away from the scene that erupted only a short time before when members of the Stalo [*sic*] Indian band decided to stand ground and disobey military and RCMP orders to vacate the Co-qualeetza facility."[64] The Coqualeetza Cultural Education website notes that the occupation was an attempt to "publicize the lack of action on achieving reserve status and ownership of the Coqualeetza Property." The occupation succeeded in bringing more attention to the Stó:lō First Nation's claims to the land, and eventually the Stó:lō Nation won back the site (figures 4.14 and 4.15). The buildings, now being used as the headquarters for the Stó:lō Nation and other cultural, health, and educational initiatives, still show traces of that past, but they also reveal a promising future.

FIGURE 4.14 Traces of the Coqualeetza Industrial Institute, now being used as the Stó:lō Nation headquarters, May 2011. Photo by Naomi Angel.

FIGURE 4.15 A new sign outside the Stó:lō Nation headquarters and cultural center, May 2011. Photo by Naomi Angel.

"A Beating Heart of Episodes"

When I first envisioned the research for this chapter, I had Michel-Rolph Trouillot's *Silencing the Past* in mind as a starting point. Trouillot writes that where there is silence, there is also *a silencing*, a process by which such silences are both created and enforced. With reference to how such processes relate to the material trace, he writes:

> The bigger the material mass, the more easily it entraps us: mass graves and pyramids bring history closer while they make us feel small. A castle, a fort, a battlefield, a church, all these things bigger than we that we infuse with the reality of past lives, seem to speak of an immensity of which we know little except that we are part of it. Too solid to be unmarked, too conspicuous to be candid, they embody the ambiguities of history. They give us the power to touch it, but not that to hold it firmly in our hands—hence the mystery of their battered walls. We suspect that their concreteness hides secrets so deep that no revelation may fully dissipate their silences. We imagine the lives under the mortar, but how do we recognize the end of a bottomless silence?[65]

Trouillot draws our attention to the "ambiguities of history" represented by these material traces, encouraging us to see them as productive sites for conjuring images of the past. In conceptualizing this chapter about the schools and their remains, I imagined my project, though vastly different in its historical context, to run parallel to Trouillot's. Like Trouillot's Haiti, Canada had produced many entanglements with silence. I expected to find this "bottomless silence" at the schools, a painful reminder of past and present hurt. I imagined buildings forgotten by time, abandoned to the ghosts of former students. But as my visits to these schools progressed, it became increasingly clear that the schools were not enveloped by silence. Instead, I found what Mi'kmaq poet and author Rita Joe has called "a beating heart of episodes." Joe has famously written about the Shubenacadie School in Nova Scotia:

HATED STRUCTURE: INDIAN RESIDENTIAL SCHOOL, SHUBENACADIE, N.S.

If you are on Highway 104
In a Shubenacadie town
There is a hill
Where a structure stands
A reminder to many senses
To respond like demented ones.

I for one looked into the window
And there on the floor
Was a deluge of a misery
Of a building I held in awe
Since the day
I walked into the ornamented door.

There was grime everywhere
As in buildings left alone or unused.
Maybe to the related tales of long ago
Where the children lived in laughter, or abused.

I had no wish to enter
Nor to walk the halls
I had no wish to feel the floors
Where I felt fear
A beating heart of episodes
I care not to recall.
The structure stands as if to say:
I was just a base for theory
To bend the will of children
I remind
Until I fall.[66]

I found that what awaited me at the schools was by no means silence or a landscape populated by ghosts. It was not a quiet stillness, nor was it a deafening noise. Sometimes it was the sound of resilience and of traditional ceremonies and languages resurrected. I imagined the schools as places where memories and experiences of former students would be felt as an excess. Following Macarena Gómez-Barris, I believed that "perhaps such excesses cannot be monumentalized in places themselves, but rather in the passage through places."[67] By passing through these spaces, I imagined that buried memories and hauntings could perhaps be excavated. What I found instead was that excavation was often unnecessary. Many of the schools I visited were not shrouded in former pain; rather, they had become vital and vibrant sites for organization and political action. The schools stand as reminders of the past, of the "beating heart of episodes" that transpired there. But they also speak of a future, one where Indigenous cultures, languages, and communities are being tended to every day.

Reconciliation as a Ghostly Encounter

In this chapter I have explored discourses of hauntings and ghosts on several levels. In particular, I have focused on how reconciliation may be seen as a ghostly encounter. Conceptualizing reconciliation as a ghostly encounter may signal the ways in which "reconciliation is never a fully realizable category; it can never be completely settled."[68] Like speaking about ghosts, the reconciliation process can often seem like a nebulous, haunted project, one where the very means of dialogue are often called into question. "We always knew that the dismantling of the colonial paradigm would release strange demons from the deep, and that these monsters might come trailing all sorts of subterranean material," writes Stuart Hall.[69] But it may also release other sorts of specters, not demons or monsters but spirits that seek to guide people and communities in navigating the past.

So I return to the questions I posed earlier in this chapter: What can narratives of hauntings tell us about reconciliation? And, in the Canadian context, what does it mean to see ghosts? The fact that former Indian residential schools have been reclaimed illustrates that reconciliation is happening on various levels and in various places. The importance of place in the Canadian context cannot be underestimated. Imagining this landscape as one populated by ghosts should not obscure the fact that it is also populated by vibrant and active political communities. It is also important to remember that hauntings, though often conceptualized as an Indigenous ghost haunting the settler, happen in many directions. The settler also haunts Indigenous peoples (and settlers too), and Indigenous ghosts commune with Indigenous peoples. Ghostly encounters can represent an anxiety, but they may also represent a soothing, an opportunity for a dialogue with the past. On the one hand, the language of haunting can open up previously unexplored issues, provoking new attention to past injustices. On the other hand, using the language of haunting can lead to a "reconciliation with ghosts rather than a reckoning with the specific and ongoing violences of colonialism."[70] In the case of Canada, perhaps the ghosts that inhabit the reconciliation process do not represent a return of the repressed but a form of continuance.[71] Perhaps the ghost is not a part of a tragic archive but one that pulses with future possibilities.

Fragments of Truth

Concluding Gestures

What I'm starting to understand is that we did not lose our language, we were severed from it. I keep being reminded of all those stolen conversations. With Nanan's passing, her stories are lost forever, back into the earth with my ancestors.

—JULES KOOSTACHIN (CREE), *Remembering Inninimowin*

In *Fragments of Truth* I have aimed to work through some of the complex intersections of visual culture, memory, and nationhood as they create meaning within the Canadian context of redress regarding the Indian residential school system. In the book's introduction, I began by recounting my conversation with Eric Large, a former student at the Blue Quills Indian Residential School. By remarking that there is no Cree word for *reconciliation*, Large foregrounded some of the many issues that have emerged through the reconciliation process. Throughout my engagement with the IRS archive—whether working with images, testimonies, or the material traces left behind by the schools—I have argued that calls to reconciliation are also calls to new ways of seeing. The process of revisiting, remembering, and revisualizing the painful history of the IRS system entails attending to experiences that can provoke unease; it requires not looking away when faced with difficult truths about Canada's past and present. Framing reconciliation as a way of seeing also allows for recognition of the fact that Indigenous peoples have been negotiating this history—often through artwork, performance, and film—long before the IRS TRC published its *Final Report*.

In chapter 1, I wrote about the CBC's *A New Future*, where, among other things, Indigenous children were shown playing hockey and learning English at the Indian residential school in Moose Factory, Ontario.[1] Set to upbeat music with a cheerful voice-over, the film projects an imagined future for Indigenous children—"for the oldest Canadians," as they say in the film, "a new future." This "new" future did not include Indigenous language or culture. I turn now to a brief discussion of another film, a documentary by Cree filmmaker Jules Koostachin, *Remembering Inninimowin*. Although certain scenes from Koostachin's film are also set in the area of Moose Factory, *Remembering Inninimowin* serves as a powerful counterstory to representations like *A New Future*, which tried to mask the devastating effects of the IRS system.[2] In some ways, Koostachin's film serves as a prism through which to observe many of the complicated dynamics at stake in reconciliation in the Canadian context.

I first met Koostachin in April 2010 at a conference on truth and reconciliation held at Nipissing University. At the time, she was finishing *Remembering Inninimowin*. The film follows Koostachin on her journey in learning to speak Cree (*Inninimowin* is Cree for "Cree language") and explores her relationships with her family, looking at how they were affected by the IRS system. In 2008 Koostachin had planned to travel to Attawapiskat, Ontario, to talk to her nanan (grandmother). She had hoped to speak with her in Inninimowin for the first time. The film was meant to document and capture this conversation, depicting language reinvigoration on the level of kin and intimate family ties. But her grandmother's sudden death changed the trajectory and scope of the project.

At Nipissing, Koostachin showed a short clip from the film and discussed her intentions for making the documentary. She conceptualized the film as a "journey of remembering" and an exploration of the bonds formed through language, not only between people but to culture and land as well. Koostachin also discussed the importance of Indigenous media. These are themes that Koostachin also addressed in an article written about the film:

> Before colonization and the assault of residential schools, the Inninuwak life and ethos abounded with respect for ceremony, family, community, and the land. Now we find ourselves in a state of fragmentation, trying to put the pieces back together. *Remembering Inninimowin*, as an indigenized form of media, sheds light on these issues and is itself an example of new approaches and cultural representation, an alternative to the Westernized practices whereby, for the most part, our stories are told from outside the community. The film is also a means of storytelling, an

oral and visual record of how we as Indigenous people can use media to sustain and preserve sacred ways and languages, as well as how we can use media to inform and create social change.[3]

As Koostachin makes clear, Indigenous film has the potential to engage audiences as both an aesthetic and political tool. As a storytelling device, film can speak to the fragmentation created by colonial policies, including but not limited to the Indian residential schools.

Koostachin's film is complex in its weaving together of several narratives. Her own journey is tied to the larger historical background of the IRS system as well as the histories of Indigenous relationships to the land, to one another, and to the federal government. The film begins with Koostachin narrating footage featuring three generations of Cree women. Koostachin is sitting between her mother, a survivor of the residential school system, and her grandmother, a woman who lived off the land. The filmmaker explains that even though her mother's first language was Inninimowin, it had never been spoken between them. At the residential school, her mother had been forbidden from speaking her native tongue, so it was not passed on to her children. The film shifts back and forth, oscillating between scenes of the filmmaker's journey to her grandmother's funeral (and later to her grave) and her life in Toronto, where she takes Cree lessons with two of her sons.

Throughout the film Koostachin uses both archival images and interviews with community members to convey what life was like in the region during the IRS era and also to offer a sense of life in the community now. The images in the film are drawn from a variety of sources. Some are from the Hudson's Bay archives, and others are from personal collections. Speaking of these images, Koostachin has remarked that "when [outsiders] took photos, they didn't use names. Instead, they labeled images with captions like 'Indian woman with no leg.' The ones of Indians were so impersonal. The white people all had names. The Indians were nameless. Some of the photos in the film were ones that my mom took—the church provided a camera or something. So, I used a mix of archival images and personal ones in the film."[4] By blurring the lines between personal and archival images, and by bringing together photographs that were taken both by students and staff or colonial officials, Koostachin stages an important intervention into the logic of the archive.

Perhaps the most powerful scene in the film is its conclusion. Koostachin has been preparing to speak to her mother in Cree for the first time. "I'm going to be reading," she explains, "but you have to start somewhere." Mother and daughter sit in chairs facing each other. They are in a living room. Traditional drums are perched on a shelf behind Koostachin's mother. Koostachin herself sits beside a piano and fresh-cut flowers. She holds her notes in her hands and begins to read:

> I have never felt complete. I have always felt like I existed outside the circle. I am sure there are many of us out there who never had the chance to be part of the conversation. We listen and try hard to be part of it. No one has ever looked and spoke directly to us. In some cases we cannot seem to learn. It is like we are being ignored. I feel that I need to be honest with you. I have carried resentment for not knowing the language. I understand why you didn't teach us, your children. You wanted to protect us. Protect us from the things that have happened to you. The things that happened in residential school. It was a hard time for you. Now as a mother, I understand your need to protect us. I see now as an adult what you have gone through. I am doing this because I want to tell you how I feel. I want to tell you how this has impacted me. Not to pass on Cree was out of your control. It was not your fault. I blame the church and the government. They're responsible for trying to destroy our way of life. I am proud of you and what you have done for us. You've worked hard to instill the importance of fighting. I have been fighting my whole life. Now I am ready to heal. Nanan and I could not speak to each other. We loved each other very much. I wish that I was able to understand her stories. The stories I will never be able to hear in this life. Her stories have gone with her. I feel I am trying to put the pieces back together.[5]

When Koostachin says "It was not your fault," her mother's eyes become moist. She brushes away a tear and nods. After Koostachin finishes reading her statement, her mother speaks back to her in Cree. The words are clearly emotional. Her mother gestures with her hands, and her eyes remain teary throughout. Her voice catches. She puts her hand on her chest. But her words are left untranslated.

When I first saw the film, I thought that this moment of untranslated dialogue was a way of protecting the delicate strength of the exchange, a type of withholding, so that not everyone would be given access to the vulnerability and intimacy of the moment. I wanted to know more, to understand the director's choice to leave those words without translation. On December 9, 2012, I spoke with Koostachin.

NAOMI In the last scene, your mother's words are not translated. Can you talk about this? Is this a way to speak directly to people who speak the language and to "hold back" a form of knowledge or experience from those who don't?

JULES No. It wasn't translated because I didn't want to ask someone else to do it. I wanted to do it myself. I wanted to be at the point where I was able to understand her first. Some Cree people wanted to tell me what she said, but I told them not to. I wanted to show the audience that this was the relationship that I had with my mom, that there was pain and emotion there.

It's the first time she looked at me and spoke to me in Cree. I had heard her speak it before, but never to me. I hadn't expected her to respond. We were actually just about to shut off the tape. It was a surprise when she responded in Cree. My Cree wasn't strong enough to translate it yet, so I left it that way in the film.

N So now that some time has passed, do you know what she said? Have you done the translation?

J My understanding of it was that she was sorry. She was mourning the loss of Nanan, my grandmother. And then she did this thing where she pointed her fingers, and that's where I got the real "I'm sorry." What I was thinking was "She has her own story." And I had felt kind of resentful, but then I felt a moment of forgiveness. I understood that this hurt her as much as it hurt me.

I don't know exactly word for word what she said, but I understood that she was dealing with that loss and that she felt bad for me. In the film, we witness a powerful moment of forgiveness, a reconciliation of sorts. But it is not between Indigenous people and settlers; it is between a mother and a daughter.

As I discussed in chapter 1, reconciliation requires that people be engaged on a personal level; in this context, it requires an understanding that every Canadian, both Indigenous and non-Indigenous, is implicated in the IRS system.[6] By traveling across Canada, looking at archives, listening to testimony, and visiting former schools, I have learned about this history and about the many ways that Indigenous peoples and their allies are fighting for recognition and for justice. But perhaps the most revealing moments of my research have occurred in the conversations I have had with Indigenous and non-Indigenous people throughout the process. I share this short exchange with Koostachin as a way to draw attention to the need for dialogue.

Without our discussion, I would have never known that I had profoundly misread the last scene of her film. I read it as a withholding, as a way to protest, to keep settlers at bay. But in talking to Koostachin I learned that the untranslated scene was not a refusal or denial; it was about the filmmaker's desire to do the complicated work of translation on her own terms. It was about a commitment she made to both her language and her mother.

As the closing credits to *Remembering Inninimowin* roll, we see Koostachin walk into a tattoo parlor. She leaves some time later with two tattoos, one on each forearm. Each forearm has three Cree syllabics drawn into the skin. Around the syllabics are two small leaves, etched onto both arms, the skin slightly red and raised. Again, they are left untranslated.

"And the tattoos at the end?" I ask. "Can you share what they mean?"

"They are the names of my twin boys," she explains. "Tapwewin and Pawaken. Pawaken means totem."

"And Tapwewin?" I ask.

"Tapwewin means truth."⁷

Remembering Inninimowin has been screened around the world: in Australia, Peru, the United States, and Canada. With the film's success, Koostachin moved on to her next project. She wanted to focus on life before residential schools, so she began working on *Alive with Breath*, a multimedia installation. Her motivation for the project was to cultivate awareness about the textures and senses that made up life before the residential schools. She explains: "For people to understand the residential school experience, they have to know about the life from before, because it was beautiful. I remember the rabbit skin. I remember the smell of my grandmother. To see what the children were stolen from is important."⁸

Koostachin's work draws our attention, yet again, to some of the ways that Indigenous peoples have been negotiating the history of the IRS system outside of the commission's work and often long before the commission's mandate began. *Remembering Inninimowin* also works to remind us that issues of land, language, and restitution must be engaged if the reconciliation process in Canada is to be meaningful.

The Canadian Truth and Reconciliation Commission has officially finished its tenure and fulfilled its mandate. However, the commissioners have stated that more work is necessary for the future. They continue to be present in dialogues surrounding access to information, documents, and historical records regarding the IRS system, as well as the National Centre for Truth and Reconciliation (NCTR), which was originally conceived as under the TRC's mandate. The ninety-four recommendations made in the TRC's *Final*

Report make clear that the work of "reconciling" Canada and redressing the histories of the IRS is far from complete. The recommendations range from educational, encouraging more awareness and critical thinking surrounding education at all levels in Canada, to material and systemic, regarding the parallels between the injustices of Indian residential schools and contemporary socioeconomic and institutional contexts in Canada.

I hope that *Fragments of Truth* can be seen as one contribution to the process of reconciliation, but I recognize that many others are required. By the end of the commission's mandate in 2014, it had gathered 6,750 voluntary testimonies.[9] These testimonies are housed in the NCTRC at the University of Manitoba. The center is open to the public, to families, and to researchers, and the testimonies are also available online in varying degrees according to the wishes of the survivors who shared them.[10] The future of reconciliation remains to be seen. How will the residential schools be represented to future generations? How will settlers become more engaged in the reconciliation process as it continues to unfold? Will *talk* of reconciliation lead to the *action* of restitution?

I have conceptualized these final pages not as a conclusion but as a place to gesture to both a past that needs attention and a present that is still unfolding. *Fragments of Truth* has explored the normative orders of remembrance that surfaced during the official reconciliation process and the ways in which individuals and communities have taken up, negotiated, *and* pushed back against these demands. The success or failure of the IRS TRC did not interest me as much as what the commission mobilized, what it put into motion. As I began this book with the words of Eric Large, I would like to draw to a close with the words of Jules Koostachin: "When my mother was in residential school, she was punished for speaking Inninimowin. She was punished for being Inninuwak. I believe that history needs to be rewritten to include the truth, the truth of what happened to Native people. Read between the lines. The effects of genocide are evident. You just have to look around. If you live in this country, all you have to do is open your eyes and the truth will be revealed."[11]

Whereas Eric Large drew our attention to the loss of language and to lines of communication in need of repair, Jules Koostachin brings into focus the need to revisit our history; she beckons us to *open our eyes*. As I have argued throughout this book, relations of seeing play a fundamental role in the reconciliation process. The act of opening one's eyes, of course, is not straightforward or uncomplicated. Nor does it guarantee that the recognition of injustices will lead to actions that can rectify them. Reconciliation is a project that requires more than a reimagining of Canada's past. It also demands action that will change the course of its future.

Notes

Preface: Tracing Memory in Naomi Angel's Archive

1   Important voices in these conversations include Krista Maxwell in "Settler-Humanitarianism," Audra Simpson in "Whither Settler Colonialism," and Jill Carter's model of "survivance-intervention" in "Discarding Sympathy, Disrupting Catharsis." On resistance to reconciliation in the arts, see also Sophie McCall and Gabrielle L'Hirondelle Hill, eds., *The Land We Are*.

2   National Inquiry, *Reclaiming Power and Place*.

3   The "burden" of reconciliation as collective and shared obligation was first noted by Chief Justice Murray Sinclair, the chair of the commission; see "Reconciliation Is Not an Aboriginal Problem." More recently, the phrase *burden of reconciliation* is being used in Canadian institutions—funding bodies, universities, sites of cultural production—to draw attention to how Indigenous bodies continue to bear the burden of reconciling the nation as Indigenous intellectuals and artists are incorporated into the academy and Indigenous nations are still required to "prove" their connection to the land in court cases.

4   Deb Haaland, "My Grandparents Were Stolen from Their Families as Children. We Must Learn About This History," *Washington Post*, June 11, 2021, www.washingtonpost.com/opinions/2021/06/11/deb-haaland-indigenous-boarding-schools.

5   Angel, *Before Truth*, 17.

6   See Angel, "Text or Testimony" and "A Fragmented Reconciliation Process," for instance.

7   Angel, "On Collaboration."

8   Behar, *The Vulnerable Observer*.

9   She writes about how the experience of being pregnant and a new mother affected her research in a post titled "New Beginnings."

10   Angel, "On Writing About Illness."

11   Singh, *Unthinking Mastery*.

12   Robinson, "Enchantment's Irreconcilable Connection," 212.

13   Angel, *Before Truth*, 98–99.

14 Angel, *Before Truth*, 150.

15 Angel, *Before Truth*, 29.

16 Angel, *Before Truth*, 27.

17 Christi Belcourt's *Walking with Our Sisters*, a traveling installation of moccasin vamps sewn, beaded, and embroidered by family and community members to represent stolen sisters, was the most visible of these projects as it traveled across North America. For more, see Recollet, "Glyphing Decolonial Love."

18 Lisa Jackson, personal communication with Eugenia Kisin.

19 Angel, *Before Truth*, 235.

Introduction: Reconciliation and Remembrance

1 Audio recordings of the conference are available at https://papyrus.bib.umon-treal.ca/xmlui/handle/1866/2594.

2 The current number of schools recognized is 139. The federal recognition of Indian residential schools is significantly limited by the parameters established in Article 12 of the Indian Residential Schools Settlement Agreement (IRSSA). Since the IRSSA's establishment, 9,471 people have asked for 1,531 distinct institutions to be added to the IRSSA. The federal government has added nine. See Indigenous and Northern Affairs Canada, "Statistics on the Implementation of the Indian Residential School Agreement." More recently, a process of implementing a compensation program for attendees of day schools has been initiated for those who did not board overnight while attending a residential school.

3 In *Truth and Indignation* and "Templates and Exclusions," Ronald Niezen has explored the complexity and potential conflicts of how testimony and statement making have been shaped within the context of the truth and reconciliation events.

4 The work of testimony in relation to other atrocities is also relevant here because it has contributed to wider discourses about the role of active listening, empathy, and relations of power. See Laub and Felman, *Testimony*, and Agamben, *Remnants of Auschwitz*, for work on Holocaust testimony; and Krog, *Country of My Skull*, and Krog, Ratele, and Mpolweni, *There Was This Goat*, for work on the South African TRC. Cole, *Performing South Africa's Truth Commission*, provides an important critique of Krog's work. See Whitlock's "Active Remembrance" and Emberley's "'Epistemic Heterogeneity'" and *The Testimonial Uncanny* for Canadian context. I explore the dynamics of testimony further in chapter 3.

5 Although it is my hope that *Fragments of Truth* is of use to those working in the fields of visual and memory studies, it is not in the first instance a contribution to those fields in the sense that I seek to avoid resourcing histories of the residential schools, survivors' experiences, and the IRS TRC as knowledge that primarily contributes to advancing those fields. Instead, throughout the text I seek a textual ethics that situates survivors' and intergenerational survivors' words

in relationship with other discourses without making them subject to such discourse. This choice is made in an attempt to put knowledge in relationship, rather than in service to. For further critical discussion of performance studies' colonial tendencies toward "field building" through Indigenous knowledge extraction, see Robinson, "Enchantment's Irreconcilable Connection."

6 Anderson and Robertson, *Seeing Red*, 3.

7 Alfred and Corntassel, "Being Indigenous," 599.

8 This shift includes the return to names that misidentified First Nations, like the Nuu-chah-nulth being misidentified as "Nootka"; the use of the international phonetics alphabet to convey the proper pronunciation of *nations*, for example, with the xʷməθkʷəy̓əm (Musqueam) and Sḵwx̱wú7mesh (Squamish) people; and the use of Halq'emeylem words *xwelmexw* and *xwelitem* to identify Stó:lō people and settlers, respectively. See Statistics Canada, "Census of Population."

9 Sanderson notes that a primary motivation in coming up with the term was "because our people didn't want to talk about sovereignty—they were afraid to even say the word. So I had to find a way of planting the seed that we are nations, and we have sovereignty." Quoted in Susan Methot, "Sol Sanderson."

10 See Anderson, "Métis," and Vowel, "You're Métis? Which of Your Parents Is an Indian?," in *Indigenous Writes*.

11 Wolfe, "Settler Colonialism," 388.

12 Garneau, "Imaginary Spaces of Conciliation," 38.

13 See Morgensen, "The Biopolitics of Settler Colonialism"; Snelgrove, Dhamoon, and Corntassel, "Unsettling Settler Colonialism"; and Day, *Alien Capital*.

14 Coombes, "Introduction: Memory and History in Settler Colonialism," 2.

15 Epp, *We Are All Treaty People*, 4.

16 This "year of reconciliation" model was subsequently implemented by cities (Vancouver, BC, June 2013–June 2014; Nanaimo, BC, June 2013–2014; Toronto, ON, November 2013–November 2014; Calgary, AB, 2014; Edmonton, AB, 2014–2015; Sioux Lookout, ON, 2017; Winnipeg, MB, 2016; Victoria, BC, 2017) and countries (in Africa, July 2015–July 2016, whereas China and Taiwan's year of reconciliation took place one year before the UN year of reconciliation in 2008).

17 For comparative analyses of apologies within Canada, situated within the global "culture of redress," see Henderson and Wakeham, eds., *Reconciling Canada*.

18 Although both "full-" and "half-caste" children were taken from their homes without the consent of their parents, particular attention was paid to the "half-caste" children in the early 1900s. They occupied a liminal space in the racial hierarchy and so posed a particular threat to white Australia. For more, see McGregor, *Imagined Destinies*.

19 Short, *Reconciliation and Colonial Power*, 177.

20 Short, *Reconciliation and Colonial Power*.

21 Auguste, "Rethinking the Nation."

22 Healy, *Forgetting Aborigines.*

23 Hayner, *Unspeakable Truths*, 24.

24 For general information on many of these commissions, see Hayner, *Unspeakable Truths*; Chapman and Ball, "The Truth of Truth Commissions"; and Grandin, "The Instruction of Great Catastrophe." Both Uganda and Chile had two truth commissions.

25 For example, the Zimbabwean commission, established in 1985, was meant to deal with human rights abuses committed under President Robert Mugabe's rule. But because it was established while Mugabe was still in power, any real investigation or disclosure of crimes committed was both dangerous and ineffective for those seeking justice. Its findings were never made public, and Mugabe's opponents continue to request a new and unbiased truth commission. See Hayner, *Unspeakable Truths*, 242–43.

26 Hayner, *Unspeakable Truths.*

27 VanAntwerpen, "Reconciliation Reconceived," 34.

28 Krog, *Country of My Skull*, 143.

29 See also Kymlicka and Bashir, "Introduction: Struggles for Inclusion," 19.

30 Garneau, "Imaginary Spaces of Conciliation and Reconciliation," 30.

31 Roland Chrisjohn, among others, has been a vocal critic of the Canadian TRC, especially since Justice LaForme stepped down as chair. To hear an interview with Dr. Chrisjohn, visit www.rabble.ca. See also Garneau, "Imaginary Spaces of Conciliation and Reconciliation."

32 For a description of how survivors resisted norms for confession and sharing traumatic experience, as well as used the TRC as a forum for expressing political messages and coming together with family, see Robinson, "Reconciliation Relations."

33 Smith, *Decolonizing Methodologies*, 5.

34 Absolom and Willett, "Putting Ourselves Forward," 98.

35 King, "Coyote and the Enemy Aliens."

36 King, "Coyote and the Enemy Aliens," 158.

37 Trouillot, *Silencing the Past*, xix.

38 See Episkenew, *Taking Back Our Spirits*, and McKegney, *Magic Weapons*, for discussion of Indigenous storytelling. Storytelling will also be discussed further in chapters 3 and 4.

39 Rothberg, *Multidirectional Memory*, 3.

40 Miller, "Reading Photographs," 461.

41 Stoler, *Along the Archival Grain.*

42 For more on these ideas, see Taylor, "Trauma as Durational Performance"; and Trouillot, *Silencing the Past.*

43 Marie Wilson, lecture at St. Regis, University of Toronto, April 6, 2011.

44 Regan, "A Transformative Framework," 7. Regan further develops this argument in her book *Unsettling the Settler Within*.

Chapter 1: Reconciliation as a Way of Seeing

Epigraph: Quoted in Titley, *A Narrow Vision*, 50.

1 Quoted in Titley, *A Narrow Vision*, 34.

2 John Paul Tasker, "Conservative Senator Defends 'Well-Intentioned' Residential School System," CBC *News*, March 8, 2017, www.cbc.ca/news/politics /residential-school-system-well-intentioned-conservative-senator-1.4015115.

3 Prager and Glover, eds., *Dilemmas of Reconciliation*.

4 Canadian history is often split into five distinct stages. The first comprises a long period where Indigenous peoples lived and interacted with one another on the land now known as Canada. The second historical period begins with the founding of New France in 1607. This period was also marked by conflicts between the British and the French for control in Canada, with the British eventually establishing themselves as the victor. With the Royal Proclamation of 1763, the third stage in Canadian history, commonly known as the colonial period, began. Confederation, which marks the fourth period of Canadian history, signals the epoch of nation building: completion of the national railway occurred during this stage, uniting the country both physically and symbolically. Historians define the fifth stage as the modern period, beginning in the twentieth century. For more on this history, see Mookerjea, Szeman, and Faurschou, "Introduction: Between Empires."

5 Quoted in Dickason and Newbigging, *A Concise History of Canada's First Nations*, 355n1.

6 The practices of orality and the skill of storytelling have been thought inferior to written documentation about the past. This has slowly begun to change. One major turning point was the landmark court case *Delgamuukw v. British Columbia* (1997). The case, after several appeals, established that Indigenous oral histories could be submitted as evidence in land claims cases in Canada. For a brief summary of the Delgamuukw case, see "A Lay Person's Guide to Delgamuukw."

7 Bain Attwood writes of a parallel situation in Australia where Aborigines were not considered to be the proper subjects of history. As an "ancient" people, they belonged to the discipline of anthropology, not history. See Attwood, *Telling the Truth About Aboriginal History*, 16.

8 Mackey, *The House of Difference*, 9.

9 See Hanson, "The Sixties Scoop & Aboriginal Child Welfare"; and Cardinal, *Ohpikiihaakan-Ohpihmeh (Raised Somewhere Else)*.

10 Scholars have both built upon and critiqued Anderson's work as different models of nationhood became apparent. Notably, Partha Chatterjee's work on anticolonial ideas of nationhood has complicated Anderson's work. Focusing on Bengali drama in India, Chatterjee objects to Anderson's treatment of ideas

of the "nation" "as part of the universal history of the modern world" and laments that if this is the case, then even the realm of imagination will remain "forever colonized." See Chatterjee, *The Nation and Its Fragments*, 5. See also Anderson, *Imagined Communities*.

11 Gómez-Barris, *Where Memory Dwells*, 14.

12 Archibald, Castellano, and DeGagné, "Introduction," 1.

13 LaRocque, *When the Other Is Me*, 104.

14 Francis, *National Dreams*, 29.

15 Francis, *National Dreams*, 24. For example, *The Dudley Do-Right Show* was a popular children's show in the 1960s. Created by US cartoonists Alex Anderson and Chris Hayward, the show capitalized on the idea of the Mountie as a conscientious (if somewhat bumbling) crime fighter.

16 Sarah Vowell includes a short essay that compares stereotypical imaginings of Mounties and cowboys in *The Partly Cloudy Patriot*.

17 Mackey, *The House of Difference*, 1, 2.

18 Mackey, *The House of Difference*, 2.

19 At the events and conferences that I attended about the IRS TRC, skepticism on the part of former students is common. Some survivors of the school believe that they are being called to perform their traumatic past for the nation, while little emphasis is given to personal and community healing or to the restitution of land and resources.

20 Niezen, *Truth and Indignation*.

21 Mookerjea, Szeman, and Faurschou, "Introduction: Between Empires," 6.

22 Mackey, *The House of Difference*, 27.

23 Milloy, *A National Crime*, 20.

24 Milloy, *A National Crime*, 21.

25 Miller, *Shingwauk's Vision*, 112–20.

26 Thobani, *Exalted Subjects*, 81.

27 Kulchyski, "Subversive Identities," 5. Lowercase is in original.

28 Stoler, *Along the Archival Grain*.

29 Kulchyski, "Subversive Identities," 5.

30 See Miller, *Shingwauk's Vision*, 343–75, for more on strategies of resistance during the IRS era. See also Furniss, *Victims of Benevolence*.

31 Truth and Reconciliation Commission, *Honouring the Truth, Reconciling for the Future*, 116–23.

32 It should be noted that residential schooling was also practiced in the seventeenth century in what was then known as "New France." However, the current focus on reconciliation generally focuses on the period from 1876 onward.

33 Indian Act, section 118, https://laws-lois.justice.gc.ca/eng/acts/i-5/section-118-20021231.html.

34 McKegney, *Magic Weapons*, 26.

35 Miller, *Shingwauk's Vision*, 90.

36 Miller, "Reading Photographs," 461. Niezen echoes this sentiment in *Truth and Indignation*, choosing to supplement his event research with interviews of priests and nuns formerly employed in residential schools.

37 Maurice Halbwachs has written that memory is mediated through many social frameworks, including the family, religion, and language. However, the construct of the family in Halbwachs's writing is of a particular sort. Largely, he focuses on the nuclear family and its gendered roles of father, mother, son, and daughter. Halbwachs discusses the role between the family and legal authority, emphasizing the bonds of family ties and the traces of these bonds even when they are broken. However, Halbwachs's theories of kinship are not universal, for the construct of the family is produced through various means. See Halbwachs, *On Collective Memory*. Halbwachs also notes that the legal system influences, and is influenced by, these same social frameworks. See Karstedt, *Legal Institutions and Collective Memories* (especially the introduction), for a more in-depth discussion of legal institutions and collective memories.

38 Emberley, *Defamiliarizing the Aboriginal*, xvi.

39 See reports and publications from the Aboriginal Healing Foundation, www.ahf.ca/publications/research-series.

40 Johnston, *Indian School Days*, 137.

41 Truth and Reconciliation Commission, "School Meals," in *The Survivors Speak*, 71; Truth and Reconciliation Commission, *Honouring the Truth*, 91.

42 Quoted in Jack, ed., *Behind Closed Doors*, 126.

43 Starr, "Foreword," ix.

44 Blondin-Perrin, *My Heart Shook Like a Drum*, 35.

45 Johnston, *Indian School Days*, 28, 53. Although it is much less common to hear survivors recount positive memories of their experience at the Truth and Reconciliation Commission events at the Indian residential schools, this camaraderie was notable in several of the TRC national events. Survivors who shared positive memories often noted individual teachers who had a significant impact on their lives. See Truth and Reconciliation Commission, *The Survivors Speak*, 125–27.

46 Wagamese, "Returning to Harmony," 141.

47 Hirsch, "The Generation of Postmemory," 106, and *The Generation of Postmemory*, 5.

48 Furniss, *Victims of Benevolence*.

49 Koostachin, dir., *Remembering Inninimowin*.

50 Thobani, *Exalted Subjects*, 141.

51 Mackey, *The House of Difference*, 16; Thobani, *Exalted Subjects*, 144.

52 Barker, "For Whom Sovereignty Matters," 16–17.

53 The conflict over land and resources sets Indigenous issues apart from those of recent immigrant communities in relation to multicultural policies. To learn more, for instance, about the creation of Nunavut, the first Inuit self-governing territory, in 1999, see Henderson, *Nunavut*. Although significant for its

implications on Indigenous sovereignty, the creation of Nunavut has not resonated with the general Canadian public as a way to deal with colonial legacies and land rights. See also Turner, "On the Idea of Reconciliation"; Kalant, *National Identity*; and Champagne, "Rethinking Native Relations." For information on the Australian context, see Povinelli, *The Cunning of Recognition*.

54 I have simplified the definitions of *state* and *nation* here. For a more in-depth discussion, see Anderson, *Imagined Communities*, or Hobsbawm, *Nations and Nationalism*. For a discussion more specific to the Canadian case, which in some ways challenges the historical framing put forward by Anderson and Hobsbawm, see Kalant, *National Identity*.

55 Saul, *A Fair Country*.

56 Kalant, *National Identity*, 4.

57 See York and Pindera, *People of the Pines*; and Kalant, *National Identity*.

58 Smyth, "The Mohawk Warrior," 58–80; Kalant, *National Identity*.

59 Webb, "Standoff at Oka," 191.

60 Wheeler, "Act of Defiance," 186.

61 It is interesting to note that during this time, Canada was one of four nations (along with New Zealand, Australia, and the United States) that did not sign the United Nations Declaration on Rights of Indigenous Peoples. The wording surrounding land and resources was noted as the primary reason for Canada's objection to the declaration. Canada ratified the document in 2010.

62 Under the aegis of the Indian Residential Schools Settlement Agreement (IRSSA), there have been more than 38,096 individual IAP and 105,530 CEP claims lodged. In addition, progress has begun toward a similar compensation regime for those who attended Indian day schools. See Indigenous and Northern Affairs Canada, "Statistics on the Implementation of the Indian Residential Schools Settlement Agreement."

63 Indian Residential Schools Settlement Agreement (IRSSA): Schedule A.

64 IRSSA: Schedule D.

65 IRSSA: Schedule N, Section 1.

66 Hayner, *Unspeakable Truths*.

67 IRSSA: Schedule D, Section 1d.

68 See "Justice Harry S. LaForme Resigns."

69 As with the previous commission, two of the three commissioners (Sinclair and Littlechild) and the entirety of the ten-member Advisory Committee to the commission are of Indigenous descent. Chief Wilton Littlechild is a former IRS student. Justice Murray Sinclair and Marie Wilson have family members who attended the schools.

70 See Halbwachs, *On Collective Memory*; and Olick, *The Politics of Regret*. For some of the key approaches to the study of memory, see the edited collection by Michael Rossington and Anne Whitehead, *Theories of Memory*. Their introduction offers a brief discussion of the "memory boom" and explores some early critiques of the emerging field of memory studies.

71 Debates about the methods to remember such pasts increasingly became part of public discourse; see Young, *At Memory's Edge*; and Huyssen, *Present Pasts*. Survivors of the Holocaust played a pivotal role in these discourses, and remembering the atrocities of World War II began to occupy a central role in the burgeoning field of memory studies. For more on this, see Huyssen, *Present Pasts*; Olick, *The Politics of Regret*; and Rothberg, *Multidirectional Memory*. Other contributing factors to the field included the rise of identity politics as well as crises within several academic disciplines, including history and anthropology. See also Sturken, "Memory, Consumerism and Media."

72 This is not to suggest that the concepts of history and memory can be disentangled; in fact, it is in the tensions within and between memory and history that some of the most productive work gets done. See Jelin, *State Repression and the Labors of Memory*.

73 See Huyssen, "International Human Rights and the Politics of Memory."

74 Truth and Reconciliation Commission, *The Survivors Speak*, 47–58.

75 On "nonmemory," see Freeman, *Distant Relations*, xvii; on "willful amnesia," see Epp, *We Are All Treaty People*, 228; on "induced amnesia," see Chandler, "Coming to Terms," 307.

76 Sturken, *Tangled Memories*, 2.

77 Irwin-Zarecka, *Frames of Remembrance*, 37.

78 "Indian Residential Schools."

79 Wakeham, "Reconciling 'Terror,'" 3, 24.

80 For Canadian context, see Turner, *This Is Not a Peace Pipe*; and Alfred, *Wasáse*. For American context, see Deloria, *Playing Indian*.

81 Turner, "On the Idea of Reconciliation."

82 Robinson, "Reconciliation Relations."

83 McKegney, *Magic Weapons*, 6; Alfred, *Wasáse*.

84 This clip is available at https://www.cbc.ca/player/play/2565484259.

85 This event has nation-specific names that vary across Indigenous communities along the northwest coast of Canada and the United States.

86 For a detailed examination of Coast Salish economies of affection, see Kelly and Kelly, "An Ethic of Reciprocity."

87 Quoted in McKegney, *Magic Weapons*, 12.

88 Mirzoeff, *The Right to Look*, xv, 14.

89 Atleo, "First Nations," 33.

90 Coulthard, "The Subjects of Empire," 439. Coulthard further develops this argument as well as his own theory of successful self-recognition for Indigenous self-determinacy in *Red Skin, White Masks*.

91 Rose, *An Introduction to the Interpretation of Visual Materials*, 20.

92 Hirsch, *Family Frames*, 6.

93 Schwartz, "Un beau souvenir de Canada," 16.

94 Lewis, *Alanis Obomsawin*, 174.

95   Lewis, *Alanis Obomsawin*, 175.

96   Burant, "'Between Two Worlds,'" 5.

97   Much of this historical background is based on the work in Burant's "'Between Two Worlds'" and Mulvey's "Among the Sag-a-noshes."

98   Mulvey, "Among the Sag-a-noshes."

99   Tsinhnahjinnie, "When Is a Photograph Worth a 1000 Words?," 42.

100 Lydon, *Eye Contact*, xxiii.

101 Ginsburg and Myers, "A History of Aboriginal Futures," 43.

102 Lydon, *Eye Contact*, xxi.

103 For a discussion of IsumaTV, see Ginsburg, "Native Intelligence"; and Cache Collective, "Cache."

104 Bredin, "The Learning Path," 154.

105 Rajagopal, "Notes on Postcolonial Visual Culture," 16.

106 Hariman and Lucaites, *No Caption Needed*, 289.

107 Atleo, "First Nations," 34.

Chapter 2: Images of Contact

1   Barthes, *Camera Lucida*, 53.

2   Debord, *The Society of the Spectacle*, 12.

3   Pinney, *Camera Indica*.

4   This phrase, "to kill the Indian in the child," has been used by several government officials in describing the goals of the residential school system. Prime Minister Harper, in his official apology, quoted these now-infamous words.

5   Debord, *The Society of the Spectacle*, 19.

6   Hirsch and Spitzer, "About Class Photos" and *School Photos in Liquid Time*.

7   Hirsch and Spitzer, "About Class Photos."

8   McMaster, "Colonial Alchemy," 79.

9   Pinney, "Introduction," 4.

10   Pinney, "Introduction," 6.

11   LaRocque, *When the Other Is Me*, 121.

12   Pratt, *Imperial Eyes*, 4.

13   Pratt, *Imperial Eyes*, 4.

14   Emberley, *Defamiliarizing the Aboriginal*, 3.

15   Angel and Wakeham, "Witnessing *in Camera*," 100.

16   Tagg, *The Burden of Representation*.

17   Malmsheimer, "Photographic Analysis," 23, 25.

18   Hirsch and Spitzer, *School Photos in Liquid Time*, 86.

19   Milloy, *A National Crime*, 6.

20   It was not uncommon in colonial societies to use before-and-after images to communicate the efficacy of assimilationist policies. In Laura Wexler's

discussion of a before-and-after image of three young girls from the Hampton Institute in the United States, she describes how such images were used: "[The photograph intimates] that institutions like Hampton would be able to accomplish what the entire U.S. Cavalry had tried and failed to do: to persuade the western tribes to abandon their communal, nomadic way of life; adopt the prizes, mores, and values of consumer culture; and turn their little girls into desirable women on the middle-class-commodity plan." See Wexler, *Tender Violence*, 112–13.

21 Interestingly, just as Thomas Moore's staged transformation is used to represent American residential schools as well as Canada's in current historical scholarship, this phrase has been traced to American, not Canadian, origins.

22 Legacy of Hope Foundation, "Where Are the Children?," accessed February 26, 2021, https://legacyofhope.ca/wherearethechildren.

23 Fullenwieder, "Unsettling Histories," 185.

24 Anglican Church of Canada General Synod Archives. 6575-103, box 137 9-14.13. Circa 1940.

25 Anglican Church of Canada General Synod Archives. 6575-104, box 137 9-14.13. Circa 1954.

26 For a detailed analysis of the symbolic work of totem poles, see Jonaitis and Glass, *The Totem Pole*.

27 Quoted in LaRocque, *When the Other Is Me*, 121–22.

28 Quoted in LaRocque, *When the Other Is Me*, 129.

29 Quoted in Miller, *Shingwauk's Vision*, 194.

30 Miller, *Shingwauk's Vision*, 195.

31 Raheja, *Reservation Reelism*, 22.

32 Deloria, *Playing Indian*, 7.

33 "The Ballroom Costumes," Canadian Museum of History, www.historymuseum .ca/cmc/exhibitions/hist/balls/b-3eng.html.

34 Francis, *National Dreams*, 229.

35 Green, "Rosebuds of the Plateau," 50.

36 LaRocque, *When the Other Is Me*, 129.

37 I was told that Kusick was his mother's maiden name. Email exchange with archivist Tim Novak at Reference Services, Saskatchewan Archives Board, September 24, 2010.

38 I spoke to archivists at the National Archives in Ottawa, the Saskatchewan Archives, and the Presbyterian and Anglican archives. I also discussed this with historian John Milloy, who, as mentioned, wrote *A National Crime*. Milloy was also unable to find more information about Moore.

39 Email exchange with Novak.

40 In 2017 the site of the cemetery received heritage status, and in 2019 the land was officially transferred to the Regina Indian Industrial School Commemorative Association. See Ethan Williams, "'We're Honouring the Children:' Industrial School Cemetery Land Transferred to Commemorative Association,"

Regina Leader-Post, June 25, 2019, https://leaderpost.com/news/local-news
/were-honouring-the-children-industrial-school-cemetery-land-transferred-to
-commemorative-association.

41 BigEagle's short documentary, *I Am a Boy: Thomas Moore Keesick*, premiered
in March 2015 and is available for viewing at https://www.youtube.com/
watch?v=74qL_OomdeE.

42 Angel and Wakeham, "Witnessing *in Camera*," 104–5.

43 Thompson, "The Missing Children."

44 Neu and Therrien, *Accounting for Genocide*.

45 Trouillot, *Silencing the Past*.

46 Derrida, *Archive Fever*, 4.

47 Miles, "On Canadian Archives," 53.

48 Library and Archives Canada, https://www.bac-lac.gc.ca/eng/Pages/home.aspx.

49 Wallot, "Foreword," v.

50 Wilson, "Peace, Order and Good Governance," 237.

51 McBryde, *Who Owns the Past?*, 6.

52 Feldman, "The Structuring Enemy," 1707.

53 Fourmile, "Who Owns the Past?," 1.

54 Azoulay, *The Civil Contract of Photography*, 18.

55 Azoulay, *The Civil Contract of Photography*, 14.

56 Emberley, *Defamiliarizing the Aboriginal*, 179.

57 McCallum, *Cultural Memories and Imagined Futures*, 114.

58 Bell, "Unsettling Acts," 169.

59 In the United States, artists such as Carrie Mae Weems and Stephen Deo
have taken up photographs from the Carlisle and Hampton schools, where
attempts to assimilate Native Americans took place. See Hirsch and Spitzer,
School Photos in Liquid Time, 118–23. In Canada, Indigenous artists Edward
Poitras, Jeff Thomas, and Dana Claxton have also used images from the IRS
system in their work.

60 Gómez-Barris, *Where Memory Dwells*, 6.

61 Barthes, *Camera Lucida*, 38, 27, 48.

62 Edwards, *Raw Histories*, 22.

63 Todd, dir., *The Learning Path*.

64 Gordon, *Ghostly Matters*, 63.

65 Neitch, "Indigenous Persistence."

66 Stoler, "Tense and Tender Ties," 4.

67 Hirsch and Spitzer, "About Class Photos."

68 Nora, "Between Memory and History," 1.

69 Trouillot, *Silencing the Past*, 29.

70 Derrida, *Archive Fever*, 36.

71 Freud, "Screen Memories," 306, 309.

72 Veracini, "Settler Collective, Founding Violence and Disavowal."

73 Ginsburg, "Screen Memories," 40.

74 See also the work done by the Children of Shingwauk Alumni Association at Algoma University (formerly the Shingwauk Residential School). The school now houses the Shingwauk Residential Schools Centre, which includes a large archive of old photographs from its residential school past. Former students are able to donate, look through, and identity themselves or others in these photographs.

75 After I presented a paper that included this image at the ACLA conference in Toronto in 2013, Marianne Hirsch suggested this connection between the "post"-theories and the Post-It. See also a short discussion of this connection in Hirsch's *The Generation of Postmemory*, 5. Pauline Wakeham has also contributed to my thinking on the use of these Post-It Notes.

76 Emberley, *Defamiliarizing the Aboriginal*, 158.

77 Simpson, "Captivating Eunice," 106.

78 Hirsch, *Family Frames*, 83.

79 Sassoon, "Photographic Materiality," 196.

80 Schwartz, "'Having New Eyes,'" 339.

Chapter 3: Nations Gather

Epigraphs: The full text is available at https://www.cbc.ca/archives; see also Kusugak, "On the Side of Angels," 25.

1 For writing about these two registers in relation to multicultural rhetoric in Australia, see Povinelli, *The Cunning of Recognition*, 29.

2 In addition to these national gatherings, the IRS TRC included community events that were "designed by communities and respond to the needs of the former students, their families and those affected by the IRS legacy including the special needs of those communities where Indian Residential Schools were located." In total, there were 238 days of local hearings held across 77 community events with the purpose of "acknowledging the capacity of communities to develop reconciliation practices, respecting the goal of witnessing in accordance with Aboriginal principles," as stated in Schedule N of the IRSSA. Two regional events, one in Victoria, BC, and the other in Yellowknife, in the Northwest Territories, also took place. For a further discussion of witnessing, see Gaertner, "'Aboriginal Principles of Witnessing.'"

3 Truth and Reconciliation Commission of Canada, *Honouring the Truth, Reconciling for the Future*, 25.

4 As Catherine Cole explains in *Performing South Africa's Truth Commission*, to call these national gatherings a performance is not to judge them negatively; it is to recognize their performative aspects. Cole builds on Diana Taylor's work, which distinguishes between the archive and the repertoire, or "embodied memory." See Taylor, *The Archive and Repertoire*, 20.

5 Nagy, "The Truth and Reconciliation Commission of Canada."

6 Thrift, "Intensities of Feeling," 60.

7 For excellent contributions to the literature, see *Reconciling Canada*. In this edited volume, both Amber Dean and Roger Simon explore the role of mourning and public emotions. Dean asserts that powerful affect might be a distraction, drawing attention away from injustices that require concrete political changes. See Dean, "Public Mourning and the Culture of Redress"; and Simon, "Toward a Hopeful Practice of Worrying." Dylan Robinson illustrates the ways in which communal affective engagement through musical performance and cultural events may result in individuals "feeling reconciled" yet "remaining settled." Robinson's assertion conveys how the sensory perception associated with these national events evokes an immediacy easily confused with veracity. See Robinson, "Feeling Reconciliation, Remaining Settled." Finally, Lara Fullenwieder asserts that the TRC national events engage in an economy of affect, whereby the powerful affective sensations associated with both sharing and witnessing testimony work to legitimize existing power asymmetries associated with settler governance. See Fullenwieder, "Settler Biopower."

8 Berlant, "Intimacy," 1.

9 See Robinson, "Intergenerational Sense, Intergenerational Responsibility," and "Reconciliation Relations."

10 See Finlay, "Negotiating the Swamp"; and Robinson, "Feeling Reconciliation, Remaining Settled."

11 McAllister uses the term *elder* to draw comparisons between elders in the Japanese community and elders in Indigenous communities. There has also been collaboration between the Japanese and Indigenous Canadian communities in Canada as they each sought redress for historical injustices. See McAllister, *Terrain of Memory*, 256n1.

12 See Krog, "Fact Bordering Fiction."

13 Krog, *Country of My Skull*, 170–71.

14 Krog, "Fact Bordering Fiction," 4.

15 LaRocque, *When the Other Is Me*, 23–35.

16 See Lippard, "Introduction," for a discussion on the productive spaces of fragmented or partial readings.

17 Episkenew, *Taking Back Our Spirits*, 108.

18 Dion, "(Re)telling to Disrupt," 64.

19 Corntassel, Chaw-win-is, and T'lakwadzi, "Indigenous Storytelling."

20 Maracle, *Bent Box*, 107.

21 Maracle, "Oratory," 8.

22 Sontag, *Regarding the Pain of Others*.

23 The field notes throughout this chapter are excerpts that have been edited. They are italicized. The excerpts from survivor testimony are not italicized.

24 Volume I, part I: *The History, Origins to 1939/Canada's Residential Schools*. Volume I, part 2: *The History, 1939 to 2000/Canada's Residential Schools*. Volume 2: *The Inuit and Northern Experience/Canada's Residential Schools*. Volume 3:

The *Métis Experience/Canada's Residential Schools*. Volume 4: *Missing Children and Unmarked Burials/Canada's Residential Schools*. Volume 5: *The Legacy/ Canada's Residential Schools*. Volume 6: *Reconciliation*. All volumes are free and available online through the National Centre for Truth and Reconciliation at https://nctr.ca.

25 Spivak, "The Politics of Translation," 397.

26 Dewar, "Interview with Alexander Javier," 16.

27 Bassnett and Trivedi, "Introduction," 2.

28 Apter, *The Translation Zone*, 6.

29 Appiah, "Thick Translation."

30 Laub and Felman, *Testimony*, 70–71, emphasis in original. For the most part I have focused specifically on the Indigenous or Canadian issues in dealing with testimony. However, the literature on testimony has largely taken shape through studies on trauma, narrative, and the Holocaust. See also Miller and Tougaw, "Introduction: Extremities"; Caruth, *Trauma*; and Derrida, *Demeure*.

31 See Simon, *The Touch of the Past*, for more on listening and engaging a shared but contested past in the Canadian context.

32 Regan, *Unsettling the Settler Within*, 12, 13.

33 Williams, *Marxism and Literature*.

34 In "Settler Biopower," Fullenwieder explores the IRS TRC as it works to structure settler "structures of feeling." See also Rifkin's "Settler States of Feeling."

35 On the "memory boom," see Winter, *Remembering War*. On "memorial mania," see Doss, *Memorial Mania*. Additionally, some scholars have focused on the ways in which memories of traumatic pasts in national histories now haunt the construct of citizen and nation; see Sturken, *Tangled Memories*; Jelin, *State Repression and the Labors of Memory*; and Gómez-Barris, *Where Memory Dwells*. For work on how memory gets passed from generation to generation, see Hirsch, *Family Frames*. For work on how public spaces have become sites of memorialization, see Huyssen, *Present Pasts*; Nora, "Between Memory and History"; Taylor, *The Archive and Repertoire*; and Young, *At Memory's Edge*.

36 The literature on truth and reconciliation commissions encompasses a diverse range of work. Some of the relevant literature focuses on comparative analysis—for example, Hayner, *Unspeakable Truths*; and Grandin, "The Instruction of Great Catastrophe." Others focus on literature and narrative—for example, Krog, *Country of My Skull*; Sanders, *Ambiguities of Witnessing*; Slaughter, *Human Rights Inc.*; and Corntassel, Chaw-win-is, and T'lakwadzi, "Indigenous Storytelling." Others focus on memory studies: Gómez-Barris, for example, in *Where Memory Dwells*. There are also scholars interested in broader legal frameworks and transitional justice, such as Regan in *Unsettling the Settler Within* and Murdocca in *To Right Historical Wrongs*.

37 In response to theorists who believe that trauma culture can represent "the failure of political culture and its displacement by a sentimental culture of feeling or voyeuristic culture of spectacle," Cvetkovich's *An Archive of Feelings* (on

queer trauma) focuses instead on "how trauma can be a foundation for creating counterpublic spheres rather than evacuating them" (15). Like Cvetkovich, I recognize both the dangers and possibilities of political agency that coalesces around cultures of trauma.

38 Van Styvendale, "The Trans/Historicity of Trauma," 204.

39 Gone, "'So I Can Be Like a Whiteman,'" 387.

40 See Johnston's foreword in McKegney's *Magic Weapons* for a personal account of an IRS survivor's frustrations with clinical psychology's approaches to healing.

41 Coulthard, *Red Skin, White Masks*; Niezen, *Truth and Indignation*; Simon's and Dean's individual essays in *Reconciling Canada*; Fullenwieder, "Unsettling Histories" and "Settler Biopower"; and Fullenwieder and Molnar, "Settler Governance and Privacy."

42 Vizenor, *Survivance*.

43 See Slaughter, *Human Rights Inc.*; Whitlock, "Active Remembrance"; and Jelin, *State Repression and the Labors of Memory* for broader discussions of TRCs. See Niezen's *Truth and Indignation* for the Canadian example.

44 Many of the discourses of collective trauma focus on the Holocaust as the paradigmatic site of the ethical and moral questions of bearing witness—for example, Agamben's *Remnants of Auschwitz* and Laub's "On Holocaust Testimony." Other authors question this emphasis and draw attention to the ways in which the Holocaust has produced a discourse that has influenced the way in which other genocides or cases of extreme human suffering are discussed. See, for example, Miller and Tougaw's "Introduction: Extremities" and Rothberg's *Multidirectional Memory*.

45 At the events I attended, I spoke informally to some people who were taking testimonies. One man noted that out of the handful of people trained to take testimony at this particular event, he was the only male. For this reason, his days were particularly long because he had to take testimony from anyone who requested to give testimony to a man. The commission attempted to accommodate different languages and requests whenever possible.

46 Kelm, *Colonizing Bodies*; Kelly, "Confessions of a Born Again Pagan."

47 Jelin, *State Repression and the Labors of Memory*, 75.

48 Feldman, "Memory Theaters," 167.

49 In contrast, in one of the most celebrated (and criticized) TRCs, in South Africa, there was a strong emphasis on both oppressed and oppressors giving their accounts of life under the apartheid regime. Although perpetrators in South Africa also voluntarily participated, amnesty could be requested and granted. For more, see Mamdani, "Amnesty or Impunity?"

50 Truth and Reconciliation Commission, *Honouring the Truth*, 342.

51 Kulchyski, "What Is Native Studies," 13.

52 Commissioner Wilton Littlechild (Cree) is a survivor of the IRS system. Both the chair of the commission, Justice Murray Sinclair (Ojibwe), and Commissioner Marie Wilson have family members who attended the schools.

53   Gaertner, "'Aboriginal Principles of Witnessing,'" 135.

54   It may also be noted that the much of the TRC's mandate was developed before any iteration of the commission and its Indigenous leadership was realized. That is, the mandate developed out of a legal settlement that at times, as Rosemary Nagy has pointed out, had more than seventy lawyers negotiating, almost none of whom were Indigenous. See Nagy, "The Truth and Reconciliation Commission of Canada."

55   Gaertner argues that the TRC's notion of Indigenous witnessing mirrors similar definitions developed for the Vancouver Olympics in 2009 from Musqueam elder Larry Grant, which also focused on sharing and carrying the burden of witnessing. Gaertner asserts that the TRC relied heavily on this Coast Salish/Musqueam framework but, ultimately, that representing this framework as pan-Indigenous is in direct conflict with the nation-specific approaches outlined in Schedule N. See Gaertner, "'Aboriginal Principles of Witnessing.'"

56   Younging, "Inherited History," 341.

57   See McKegney's *Magic Weapons*.

58   Taiaiake Alfred and Jeff Corntassel have expressed something similar in writing that colonization cannot be the central story of Indigenous lives: "It must be recognized that colonialism is a narrative in which the Settler's power is the fundamental reference and assumption, inherently limiting Indigenous freedom and imposing a view of the world that is but an outcome or perspective on that power." See Alfred and Corntassel, "Being Indigenous," 601.

59   Robinson, "Reconciliation Relations," 63.

60   See Robinson, "Reconciliation's Senses," for more on the role of songs and the act of singing at reconciliation events.

61   This protest was organized by Kevin Annett, a former Anglican minister who has broken from the church. He is a vocal and controversial critic of the IRS TRC.

62   Quoted in Andrew Stobo Sniderman, "A Shameful Chapter Aired," *Montreal Gazette*, accessed May 10, 2011, https://www.bishop-accountability.org/news2011/05_06/2011_05_07_Stobo_AShameful.htm.

63   As discussed in chapter 1, Harper held up his eagle feather in the Manitoba legislature as a symbolic gesture in blocking the Meech Lake Accord.

64   For a discussion of a similar dynamic at the TRC's regional event in Victoria, BC, see Robinson, "Reconciliation's Senses." Robinson looks at the aestheticization of reconciliation through the use of song, and he discusses Susan Aglukark's song "O Siem" during that event's closing concert.

65   hooks, *Black Looks*, 39.

66   At the TRC's Victoria regional event, a Catholic priest was repeatedly heckled by Indigenous audience members during his presentation on behalf of the church, as two different Indigenous women demanded multiple times that he "Tell the truth!" This continued until Justice Murray Sinclair asked the audience to let the priest continue without interruption.

67 Quoted in Peter White, "Some Former Residential School Students Struggle with Church Presence at Reconciliation Event," *Globe and Mail*, June 14, 2010, accessed June 20, 2010, www.theglobeandmail.com/news/national/some-former-residential-school-students-struggle-with-church-presence-at-reconciliation-event/article1367933.

68 Indeed, this has been the case since prior to the era of the residential schools, when missionaries, noting the centrality of song to Indigenous peoples' lives (songs have always been used as forms of law, historical documentation, and medicine), had hymnals translated into Indigenous languages to aid the process of conversion.

69 VanAntwerpen, "Reconciliation Reconceived."

70 To explain this refusal, the Catholic Church notes its decentralized structure in Canada and claims that "only 16 out of 70 dioceses in Canada were associated with the former Indian Residential Schools." Numerous statements by the Catholic Church in Canada on the schools can be found at www.cccb.ca.

71 For more on the role of official apologies in reconciliation processes, see Mackey, "The Apologizers' Apology"; Wakeham, "Rendition and Redress"; and Gooder and Jacobs, "'On the Border of the Unsayable.'"

72 The Department of Indian and Northern Affairs (INAC) changed its name to the Department of Aboriginal and Northern Affairs (ANAC) in 2011.

73 Quoted in Narine, "Indian Act Sections to Be Repealed."

74 This testimony is archived at www.nctr.ca.

75 Quoted in Swan, "Inuvalit Witness Stolen Lives."

76 Stevenson, "An Ethical Injunction to Remember," 180.

77 Stevenson, "An Ethical Injunction to Remember," 180.

78 Cvetkovich, *An Archive of Feelings*, 284.

79 I am indebted to Keavy Martin, who first suggested at the Aesthetics of Reconciliation research meeting during the Halifax TRC national event that I pursue the concept of "affective sovereignty."

80 For a discussion of "partial truths" in ethnographic writing, see Clifford, "Introduction: Partial Truths."

Chapter 4: Reconciliation as a Ghostly Encounter

1 See, for example, Cameron, "Indigenous Spectrality"; Gordon, *Ghostly Matters*; Stoler, "Intimidations of Empire"; Tuck and Ree, "A Glossary of Haunting"; and Tuck and Yang, "Decolonization Is Not a Metaphor."

2 In the areas of comparative literature, cinema studies, sociology, and memory studies, the use of haunting discourses has become one way in which the past is negotiated. The term *hauntology* was coined by Jacques Derrida in *Specters of Marx*. A play on the verb *to haunt* and the noun *ontology*, the concept has proven fertile for scholars excavating and negotiating contested histories. Der-

rida asserts that the ghost is a reminder of an "ethical injunction to remember" and that any relationship with a nation's specters should be undertaken "in the name of justice." See Derrida, *Specters of Marx*, xix.

3 Colmeiro, "A Nation of Ghosts?," 30.

4 Stoler, "Intimidations of Empire," xiii.

5 Anderson, *Imagined Communities*, 9.

6 Edwards, *Gothic Canada*, xix.

7 See Richardson, *Wacousta*; and Atwood, *Surfacing*, for example. See the anthologies edited by Sugars and Turcotte (*Unsettled Remains*) and Sugars (*Unhomely States*) for discussions about haunting narratives in the work of Canadian authors. See also Gelder and Jacobs, *Uncanny Australia*, for Australian context.

8 Gordon, *Ghostly Matters*, xvi.

9 Tuck and Ree, "A Glossary of Haunting," 643.

10 Tuck and Ree, "A Glossary of Haunting," 647. See also Tuck and Yang, "Decolonization Is Not a Metaphor."

11 Morrill, Tuck, and Super Futures Haunt Qollective, "Before Dispossession, or Surviving It," 7.

12 For examples, see Glavin et al., *Amongst God's Own*; and Knockwood, *Out of the Depths*. For reports of paranormal activity, see Jody Porter, "Remains Found Near Residential School Are Non-human. Ontario Families Vow to Continue Search for 15 Children Missing from 1926–1973," *CBC News*, accessed July 15, 2012, www.cbc.ca/news/canada/sudbury/story/2012/07/12/tbay-remains -residential-school.html.

13 Krog, Ratele, and Mpolweni, *There Was This Goat*, 100.

14 In *Uncanny Australia*, Gelder and Jacobs do an excellent job of exploring these relationships in an Australian context, detailing how "Aboriginal sacredness is also a fact of modern, bureaucratic life: worldly, rather than other-worldly. It is continually being dealt with by governments, businesses, mining companies and mediators." Marita Sturken also looks at the role of human remains in the making of meaning at Ground Zero after 9/11. She notes that the search for the "tiniest traces of those lost" is also a search "for a narrative, not only for proof that someone died at the World Trade Center, but the belief that those traces will tell the story of how someone died." See Sturken, *Tourists of History*, 210.

15 Regan, *Unsettling the Settler Within*, 230.

16 Knockwood, *Out of the Depths*, 106.

17 Mitchell, *What Do Pictures Want?*, 28–29.

18 Lawrence, "Gender, Race, and the Regulation of Native Identity."

19 Osborne, "Figuring Space, Marking Time," 26.

20 Alfred, "Opening Words," 10.

21 Susan Buggey, "An Approach to Aboriginal Cultural Landscapes," Government of Canada publication, 1999, https://publications.gc.ca/site/eng/9.823720/ publicaton.html.

22 Morin, "this is what happens when we perform the memory of the land."

23 Alfred, *Wasáse*, 206.

24 de Leeuw, "Intimate Colonialisms," 341, 344–45.

25 Nora, "Reasons for the Current Upsurge in Memory," 4.

26 Simpson, "Captivating Eunice," 114–16.

27 Todd, dir., *The Learning Path*.

28 Abbot, "Interviews with Loretta Todd," 338.

29 Abbot, "Interviews with Loretta Todd," 338–39.

30 Abbot, "Interviews with Loretta Todd," 341.

31 Henderson, "Postcolonial Ghost Dancing," 57.

32 Woo, *Ghost Dancing with Colonialism*, 3.

33 For more on ghosts as benevolent ancestors, see Cariou, "Haunted Prairie," 731.

34 Barron, "The Indian Pass System," 31.

35 Halfe, *Bear Bones and Feathers*, 2.

36 Cariou, "Haunted Prairie," 731.

37 Gingell and Borrieses, "Listening to Bones That Sing," 87.

38 Halfe, *Blue Marrow*, 75–76. I am indebted to Sam McKegney for bringing this poem to my attention through the "Aesthetics of Reconciliation in Canada" research group.

39 The Blue Quills Board comprises representatives from Beaver Lake, Cold Lake, Frog Lake, Whitefish Lake, Hart Lake, Kehewin, and Saddle Lake.

40 Blue Quills First Nations College, *Blue Quills Commemoration Edition*, vi.

41 Blue Quills First Nations College, *Blue Quills Commemoration Edition*, 2–3.

42 Blue Quills First Nations College, *Blue Quills Commemoration Edition*, 31.

43 De Leeuw, "Intimate Colonialisms," 351.

44 Blondin-Perrin, *My Heart Shook Like a Drum*, 29.

45 Sturken, *Tangled Memories*, 8.

46 Fanon, *Black Skin, White Masks*, 114.

47 Taylor, *Multiculturalism*, 27.

48 See Deloria, *Playing Indian*. Some of his ideas are discussed in chapter 1.

49 Rumors suggest that some of the funding moved to the controversial Canadian Museum for Human Rights (CMHR) in Winnipeg.

50 The Indian Residential School Museum of Canada opened to the public in October 2019 in the Rufus Prince Building in Portage with plans for expansion into 2020. See Long Plain First Nation, "Residential School Museum Becomes a Reality," October 5, 2019, www.lpband.ca/residential-school-museum-becomes-a-reality.

51 The person who sent the photos requested not to be identified by name.

52 Quoted in Stephen LaRose, "Wrecker's Ball Claims White Calf Collegiate," AMMSA.com, 1999, www.ammsa.com/publications/saskatchewan-sage/wreckers-ball-claims-white-calf-collegiate-0.

53 While attending the national gathering in Inuvik and at subsequent TRC events, I've heard rumors of ghostly sightings at the sites of IRS demolitions. I'm not sure how to properly cite these rumors, or even how to make sense of them, as they were often mentioned quickly, sometimes in hushed tones by people uncertain about repeating what they had heard or seen.

54 Deborah Steel, "Tseshaht Hosts Survivors for Demolition of Peake Hall," *Ha-Shilth-Sa*, November 13, 2012, www.hashilthsa.com/news/2012-11-13/tseshaht -hosts-survivors-demolition-peake-hall.

55 Porter, "Remains Found Near Residential School."

56 Truth and Reconciliation Commission, *Honouring the Truth*, 309.

57 Peter Edwards, "Charlie Hunter's Finally Home with His Family," *Toronto Star*, accessed August 19, 2011, https://www.thestar.com/news/canada/2011/08/19 /charlie_hunters_finally_home_with_his_family.html.

58 Suzy Thompson, "The Missing Children: The Legacy of Residential Schools Includes Unmarked Graves," *Fast Forward Weekly*, accessed March 10, 2012, http://archive.altweeklies.com/aan/the-missing-children/Story?oid=5970263.

59 Thompson, "The Missing Children."

60 In 2019 the land of Red Deer's cemetery was purchased by the Alberta Historical Resource Foundation and has since been designated for preservation. This preservation is the result of several decades of Indigenous activism and has happened in conversation with the Remembering the Children Society. See Lana Michelin, "Red Deer Indian Industrial School Cemetery Purchased by Province for Preservation," *Red Deer Advocate*, March 14, 2019, www .reddeeradvocate.com/news/red-deer-indian-industrial-school-cemetery -purchased-by-province-for-preservation.

61 Quoted in Glavin et al., *Amongst God's Own*, 69.

62 Glavin et al., *Amongst God's Own*, 25.

63 I am indebted to Patricia Raymond-Adair and Karen Bonneau at the Coqualeetza Cultural Education Centre for giving me access to the Coqualeetza archives.

64 Barb Stanbrook and Mike Doyle, "Stalo Band Lays Claim to Former Hospital," *Chilliwack Progress*, May 5, 1976, https://theprogress.newspapers.com/image /77090006.

65 Trouillot, *Silencing the Past*, 29–30.

66 Joe, *Song of Eskasoni*, 75.

67 Gómez-Barris, *Where Memory Dwells*, 72.

68 Gelder, *Edge of Empire*, xvi.

69 Hall, "'When Was the Post-colonial?,'" 259.

70 Cameron, "Indigenous Spectrality," 389.

71 Peter Morin explored ways of communing with the ancestors and former IRS students in his 2013 performance *this is what happens when we perform the memory of the land*. He writes about this performance, the memory of the land, and the body as a resonance chamber in his contribution to *Arts of Engagement* by the same title: "this is what happens when we perform the memory of the land."

Conclusion: Fragments of Truth

Epigraph: Koostachin, dir., *Remembering Inninimowin*, 7:53.

1   *A New Future*.

2   Koostachin was born in Moose Factory and grew up in nearby Attawapiskat. For other Indigenous films that look at this region, see also Alanis Obomsawin (Abenaki), *Christmas at Moose Factory* and *The People of the Kattawapiskak River*.

3   Koostachin, "Remembering Inninimowin: The Language of the Human Beings," 76–77.

4   Koostachin, telephone interview with author, December 9, 2012.

5   Koostachin, dir., *Remembering Inninimowin*, 1:07:54. I have quoted Koostachin at length here in accord with her own interviewing style, which deploys minimal editing in order to more closely conform to modes of Indigenous storytelling. For more on this, see "Remembering Inninimowin: The Language of the Human Beings," 77.

6   Dylan Robinson argues that the intergenerational effects of the IRS system are felt not only by Indigenous peoples; settler Canadians should also acknowledge an "intergenerational responsibility." Robinson suggests the term *intergenerational perpetration* to name "the continued ignorance of Indigenous histories and the lack of civic responsibility" on the part of settler Canadians. See Robinson, "Reconciliation's Senses," 16.

7   Koostachin, telephone interview with author, December 9, 2012.

8   Koostachin, telephone interview with author, December 9, 2012.

9   Truth and Reconciliation Commission of Canada, *Honouring the Truth*, 25.

10   "Privacy and Access," https://nctr.ca/research.

11   Koostachin, dir., *Remembering Inninimowin*, 49:40.

Bibliography

Abbott, Lawrence. "Interviews with Loretta Todd, Shelley Niro and Patricia Dead-
man." *Canadian Journal of Native Studies* 18, no. 2 (1998): 335–73.

Absolom, Kathy, and Cam Willett. "Putting Ourselves Forward: Location in Aborig-
inal Research." In *Research as Resistance: Critical, Indigenous and Anti-oppressive
Approaches*, edited by Leslie Brown and Susan Strega, 255–86. Toronto: Canadian
Scholars' Press, 2005.

Agamben, Georgio. *Remnants of Auschwitz: The Witness and the Archive.* New York:
Zone, 2002.

Alfred, Taiaiake. "Opening Words." In *Lighting the Eighth Fire: The Liberation, Resurgence, and Protection of Indigenous Nations*, edited by Leanne Simpson, 9–11.
Winnipeg: Arbeiter Ring, 2008.

Alfred, Taiaiake. *Wasáse: Indigenous Pathways of Action and Freedom.* Toronto: University of Toronto Press, 2005.

Alfred, Taiaiake, and Jeff Corntassel. "Being Indigenous: Resurgences against
Contemporary Colonialism." *Government and Opposition* 9 (2005): 597–614.
https://doi.org/10.1111/j.1477-7053.2005.00166.x.

Andersen, Chris. *"Métis": Race, Recognition, and the Struggle for Indigenous People-
hood.* Vancouver: University of British Columbia Press, 2014.

Anderson, Benedict. *Imagined Communities: Reflections on the Spread of Nationalism.*
London: Verso, 1983.

Anderson, Mark Cronlund, and Carmen L. Robertson. *Seeing Red: A History of
Natives in Canadian Newspapers.* Winnipeg: University of Manitoba Press, 2011.

Angel, Naomi. *Before Truth: Memory, History and Nation in the Context of Truth and
Reconciliation in Canada.* PhD diss., New York University, 2013.

Angel, Naomi. "A Fragmented Reconciliation Process?" *Tracing Memory* (blog).
July 9, 2009. https://tracingmemory.wordpress.com/2009/07/09/a-fragmented
-reconciliation-process.

Angel, Naomi. "New Beginnings." *Tracing Memory* (blog). January 13, 2012. https://
tracingmemory.wordpress.com/2012/01/13/new-beginnings.

Angel, Naomi. "On Collaboration." *Tracing Memory* (blog). October 3, 2012.
https://tracingmemory.wordpress.com/2012/10/03/on-collaboration.

Angel, Naomi. "On Writing about Illness." *Everybody Hearts* (blog). April 23, 2013. https://everybodyhearts.com/2013/04/23/on-writing-about-illness.

Angel, Naomi. "Text or Testimony?" *Tracing Memory* (blog). November 14, 2011. https://tracingmemory.wordpress.com/2011/11/14/text-or-testimony.

Angel, Naomi, and Pauline Wakeham. "Witnessing *in Camera*: Photographic Reflections on Truth and Reconciliation." In *Arts of Engagement: Taking Aesthetic Action in and beyond the Truth and Reconciliation Commission of Canada*, edited by Dylan Robinson and Keavy Martin, 93–134. Waterloo, ON: Wilfred Laurier University Press, 2016.

Appiah, Anthony. "Thick Translation." *Callaloo* 16, no. 4 (1993): 808–19. https://doi .org/10.2307/2932211.

Apter, Emily. *The Translation Zone: A New Comparative Literature*. Princeton, NJ: Princeton University Press, 2006.

Archibald, Linda, Marlene Brant Castellano, and Michael DeGagné. "Introduction." In *From Truth to Reconciliation: Transforming the Legacy of Residential Schools*, edited by Linda Archibald, Marlene Brant Castellano, and Michael DeGagné, 1–10. Ottawa: Aboriginal Healing Foundation, 2008.

Atleo, Shawn. "First Nations." In *Imagining Canada: A Century of Photographs Preserved by the* New York Times, edited by William Morassutti. Toronto: Doubleday Canada, 2012.

Attwood, Bain. *Telling the Truth About Aboriginal History*. Crows Nest, NSW: Allen and Unwin, 2005.

Atwood, Margaret. *Surfacing*. Toronto: McClelland and Stewart, 1972.

Auguste, Isabelle. "Rethinking the Nation: Apology, Treaty and Reconciliation in Australia." *National Identities* 12, no. 4 (2010): 425–63. https://doi.org/10.1080 /14608944.2010.520984.

Azoulay, Ariella. *The Civil Contract of Photography*. New York: Zone, 2008.

Barker, Joanne. "For Whom Sovereignty Matters." In *Sovereignty Matters: Locations of Contestation and Possibility in Indigenous Struggles for Self-Determination*, edited by Joanne Barker, 1–31. Lincoln: University of Nebraska Press, 2006.

Barron, Laurie F. "The Indian Pass System in the Canadian West, 1882–1935." *Prairie Forum* 13, no. 1 (1988): 25–42.

Barthes, Roland. *Camera Lucida: Reflections on Photography*, trans. Richard Howard. New York: Hill and Wang, 1981.

Bassnett, Susan, and Harish Trivedi. "Introduction: Of Colonies, Cannibals and Vernaculars." In *Post-colonial Translations: Theory and Practice*, edited by Susan Bassnett and Harish Trivedi, 1–18. London: Routledge, 1999.

Behar, Ruth. *The Vulnerable Observer: Anthropology That Breaks Your Heart*. Boston: Beacon, 1996.

Bell, Lynne. "Unsettling Acts: Photography as Decolonizing Testimony in Centennial Memory." In *The Cultural Work of Photography in Canada*, edited by Carol Payne and Andrea Kunard, 165–81. Montreal: McGill-Queen's University Press, 2011.

Berlant, Lauren. "Intimacy: A Special Issue." In *Intimacy*, edited by Lauren Berlant. Chicago: University of Chicago Press, 2000.

BigEagle, Louise, dir. *I Am a Boy: Thomas Moore Keesick*. 2015. www.youtube.com
/watch?v=74qL_OomdeE.

Blondin-Perrin, Alice. *My Heart Shook Like a Drum: What I Learned at the Indian
Mission Schools, Northwest Territories*. Ottawa: Borealis, 2009.

Blue Quills First Nations College. *Blue Quills First Nations College: Commemoration
Edition*. Blue Quills First Nations College, 2002. www.bluequills.ca/wp-content
/uploads/2012/02/BQ-30th-Anniversary-Book.pdf.

Bredin, Marian. "The Learning Path." In *The Cinema of Canada*, edited by Jerry
White, 153–61. London: Wallflower, 2006.

Burant, Jim. "'Between Two Worlds': The Man Who Struggled to Know Himself."
In *100 Photos That Changed Canada*, edited by Mark Reid, 4–5. Toronto: Harper
Collins, 2009.

Cache Collective. "Cache: Provisions and Productions in Contemporary Igloolik
Video." In *Global Indigenous Media: Cultures, Poetics, and Politics*, edited by Pamela
Wilson and Michelle Steward, 74–88. Durham, NC: Duke University Press, 2008.

Cameron, Emilie. "Indigenous Spectrality and the Politics of Postcolonial Ghost
Stories." *Cultural Geographies* 15, no. 3 (2008): 383–93. https://doi.org/10.1177
/1474474008091334.

Cardinal, Colleen. *Ohpikiihaakan-Ohpihmeh (Raised Somewhere Else): A 60s Scoop
Adoptee's Story*. Nova Scotia: Roseway, 2018.

Cardinal, Harold. "Buckskin Curtain: The Indian-Problem Problem." In *Canadian
Cultural Studies*, edited by Sourayan Mookerjea, Imre Szeman, and Fail Faurschou, 200–209. Durham, NC: Duke University Press, 2009.

Cariou, Warren. "Haunted Prairie: Aboriginal 'Ghosts' and the Spectres of Settlement." *University of Toronto Quarterly* 75, no. 2 (2006): 727–34. https://doi.org
/10.1353/utq.2006.0245.

Carter, Jill. "Discarding Sympathy, Disrupting Catharsis: The Mortification of Indigenous Flesh as Survivance-Intervention." *Theatre Journal* 67, no. 3 (2015): 413–32.

Caruth, Cathy, ed. *Trauma: Explorations in Memory*. Baltimore: Johns Hopkins
University Press, 1995.

Champagne, Duane. "Rethinking Native Relations with Contemporary Nation-
States." In *Indigenous Peoples and the Modern State*, edited by Duane Champagne, Susan Steiner, and Karen J. Torjeson, 3–23. New York: Altamira, 2005.

Chandler, David. "Coming to Terms with the Terror and History of Pol Pot's
Cambodia (1975–79)." In *Dilemmas of Reconciliation: Cases and Concepts*, edited
by Carol Prager and Trudy Glover, 307–26. Waterloo, ON: Wilfred Laurier
University Press, 2003.

Chapman, Audrey R., and Patrick Ball. "The Truth of Truth Commissions: Comparative Lessons from Haiti, South Africa, and Guatemala." *Human Rights
Quarterly* 23, no. 1 (2001): 1–43. https://doi.org/10.1353/hrq.2001.0005.

Chatterjee, Partha. *The Nation and Its Fragments: Colonial and Postcolonial Histories*.
Princeton, NJ: University of Princeton Press, 1993.

Churchill, Ward. *Kill the Indian, Save the Man: The Genocidal Impact of American
Indian Residential Schools*. San Francisco: City Lights, 2004.

Clifford, James. "Introduction: Partial Truths." In *Writing Culture: The Poetics and Politics of Ethnography*, edited by James Clifford and George E. Marcus, 1–26. Berkeley: University of California Press, 1986.

Cole, Catherine M. *Performing South Africa's Truth Commission: Stages of Transition*. Bloomington: Indiana University Press, 2010.

Colmeiro, José. "A Nation of Ghosts? Haunting, Historical Memory and Forgetting in Post-Franco Spain." *452°F* 4 (2011): 17–34.

Coombes, Annie. "Introduction: Memory and History in Settler Colonialism." In *Rethinking Settler Colonialism History and Memory in Australia, Canada, Aotearoa New Zealand and South Africa*, edited by Annie Coombes, 1–12. Manchester, UK: Manchester University Press, 2005.

Corntassel, Jeff, Chaw-win-is, and T'lakwadzi. "Indigenous Storytelling, Truth-Telling, and Community Approaches to Reconciliation." *English Studies in Canada* 35, no. 1 (2009): 137–59. https://doi.org/10.1353/esc.0.0163.

Coulthard, Glen S. *Red Skin, White Masks: Rejecting the Colonial Politics of Recognition*. Minneapolis: University of Minnesota Press, 2014.

Coulthard, Glen S. "The Subjects of Empire: Indigenous Peoples and the 'Politics of Recognition' in Canada." *Contemporary Political Theory* 6 (2007): 437–60. https://doi.org/10.1057/palgrave.cpt.9300307.

Crosby, Marcia. 1997. "Lines, Lineage and Lies, or Borders, Boundaries and Bullshit." In *Nations in Urban Landscapes*, edited by Faye Heavy Shield, Shelley Niro, and Eric Robertson, 23–30. Vancouver: Contemporary Art Gallery, 1997.

Cvetkovich, Ann. *An Archive of Feelings: Trauma, Sexuality, and Lesbian Public Cultures*. Durham, NC: Duke University Press, 2003.

Day, Iyko. *Alien Capital: Asian Racialization and the Logic of Settler Colonial Capitalism*. Durham, NC: Duke University Press, 2016.

de Leeuw, Sarah. "Intimate Colonialisms: The Material and Experienced Places of British Columbia's Residential Schools." *Canadian Geographer* 51, no. 3 (2007): 339–59. https://doi.org/10.1111/j.1541-0064.2007.00183.x.

Dean, Amber. "Public Mourning and the Culture of Redress: Mayerthorpe, Air India, and Murdered or Missing Aboriginal Women." In *Reconciling Canada: Critical Perspectives on the Culture of Redress*, edited by Jennifer Henderson and Pauline Wakeham, 278–95. Toronto: University of Toronto Press, 2013.

Debord, Guy. *The Society of the Spectacle*. New York: Zone, 1995.

Deloria, Philip J. *Playing Indian*. New Haven, CT: Yale University Press, 1998.

Derrida, Jacques. *Archive Fever: A Freudian Impression*, trans. Eric Prenowitz. Chicago: University of Chicago Press, 1998.

Derrida, Jacques. *Demeure: Fiction and Testimony*, trans. Elizabeth Rottenberg. Stanford, CA: Stanford University Press, [1998] 2000.

Derrida, Jacques. *Specters of Marx: The State of the Debt, the Work of Mourning and the New International*, trans. Peggy Kamuf. New York: Routledge, 1994.

Dewar, Jonathan. "Interview with Alexander Javier, October 7, 2011, Kamloops, BC." *Westcoast Line* (Summer 2012).

Dickason, Olive Patricia, and William Newbigging. *A Concise History of Canada's First Nations*, 2nd ed. Oxford: Oxford University Press, 2010.

Dion, Susan D. "(Re)telling to Disrupt: Aboriginal People and Stories of Canadian History." *Journal for the Association of Curriculum Studies* 2, no. 1 (2004): 55–76.

Doss, Erika. *Memorial Mania: Public Feeling in America*. Chicago: University of Chicago Press, 2010.

Du Bois, William E. B. *The Souls of Black Folk*. [1903]. New York: Bantam, 1994.

Edwards, Elizabeth. *Raw Histories: Photographs, Anthropology and Museums*. Oxford: Berg, 2001.

Edwards, Justin D. *Gothic Canada: Reading the Spectre of a National Literature*. Edmonton: University of Alberta Press, 2005.

Emberley, Julia. *Defamiliarizing the Aboriginal: Cultural Practices and Decolonization in Canada*. Toronto: University of Toronto Press, 2007.

Emberley, Julia. "'Epistemic Heterogeneity': Indigenous Storytelling, Testimonial Practices, and the Question of Violence in Indian Residential Schools." In *Reconciling Canada: Critical Perspectives on the Culture of Redress*, edited by Jennifer Henderson and Pauline Wakeham, 143–58. Toronto: University of Toronto Press, 2013.

Emberley, Julia. *The Testimonial Uncanny: Indigenous Storytelling, Knowledge, and Reparative Practices*. Albany: State University of New York Press, 2014.

Episkenew, Jo-Ann. *Taking Back Our Spirits: Indigenous Literature, Public Policy, and Healing*. Winnipeg: University of Manitoba Press, 2009.

Epp, Roger. *We Are All Treaty People: Prairie Essays*. Edmonton: University of Alberta Press, 2008.

Fanon, Frantz. *Black Skin, White Masks*, trans. Charles Lam Markmann. New York: Grove, 1967.

Feldman, Allen. "Memory Theaters, Virtual Witnessing, and the Trauma-Aesthetic." *Biography* 27, no. 1 (2004): 163–202. www.jstor.org/stable/23540434.

Feldman, Allen. "The Structuring Enemy and Archival War." *PMLA* 124, no. 5 (2009): 1704–13. www.jstor.org/stable/25614394.

Finlay, Linda. "Negotiating the Swamp: The Opportunity and Challenge of Reflexivity in Research Practice." *Qualitative Research* 2, no. 2 (2002): 209–30. https://doi.org/10.1177/146879410200200205.

Fourmile, Henrietta. "'Who Owns the Past?' Aborigines as Captives of the Archives." *Aboriginal History* 13 (1989): 1–8.

Francis, Daniel. *National Dreams: Myth, Memory, and Canadian History*. Vancouver: Arsenal Pulp, 1997.

Freeman, Victoria. *Distant Relations: How My Ancestors Colonized North America*. Toronto: McClelland and Stewart, 2002.

Freud, Sigmund. "Screen Memories." In *The Standard Edition of the Complete Psychological Works of Sigmund Freud*, vol. 3, *1893–1899*, 299–322. London: Hogarth, 1899.

Fullenwieder, Lara E. C. "Settler Biopower: Accumulation and Dispossession in the Indian Residential School Settlement Agreement." In *Reconciling Canada: Critical Perspectives on the Culture of Redress*, edited by Jennifer Henderson and Pauline Wakeham, 100–114. Toronto: University of Toronto Press, 2013.

Fullenwieder, Lara E. C. "Unsettling Histories: Representation and Indigenous Creative Art Praxis in Official Indian Residential School Redress." PhD diss., Queens University, 2016.

Fullenwieder, Lara E. C., and Adam Molnar. "Settler Governance and Privacy: Canada's Indian Residential School Settlement Agreement and the Mediation of State-Based Violence." *International Journal of Communication* 12 (2018): 1332–49. http://ijoc.org/index.php/ijoc/article/view/7042.

Furniss, Elizabeth. *Victims of Benevolence: The Dark Legacy of the Williams Lake Residential School*. Vancouver: Arsenal Pulp, 1992.

Gaertner, David. "'Aboriginal Principles of Witnessing' and the Truth and Reconciliation Commission of Canada." In *Arts of Engagement: Taking Aesthetic Action in and beyond the Truth and Reconciliation Commission of Canada*, edited by Dylan Robinson and Keavy Martin, 135–56. Waterloo, ON: Wilfred Laurier University Press, 2016.

Garneau, David. "Imaginary Spaces of Conciliation and Reconciliation." *Westcoast Line* 74, no. 2 (2012): 28–38.

Gathering Strength: Canada's Aboriginal Action Plan. 1997. Accessed February 14, 2021. https://files.eric.ed.gov/fulltext/ED450974.pdf.

Gelder, Jane. *Edge of Empire: Postcolonialism and the City*. London: Routledge, 2002.

Gelder, Ken, and Jane M. Jacobs. *Uncanny Australia: Sacredness and Identity in a Postcolonial Nation*. Melbourne: Melbourne University Press, 1988.

Gingell, Susan, and Azalea Borrieses. "Listening to Bones That Sing: Orality, Spirituality, and Female Kinship in Louise Halfe's *Blue Marrow*." *Studies in American Indian Literatures* 23, no. 3 (2011): 69–93. https://doi.org/10.1353/ail.2011.0031.

Ginsburg, Faye. "Native Intelligence: A Short History of Debates on Indigenous Media and Ethnographic Film." In *Made to Be Seen: Perspectives on the History of Visual Anthropology*, edited by Marcus Banks and Jay Ruby, 234–55. Chicago: University of Chicago Press, 2011.

Ginsburg, Faye. "Screen Memories: Resignifying the Traditional in Indigenous Media." In *Media Worlds: Anthropology on a New Terrain*, edited by Faye Ginsburg, Lila Abu-Lughod, and Brian Larkin, 29–57. Berkeley: University of California Press, 2002.

Ginsburg, Faye, and Fred Myers. "A History of Aboriginal Futures." *Critique of Anthropology* 26, no. 1 (2006): 27–45. https://doi.org/10.1177/0308275X06061482.

Glavin, Terry, and former students of St. Mary's. *Amongst God's Own: The Enduring Legacy of St. Mary's Mission*. Mission, BC: Longhouse, 2002.

Gómez-Barris, Macarena. *Where Memory Dwells: Culture and State Violence in Chile*. Berkeley: University of California Press, 2009.

Gone, Joseph. "'So I Can Be Like a Whiteman': The Cultural Psychology of Space and Place in American Indian Mental Health." *Culture and Psychology* 14, no. 3 (2008): 369–99.

Gooder, Haydie, and Jane Jacobs. "'On the Border of the Unsayable': The Apology in Postcolonizing Australia." *Interventions* 2, no. 2 (2000): 229–47. https://doi.org/10.1080/136980100427333.

Gordon, Avery. *Ghostly Matters: Haunting and the Sociological Imagination*. Minneapolis: University of Minnesota Press, [1997] 2008.

Grandin, Greg. "The Instruction of Great Catastrophe: Truth Commissions, National History, and State Formation in Argentina, Chile and Guatemala."

American Historical Review 110, no. 1 (2005): 46–67. https://doi.org/10.1086/ahr
/110.1.46.

Grant, George. "Canadian Fate and Imperialism." In *Canadian Cultural Studies*, edited by Sourayan Mookerjea, Imre Szeman, and Fail Faurschou, 145–59. Durham, NC: Duke University Press, 2009.

Green, Rayna. "Rosebuds of the Plateau: Frank Matsura and the Fainting Couch Aesthetic." In *Partial Recall: Photographs of Native North Americans*, edited by Lucy R. Lippard, 47–54. New York: New Press, 1992.

Halbwachs, Maurice. *On Collective Memory*, trans. Lewis A. Coser. Chicago: University of Chicago Press, 1992.

Halfe, Louise. *Bear Bones and Feathers*. Regina, SK: Coteau, 1994.

Halfe, Louise. *Blue Marrow*. Toronto: McClelland and Stewart, 1998.

Hall, Stuart. "'When Was the Post-colonial'? Thinking at the Limit." In *The Postcolonial Question: Common Skies, Divided Horizons*, edited by Ian Chambers and Lidia Curti, 242–59. New York: Routledge, 1996.

Hanson, Erin. "The Sixties Scoop & Aboriginal Child Welfare." 2009. https:// indigenousfoundations.arts.ubc.ca/sixties_scoop.

Hariman, Robert, and John Lucaites. *No Caption Needed: Iconic Photographs, Public Culture, and Liberal Democracy.* Chicago: University of Chicago Press, 2007.

Hayner, Priscilla. *Unspeakable Truths: Facing the Challenges of Truth Commissions.* New York: Routledge, 2002.

Healy, Chris. *Forgetting Aborigines*. Sydney: University of New South Wales, 2008.

Henderson, Alicia. *Nunavut: Rethinking Political Culture*. Vancouver: University of British Columbia Press, 2007.

Henderson, James Youngblood. "Postcolonial Ghost Dancing: Diagnosing European Colonialism." In *Reclaiming Indigenous Voice and Vision*, edited by Marie Ann Battiste, 56–76. Vancouver: University of British Columbia Press, 2000.

Henderson, Jennifer, and Pauline Wakeham. "Introduction." In *Reconciling Canada: Critical Perspectives on the Culture of Redress*, edited by Jennifer Henderson and Pauline Wakeham, 3–27. Toronto: University of Toronto Press, 2013.

Henderson, Jennifer, and Pauline Wakeham, eds. *Reconciling Canada: Critical Perspectives on the Culture of Redress.* Toronto: University of Toronto Press, 2013.

Hirsch, Marianne. *Family Frames: Photography, Narrative, and Postmemory*. Cambridge, MA: Harvard University Press, 1997.

Hirsch, Marianne. "The Generation of Postmemory." *Poetics Today* 29, no. 1 (2008): 103–28. https://doi.org/10.1215/03335372-2007-019.

Hirsch, Marianne. *The Generation of Postmemory: Writing and Visual Culture after the Holocaust*. New York: Columbia University Press, 2012.

Hirsch, Marianne, and Leo Spitzer. "About Class Photos." Nomadikon.net. Accessed February 10, 2013. www.nomadikon.net/contentitem.aspx?ci=162.

Hirsch, Marianne, and Leo Spitzer. *School Photos in Liquid Time: Reframing Difference.* Seattle: University of Washington Press, 2020.

Hobsbawm, E. J. *Nations and Nationalism since 1780: Programme, Myth, Reality.* New York: Cambridge University Press, 1990.

hooks, bell. *Black Looks: Race and Representation*. Boston: South End, 1992.

Huyssen, Andreas. "International Human Rights and the Politics of Memory." *Criticism* 53, no. 4 (2011): 607–24. https://doi.org/10.1353/crt.2011.0037.

Huyssen, Andreas. *Present Pasts: Urban Palimpsests and the Politics of Memory.* Stanford, CA: Stanford University Press, 2003.

"Indian Act, Section 118." Canada Justice Laws. Accessed February 14, 2021. https://laws-lois.justice.gc.ca/eng/acts/i-5/section-118-20021231.html.

"Indian Residential Schools." Last modified February 21, 2019.

Indian Residential Schools Settlement Agreement. 2006. Accessed February 14, 2021. www.residentialschoolsettlement.ca/settlement.html.

Indigenous and Northern Affairs Canada. "Statistics on the Implementation of the Indian Residential Schools Settlement Agreement." Accessed January 21, 2021. www.rcaanc-cirnac.gc.ca/eng/1315320539682/1571590489978.

Irwin-Zarecka, Iwona. *Frames of Remembrance: The Dynamics of Collective Memory.* Edison, NJ: Transaction, 1994.

Jack, Agnes, ed. *Behind Closed Doors: Stories from the Kamloops Indian Residential School.* Penticton, BC: Theytus, 2006.

Jelin, Elizabeth. *State Repression and the Labors of Memory*, trans. Judy Rein and Marcial Godoy-Anativia. Minneapolis: University of Minnesota Press, 2003.

Joe, Rita. *Song of Eskasoni: More Poems of Rita Joe.* Charlottetown: Ragweed, 1988.

Johnston, Basil. *Indian School Days.* Norman: University of Oklahoma Press, 1995.

Jonaitis, Aldona, and Aaron Glass. *The Totem Pole: An Intercultural History.* Seattle: University of Washington Press, 2010.

"Justice Harry S. LaForme Resigns." CNW Newsgroup. Accessed December 12, 2008. https://www.bishop-accountability.org/news2008/09_10/2008_10_20_CNW_JusticeHarry.htm.

Kalant, Amelia. *National Identity and the Conflict at Oka: Native Belonging and Myths of Postcolonial Nationhood in Canada.* New York: Routledge, 2004.

Karstedt, Suzanne, ed. *Legal Institutions and Collective Memories.* Oxford: Hart, 2009.

Kelly, Dara, and Patrick Kelly. "An Ethic of Reciprocity: Illuminating the Stó:lō Gift Economy." *Indigenous Spiritualities at Work: Transforming the Spirit of Enterprise*, edited by Chellie Spiller and Rachel Wolfgramm, 191–208. Charlotte, NC: Information Age, 2015.

Kelly, Fred. "Confessions of a Born Again Pagan." In *From Truth to Reconciliation: Transforming the Legacy of Residential Schools*, edited by Linda Archibald, Marlene Brant Castellano, and Michael DeGagné, 11–42. Ottawa: Aboriginal Healing Foundation, 2008.

Kelm, Mary-Ellen. *Colonizing Bodies: Aboriginal Health and Healing in British Columbia, 1900–50.* Vancouver: University of British Columbia Press, 1998.

King, Thomas. "Coyote and the Enemy Aliens." In *Our Story: Aboriginal Voices on Canada's Past*, edited by Rudyard Griffiths, 159–74. Toronto: Anchor, 2005.

Knockwood, Isabelle. *Out of the Depths: The Experience of Mi'kmaw Children at the Indian Residential School at Shubenacadie, Nova Scotia.* Lokeport, NS: Roseway, 1992.

Koostachin, Jules, dir. *Remembering Inninimowin.* DVD. Vancouver: VisJuelles Productions, 2010.

Koostachin, Jules. "Remembering Inninimowin: The Language of the Human Beings." *Canadian Journal of Law and Society* 27, no. 1 (2012): 75–80. https://doi .org/10.1353/jls.2012.0001.

Krog, Antjie. *Country of My Skull: Guilt, Sorrow and the Limits of Forgiveness in the New South Africa*. New York: Three Rivers, 2000.

Krog, Antjie. "Fact Bordering Fiction and the Honesty of 'I.'" *River Teeth* 8, no. 2 (2007): 33–43. https://doi.org/10.1353/rvt.2007.0008.

Krog, Antjie, Kopano Ratele, and Nosisi Mpolweni. *There Was This Goat: Investigating the Truth Commission Testimony of Notrose Nobomvu Konile*. Pietermaritzburg, South Africa: University of KwaZulu-Natal Press, 2009.

Kulchyski, Peter. "Subversive Identities: Indigenous Cultural Politics and Canadian Legal Frameworks, or Indigenous Orphans of the State." *e-misférica* 6, no. 2. https://hemisphericinstitute.org.

Kulchyski, Peter. "What Is Native Studies." In *Expressions in Canadian Native Studies*, edited by Ron F. Laliberte, 12–27. Saskatoon: University of Saskatchewan Press, 2000.

Kusugak, Jose Amaujaq. "On the Side of Angels." In *Response, Responsibility, and Renewal: Canada's Truth and Reconciliation Journey*, edited by Gregory Youngling, Jonathan Dewar, and Mike DeGagné, 13–29. Ottawa: Aboriginal Healing Foundation, 2009.

Kymlicka, Will, and Bashir Bashir. "Introduction: Struggles for Inclusion and Reconciliation in Modern Democracies." In *The Politics of Reconciliation in Multicultural Societies*, edited by Will Kymlicka and Bashir Bashir, 1–24. Oxford: Oxford University Press, 2008.

LaRocque, Emma. *When the Other Is Me: Native Resistance Discourse, 1850–1990*. Winnipeg: University of Manitoba Press, 2010.

Laub, Dori. "On Holocaust Testimony and Its 'Reception' within Its Own Frame, as a Process in Its Own Right." *History and Memory* 21, no. 1 (2009): 127–50. https://doi.org/10.1353/ham.0.0018.

Laub, Dori, and Shoshana Felman. *Testimony: Crises of Witnessing in Literature, Psychoanalysis, and History*. New York: Routledge, 1992.

Lawrence, Bonita. "Gender, Race, and the Regulation of Native Identity in Canada and the United States: An Overview." *Hypatia* 18, no. 2 (2009): 3–31. https://doi .org/10.1111/j.1527-2001.2003.tb00799.x.

"A Lay Person's Guide to Delgamuukw." BC Treaty Commission. 1999. www.bctreaty .ca/sites/default/files/delgamuukw.pdf.

Lewis, Randolph. *Alanis Obomsawin: The Vision of a Native Filmmaker*. Lincoln: University of Nebraska Press, 2006.

Lippard, Lucy R. "Introduction." In *Partial Recall: Photographs of Native North Americans*, edited by Lucy R. Lippard, 13–43. New York: New Press, 1992.

Lydon, Jane. *Eye Contact: Photographing Indigenous Australians*. Durham, NC: Duke University Press, 2005.

Mackey, Eva. "The Apologizers' Apology." In *Reconciling Canada: Critical Perspectives on the Culture of Redress*, edited by Jennifer Henderson and Pauline Wakeham, 47–62. Toronto: University of Toronto Press, 2013.

Mackey, Eva. *The House of Difference: Cultural Politics and National Identity in Canada.* Toronto: University of Toronto Press, 2002.

Malmsheimer, Lonna M. "Photographic Analysis as Ethnohistory: Interpretive Strategies." *Visual Anthropology* 1, no. 1 (1987): 21–36. https://doi.org/10.1080/08949468.1987.9966458.

Mamdani, Mahmood. "Amnesty or Impunity? A Preliminary Critique of the Report of the Truth and Reconciliation Commission of South Africa." In *Repairing the Past? International Perspectives on Reparations for Gross Human Rights Abuses,* edited by Max du Plessis and Stephen Pete Repairing, 83–118. Oxford: Intersentia, 2007.

Maracle, Lee. *Bent Box.* Penticton, BC: Theytus, 2000.

Maracle, Lee. "Oratory: Coming to Theory." *Essays on Canadian Writing* 54 (1994): 7–11.

Maxwell, Krista. "Settler-Humanitarianism: Healing the Indigenous Child-Victim." *Comparative Studies in Society and History* 59, no. 4 (2017): 974–1007.

McAllister, Kirsten E. *Terrain of Memory: A Japanese Canadian Memorial Project.* Vancouver: University of British Columbia Press, 2010.

McBryde, Isabel. *Who Owns the Past? Papers from the Annual Symposium of the Australian Academy of the Humanities.* Oxford: Oxford University Press, 1985.

McCall, Sophie, and Gabrielle L'Hirondelle Hill, eds. *The Land We Are: Artists and Writers Unsettle the Politics of Reconciliation.* Winnipeg: ARP, 2015.

McCallum, Pamela. *Cultural Memories and Imagined Futures: The Art of Jane Ash Poitras.* Calgary: University of Calgary Press, 2011.

McGregor, Russell. *Imagined Destinies: Aboriginal Australians and the Doomed Race Theory, 1880–1939.* Melbourne: Melbourne University Press, 1998.

McKegney, Sam. *Magic Weapons: Aboriginal Writers Remaking Community after Residential School.* Winnipeg: University of Manitoba Press, 2007.

McMaster, Gerald. 1992. "Colonial Alchemy: Reading the Boarding School Experience." In *Partial Recall: Photographs of Native North Americans,* edited by Lucy R. Lippard, 77–87. New York: New Press, 1993.

Methot, Suzanne. "Canada 23/150: Sol Sanderson: First Nations Founding Father." *150 Stories: Celebrating Canada's Sesquicentennial.* Canadian Race Relations Foundation. Last modified June 19, 2017. Accessed January 28, 2021. www.crrf-fcrr.ca/en/component/flexicontent/item/25645-canada-23-150-sol-sanderson.

Miles, Henry H. "On Canadian Archives." In *Transactions of the Literary and Historical Society of Quebec: Session of 1870–1871.* Quebec: Middleton and Dawson, 1871.

Miller, James R. "Reading Photographs, Reading Voices: Documenting the History of Native Residential Schools." In *Reading Beyond Words: Contexts for Native History,* edited by Jennifer S. H. Brown and Elizabeth Vibert, 460–82. Peterborough, ON: Broadview, 2003.

Miller, James R. *Shingwauk's Vision: A History of Native Residential Schools.* Toronto: University of Toronto Press, 1996.

Miller, Nancy, and Jason Tougaw. "Introduction: Extremities." In *Extremities: Trauma, Testimony, and Community,* edited by Nancy Miller and Jason Tougaw, 1–24. Urbana: University of Illinois Press, 2002.

Milloy, John. *A National Crime: The Canadian Government and the Residential School System, 1879 to 1986*. Winnipeg: University of Manitoba Press, 1999.

Mirzoeff, Nicholas. *The Right to Look: A Counterhistory of Visuality*. Durham, NC: Duke University Press, 2011.

Mitchell, W. J. T. *What Do Pictures Want? The Lives and Loves of Images*. Chicago: University of Chicago Press, 2005.

Mookerjea, Sourayan, Imre Szeman, and Fail Faurschou. "Introduction—Between Empires: On Cultural Studies in Canada." In *Canadian Cultural Studies*, edited by Sourayan Mookerjea, Imre Szeman, and Fail Faurschou, 1–33. Durham, NC: Duke University Press, 2009.

Morgensen, Scott Lauria. "The Biopolitics of Settler Colonialism: Right Here, Right Now." *Settler Colonial Studies* 1, no. 1 (2011): 52–76. https://doi.org/10.1080 /2201473X.2011.10648801.

Morin, Peter. "this is what happens when we perform the memory of the land." In *Arts of Engagement: Taking Aesthetic Action in and beyond the Truth and Reconciliation Commission of Canada*, edited by Dylan Robinson and Keavy Martin, 67–92. Waterloo, ON: Wilfred Laurier University Press, 2016.

Morrill, Angie, Eve Tuck, and Super Futures Haunt Qollective. "Before Dispossession, or Surviving It." *Liminalities* 12, no. 1 (2016): 1–20.

Mulvey, Christopher. "Among the Sag-a-noshes: Ojibwa and Iowa Indians with George Catlin in Europe, 1843–1848." In *Indians and Europe: An Interdisciplinary Collection of Essays*, edited by Christian Feest, 253–75. Lincoln: University of Nebraska Press, 1999.

Murdocca, Carmela. *To Right Historical Wrongs: Race, Gender, and Sentencing in Canada*. Vancouver: University of British Columbia Press, 2013.

Nagy, Rosemary. "The Truth and Reconciliation Commission of Canada: Genesis and Design." *Canadian Journal of Law and Society* 29, no. 2 (2014): 199–217. https://doi.org/10.1017/cls.2014.8.

Narine, Shari. "Indian Act Sections to be Repealed in Effort of Reconciliation." *Windspeaker* 28, no. 5 (2010).

National Inquiry into Missing and Murdered Indigenous Women and Girls. *Reclaiming Power and Place: The Final Report of the National Inquiry into Missing and Murdered Indigenous Women and Girls*, vol. 1A. Accessed July 12, 2021. www .mmiwg-ffada.ca/wp-content/uploads/2019/06/Final_Report_Vol_1a-1.pdf.

Neitch, Kenna. "Indigenous Persistence: Challenging the Rhetoric of Anti-colonial Resistance." *Feminist Studies* 45, nos. 2–3 (2019): 426–54. Accessed March 20, 2020. https://doi.org/10.15767/feministstudies.45.2-3.0426.

Neu, Dean, and Richard Therrien. *Accounting for Genocide: Canada's Bureaucratic Assault on Aboriginal People*. New York: Zed, 2003.

A New Future. Canadian Broadcasting Corporation. March 13, 1955. https://www. cbc.ca/player/play/2565484259.

Niezen, Ronald. "Templates and Exclusions: Victim Centrism in Canada's Truth and Reconciliation Commission on Indian Residential Schools." *The Journal of the Royal Anthropological Institute* 22, no. 4 (2016): 920–38. https://doi.org/10.1111 /1467-9655.12497.

Niezen, Ronald. *Truth and Indignation: Canada's Truth and Reconciliation Commission on Indian Residential Schools.* Toronto: University of Toronto Press, 2013.

Nora, Pierre. "Between Memory and History: Les Lieux de Mémoire." *Representations* 26 (Spring 1989): 7–25. https://doi.org/10.2307/2928520.

Nora, Pierre. "Reasons for the Current Upsurge in Memory." *Eurozine*, April 19, 2002. https://www.eurozine.com/reasons-for-the-current-upsurge-in-memory.

Obomsawin, Alanis, dir. *Christmas at Moose Factory.* 1971. National Film Board. https://www.nfb.ca/film/christmas_at_moose_factory/.

Obomsawin, Alanis, dir. *The People of the Kattawapiskak River.* 2012. National Film Board. https://www.nfb.ca/film/people_of_kattawapiskak_river/.

Olick, Jeffrey K. *The Politics of Regret: On Collective Memory and Historical Responsibility.* New York: Routledge, 2007.

Osborne, Brian S. "Figuring Space, Marking Time: Contested Identities in Canada." *International Journal of Heritage Studies* 2, nos. 1–2 (1996): 23–40.

Pinney, Christopher. *Camera Indica: The Social Life of Indian Photographs.* London: Reaktion, 1997.

Pinney, Christopher. "Introduction: 'How the Other Half….'" In *Photography's Other Histories*, edited by Christopher Pinney and Nicolas Peterson, 1–14. Durham, NC: Duke University Press, 2003.

Povinelli, Elizabeth A. *The Cunning of Recognition: Indigenous Alterities and the Making of Australian Multiculturalism.* Durham, NC: Duke University Press, 2002.

Prager, Carol, and Trudy Glover, eds. *Dilemmas of Reconciliation: Cases and Concepts.* Waterloo, ON: Wilfred Laurier University Press, 2003.

Pratt, Mary Louise. *Imperial Eyes: Travel Writing and Transculturation.* New York: Routledge, 1992.

"Prime Minister Stephen Harper's Statement of Apology." CBC News. June 11, 2008. Accessed November 1, 2008. www.cbc.ca/news/canada/story/2008/06/11/pm-statement.html.

Raheja, Michelle. *Reservation Reelism: Redfacing, Visual Sovereignty, and Representations of Native Americans in Film.* Lincoln: University of Nebraska Press, 2011.

Rajagopal, Arvind. "Notes on Postcolonial Visual Culture." *Bioscope* 2, no. 1 (2011): 11–22. https://doi.org/10.1177/097492761000200103.

Recollet, Karyn. "Glyphing Decolonial Love through Urban Flash Mobbing and *Walking with Our Sisters.*" *Curriculum Inquiry* 45, no. 1 (2015): 129–45.

"'Reconciliation Is Not an Aboriginal Problem, It Is a Canadian Problem.'" *As It Happens.* CBC Radio. June 2, 2015. www.cbc.ca/radio/asithappens/as-it-happens-tuesday-edition-1.3096950/reconciliation-is-not-an-aboriginal-problem-it-is-a-canadian-problem-it-involves-all-of-us-1.3097253.

Regan, Paulette. "A Transformative Framework for Decolonizing Canada: A Non-Indigenous Approach." Paper presented at Indigenous Governance (IGOV) Doctoral Student Symposium, University of Victoria, January 20, 2005.

Regan, Paulette. *Unsettling the Settler Within: Indian Residential Schools, Truth Telling, and Reconciliation in Canada.* Vancouver: University of British Columbia Press, 2010.

Renan, Ernest. "What Is a Nation?" In *Becoming National: A Reader*, edited by Jeff Ely and Ronald Grigor Suny, 41–55. New York: Oxford University Press, 1996.

Richardson, John. *Wacousta*. [1832]. Toronto: McClelland Stewart, 2008.

Rifkin, Mark. "Settler States of Feeling: National Belonging and the Erasure of Native American Presence." In *A Companion to American Literary Studies*, edited by Caroline F. Levander and Robert S. Levine, 342–55. Oxford: Wiley-Blackwell, 2011.

Robinson, Dylan. "Enchantment's Irreconcilable Connection: Listening to Anger, Being Idle No More." In *Performance Studies in Canada*, edited by Laura Levin and Marlis Schweitzer, 211–35. Montreal: McGill-Queen's University Press, 2017.

Robinson, Dylan. "Feeling Reconciliation, Remaining Settled." In *Reconciling Canada: Critical Perspectives on the Culture of Redress*, edited by Jennifer Henderson and Pauline Wakeham, 100–114. Toronto: University of Toronto Press, 2013.

Robinson, Dylan. "Intergenerational Sense, Intergenerational Responsibility." In *Arts of Engagement: Taking Aesthetic Action in and beyond the Truth and Reconciliation Commission of Canada*, edited by Dylan Robinson and Keavy Martin, 43–66. Waterloo, ON: Wilfred Laurier University Press, 2016.

Robinson, Dylan. "Reconciliation Relations." *Canadian Theatre Review* 161 (2015): 60–63. https://doi.org/10.3138/ctr.161.012.

Robinson, Dylan. "Reconciliation's Senses and the Reverberations of Redress 2012." Music, Media and Place Lecture Series. Memorial University, St. John's, NL. March 26, 2012.

Rose, Gillian. *An Introduction to the Interpretation of Visual Materials*. London: Sage, 2007.

Rossington, Michael, and Anne Whitehead. *Theories of Memory: A Reader*. Edinburgh: Edinburgh University Press, 2007.

Rothberg, Michael. *Multidirectional Memory: Remembering the Holocaust in the Age of Decolonization*. Stanford, CA: Stanford University Press, 2009.

Sanders, Mark. *Ambiguities of Witnessing: Law and Literature in the Time of a Truth Commission*. Stanford, CA: Stanford University Press, 2007.

Sassoon, Joanna. "Photographic Materiality in the Age of Digital Reproduction." In *Photographs Objects Histories: On the Materiality of Images*, edited by Elizabeth Edwards and Janice Hart, 186–202. London: Routledge, 2004.

Saul, John Ralston. *A Fair Country: Telling Truths about Canada*. Toronto: Penguin, 2008.

Schwartz, Joan M. "Un beau Souvenir du Canada: Object, Image, Symbolic Space." In *Photographs Objects Histories: On the Materiality of Images*, edited by Elizabeth Edwards and Janice Hart, 16–31. New York: Routledge, 2004.

Schwartz, Joan M. "'Having New Eyes': Spaces of Archives, Landscapes of Power." *Archives & Social Studies* 1, no. 1 (2007): 321–62.

Short, Damien. *Reconciliation and Colonial Power: Indigenous Rights in Australia*. Burlington, VT: Ashgate, 2008.

Simon, Roger. *The Touch of the Past: Remembrance, Learning, and Ethics*. New York: Palgrave Macmillan, 2005.

Simon, Roger. "Toward a Hopeful Practice of Worrying: The Problematics of Listening and the Educative Responsibilities of Canada's Truth and Reconciliation Commission." In *Reconciling Canada: Critical Perspectives on the Culture of Redress*, edited by Jennifer Henderson and Pauline Wakeham, 129–42. Toronto: University of Toronto Press, 2013.

Simpson, Audra. "Captivating Eunice: Membership, Colonialism, and Gendered Citizenships of Grief." *Wicazo Sa Review* 24, no. 2 (2009): 105–29. www.jstor.org/stable/40587783.

Simpson, Audra. "Whither Settler Colonialism?" *Settler Colonial Studies* 6, no. 4 (2016): 438–45.

Slaughter, Joseph. *Human Rights Inc.: The World Novel, Narrative Form, and International Law*. Bronx, NY: Fordham University Press, 2007.

Smith, Linda Tuhiwai. *Decolonizing Methodologies: Research and Indigenous Peoples*. New York: Zed, 1999.

Smyth, Heather. "The Mohawk Warrior: Reappropriating the Colonial Stereotype." *Topia* 3 (2000): 58–80. https://doi.org/10.3138/topia.3.58.

Snelgrove, Corey, Rita Dhamoon, and Jeff Corntassel. "Unsettling Settler Colonialism: The Discourse and Politics of Settlers, and Solidarity with Indigenous Nations." *Decolonization: Indigeneity, Education & Society* 3, no. 2 (2014): 1–32. https://jps.library.utoronto.ca/index.php/des/article/view/21166/17970.

Sontag, Susan. *Regarding the Pain of Others*. New York: Farrar, Straus and Giroux, 2002.

Spivak, Gayatri Chakravorty. "The Politics of Translation." In *The Translation Studies Reader*, edited by Lawrence Venuti, 397–416. London: Routledge, 2000.

Starr, Marlene. "Foreword." In *Finding My Talk: How Fourteen Native Canadian Women Reclaimed Their Lives*, edited by Agnes Grant. Markham, ON: Fitzhenry & Whiteside, 2004.

Statistics Canada. "Census of Population." 2006. https://www12.statcan.gc.ca/census-recensement/2006/index-eng.cfm#.

Stevenson, Lisa. "An Ethical Injunction to Remember: Memory, Cultural Survival and Ethics in Nunavut." In *Critical Inuit Studies: An Anthology of Contemporary Arctic Ethnography*, edited by Pamela R. Stern and Lisa Stevenson, 167–84. Lincoln: University of Nebraska Press, 2006.

Stoler, Ann. *Along the Archival Grain: Epistemic Anxieties and Colonial Common Sense*. Princeton, NJ: Princeton University Press, 2008.

Stoler, Ann. "Intimidations of Empire: Predicaments of the Tactile and Unseen." In *Haunted by Empire: Geographies of Intimacy in North American History*, edited by Ann Stoler, 1–22. Durham, NC: Duke University Press, 2006.

Stoler, Ann. "Tense and Tender Ties: The Politics of Comparison in North American History and (Post) Colonial Studies." In *Haunted by Empire: Geographies of Intimacy in North American History*, edited by Ann Stoler, 23–67. Durham, NC: Duke University Press, 2006.

Sturken, Marita. "Memory, Consumerism and Media: Reflections on the Emergence of the Field." *Memory Studies* 1, no. 1 (2008): 73–78. https://doi.org/10.1177/1750698007083890.

Sturken, Marita. *Tangled Memories: The Vietnam War, the AIDS Epidemic, and the Politics of Remembering*. Berkeley: University of California Press, 1997.

Sturken, Marita. *Tourists of History: Memory, Kitsch, and Consumerism from Oklahoma City to Ground Zero*. Durham, NC: Duke University Press, 2007.

Sugars, Cynthia, ed. *Unhomely States: Theorizing English-Canadian Postcolonialism*. Peterborough, ON: Broadview, 2004.

Sugars, Cynthia, and Gerry Turcotte, eds. *Unsettled Remains: Canadian Literature and the Postcolonial Gothic*. Waterloo, ON: Wilfred Laurier University Press, 2009.

Swan, Michael. "Inuvalit Witness Stolen Lives." *Catholic Register*. July 25, 2011. Accessed July 28, 2011. www.wcr.ab.ca/WCRThisWeek/Stories/tabid/61/entryid/1261/Default.aspx.

Tagg, John. *The Burden of Representation: Essays on Photographies and Histories*. Minneapolis: University of Minnesota Press, 1993.

Taylor, Charles. *Multiculturalism: Examining the Politics of Recognition*. Princeton, NJ: Princeton University Press, 1994.

Taylor, Diana. *The Archive and Repertoire: Performing Cultural Memory in the Americas*. Durham, NC: Duke University Press, 2003.

Taylor, Diana. "Trauma as Durational Performance: A Return to Dark Sites." In *Rites of Return: Diaspora Poetics and the Politics of Memory*, edited by Marianne Hirsch and Nancy K. Miller, 268–79. New York: Columbia University Press, 2011.

Thobani, Sunera. *Exalted Subjects: Studies in the Making of Race and Nation in Canada*. Toronto: University of Toronto Press, 2007.

Thrift, Nigel. "Intensities of Feeling: Towards a Spatial Politics of Affect." *Geografiska Annaler* 86, no. 1 (2004): 57–78. https://doi.org/10.1111/j.0435-3684.2004.00154.x.

Titley, Brian. *A Narrow Vision: Duncan Campbell Scott and the Administration of Indian Affairs in Canada*. Vancouver: University of British Columbia, 1986.

Todd, Loretta, dir. *The Learning Path*. DVD. First Run and Icarus Films, 1991.

Trouillot, Michel-Rolph. *Silencing the Past: Power and the Production of History*. Boston: Beacon, 1997.

Truth and Reconciliation Commission of Canada. *Honouring the Truth, Reconciling for the Future: Summary of the Final Report for the Truth and Reconciliation Commission of Canada*. 2015. www.trc.ca/assets/pdf/Honouring_the_Truth_Reconciling_for_the_Future_July_23_2015.pdf.

Truth and Reconciliation Commission of Canada. *The Survivors Speak: A Report of the Truth and Reconciliation Commission of Canada*. 2015. www.trc.ca/assets/pdf/Survivors_Speak_English_Web.pdf.

Tsinhnahjinnie, Hulleah J. "When Is a Photograph Worth a Thousand Words?" In *Photography's Other Histories*, edited by Christopher Pinney and Nicholas Peterson, 40–52. Durham, NC: Duke University Press, 2003.

Tuck, Eve, and C. Ree. "A Glossary of Haunting." In *Handbook of Autoethnography*, edited by Stacey Holman Jones, Tony E. Adams, and Carolyn Ellis, 639–58. Walnut Creek, CA: Left Coast, 2013.

Tuck, Eve, and K. Wayne Yang. "Decolonization Is Not a Metaphor." *Decolonization, Education and Society* 1, no. 1 (2012): 1–40.

Turner, Dale. "On the Idea of Reconciliation in Contemporary Aboriginal Politics." In *Reconciling Canada: Critical Perspectives on the Culture of Redress*, edited by Jennifer Henderson and Pauline Wakeham, 100–114. Toronto: University of Toronto Press, 2013.

Turner, Dale. *This Is Not a Peace Pipe: Towards a Critical Indigenous Philosophy*. Toronto: University of Toronto Press, 2006.

Van Styvendale, Nancy. "The Trans/Historicity of Trauma in Jeannette Armstrong's *Slash* and Sherman Alexie's *Indian Killer*." *Studies in the Novel* 40, nos. 1–2 (2008): 203–23. https://doi.org/10.1353/sdn.0.0002.

VanAntwerpen, Jonathan. "Reconciliation Reconceived: Religion, Secularism, and the Language of Transition." In *The Politics of Reconciliation in Multicultural Societies*, edited by Will Kymlicka and Bashir Bashir, 15–47. Oxford: Oxford University Press, 2008.

Veracini, Lorenzo. "Settler Collective, Founding Violence and Disavowal: The Settler Colonial Situation." *Journal of Intercultural Studies* 29, no. 4 (2008): 363–79. https://doi.org/10.1080/07256860802372246.

Vizenor, Gerald. *Survivance: Narratives of Native Presence*. Lincoln: University of Nebraska Press, 2008.

Vowel, Chelsea. *Indigenous Writes: A Guide to First Nations, Métis, and Inuit Issues in Canada*. Winnipeg: HighWater, 2016.

Vowell, Sarah. *The Partly Cloudy Patriot*. New York: Simon and Schuster, 2002.

Wagamese, Richard. "Returning to Harmony." In *Response, Responsibility, and Renewal: Canada's Truth and Reconciliation Journey*, edited by Gregory Young-ing, Jonathan Dewar, and Mike DeGagné, 139–48. Ottawa: Aboriginal Healing Foundation, 2009.

Wakeham, Pauline. "Reconciling 'Terror': Managing Indigenous Resistance in the Age of Apology." *American Indian Quarterly* 36, no. 1 (2012): 1–33. https://muse.jhu.edu/article/464477.

Wakeham, Pauline. "Rendition and Redress: Maher Arar, Apology, Exceptionality." In *Reconciling Canada: Critical Perspectives on the Culture of Redress*, edited by Jennifer Henderson and Pauline Wakeham, 278–95. Toronto: University of Toronto Press, 2013.

Wallot, Jean-Pierre. "Foreword." In *Facing History: Portraits from the National Archives of Canada*. Ottawa: National Archives of Canada, 1993.

Webb, Chris. "Standoff at Oka: Dramatic Confrontation Concerned All Canadians." In *100 Photos That Changed Canada*, edited by Mark Reid, 190–91. Toronto: HarperCollins, 2009.

Wexler, Laura. *Tender Violence: Domestic Visions in the Age of US Imperialism*. Chapel Hill: University of North Carolina Press, 2000.

Wheeler, Winona. "Act of Defiance: Famous 'No' Vote Sank Meech Lake Accord." In *100 Photos That Changed Canada*, edited by Mark Reid, 186–87. Toronto: HarperCollins, 2009.

Whitlock, Gillian. "Active Remembrance: Testimony, Memoir, and the Work of Reconciliation." In *Rethinking Settler Colonialism: History and Memory in*

Australia, Canada, Aotearoa New Zealand and South Africa, edited by Annie Coombes, 24–44. Manchester, UK: Manchester University Press, 2006.

Williams, Raymond. *Marxism and Literature*. Oxford: Oxford University Press, 1977.

Wilson, Ian E. "Peace, Order and Good Governance: Archives in Society." *Archival Science* 12, no. 2 (2012): 235–44. https://doi.org/10.1007/s10502-011-9168-8.

Winter, Jay. *Remembering War: The Great War between Memory and History in the Twentieth Century*. New Haven, CT: Yale University Press, 2006.

Wolfe, Patrick. "Settler Colonialism and the Elimination of the Native." *Journal of Genocide Research* 8, no. 4 (2006): 387–409. https://doi.org/10.1080/14623520601056240.

Woo, Grace Li Xiu. *Ghost Dancing with Colonialism: Decolonization and Indigenous Rights at the Supreme Court of Canada*. Vancouver: University of British Columbia Press, 2011.

York, Geoffrey, and Loreen Pindera. *People of the Pines: The Warriors and the Legacy of Oka*. Boston: Little, Brown, 1991.

Young, James E. *At Memory's Edge: After-Images of the Holocaust in Contemporary Art and Architecture*. New Haven, CT: Yale University Press, 2000.

Younging, Gregory. "Inherited History, International Law, and the UN Declaration." In *Response, Responsibility, and Renewal: Canada's Truth and Reconciliation Journey*, edited by Gregory Younging, Jonathan Dewar, and Mike DeGagné, 323–38. Ottawa: Aboriginal Healing Foundation, 2009.

Index

Page numbers followed by *f* indicate figures.

ciation and, 177–78n40; relocation of, 149–50; St. Anne's Indian Residential School and, 149; St. Eugene's Mission School and, xi; St. Mary's Indian Residential School and, 125, 150–54, 155f; Tk'emlúps te Secwépemc First Nation and, xi; United Church and, 150; unmarked graves at, 2, 149, 150, 154

Canadian Broadcasting Corporation (CBC), 40–41, 44, 45f
Canadian history: in Canadian educational system, 13, 22; confederation (1867) in, 27–28; Disney Corporation and, 24; Gradual Civilization Act (1857) in, 27–28; Indian Act of 1876 and amendments in, 28–29, 113–14; land and, x, 22, 27, 171n4; narrative and, 22, 23; New France and, 27, 171n4, 172n32; Royal Proclamation of 1763, 27, 171n4; settler symbols in, 23, 25; "Sixties and Seventies Scoop" and, 23; stages of, 171n4. See also Indigenous history; tolerance and benevolence: in Canadian national identity
Canadian Museum for Human Rights, 186n49
Cardinal, Eva, 133
Cardinal, Tantoo, 80
Cariou, Warren, 135
Carlisle Indian Industrial School, 61
Catholic Church: Grollier Hall and, 119, 148; Indian Act of 1876 and, 29; and Inuvik Truth and Reconciliation Commission national gathering, 82f, 83; in IRS system, 1; and Victoria, BC, Truth and Reconciliation Commission regional event, 183n66; and Winnipeg Truth and Reconciliation Commission national gathering, 113. See also apologies
Catholic Register, 122
Chatterjee, Partha, 171–72n10
Children of Shingwauk Alumni Association, 179n74
Chrétien, Jean, 138
Chrisjohn, Roland, 170n31

Christian churches and Christianity: Indian Act of 1876 and, 29; and Indian Residential Schools Settlement Agreement (IRSSA), 112; at Inuvik Truth and Reconciliation Commission national gathering, 84, 119; in IRS system, 1, 4f, 15, 20, 26, 28–32, 33, 35, 45, 55, 61, 65–69, 83–84, 88, 96, 111–12, 119, 121, 133–34, 135–36, 173n36, 183n66, 184n68; and IRS TRC, 1, 81; Native nationhood and, 29; and South African Truth and Reconciliation Commission (SA TRC), 113; spiritual genocide by, 112; at Winnipeg Truth and Reconciliation Commission national gathering, 111, 112, 113. See also apologies
Christian Guardian, 69
Churchill, Ward, 62
Claxton, Dana, 178n59
Cloutier, Patrick, 36–37
Coastal GasLink, x
Coast Salish, 175n86, 183n55
Colmeiro, José, 126
colonial debris, 58–59, 125
conferences, gatherings and events: "Breaking the Silence: International Conference on the Indian Residential School Commission of Canada" (Montreal), 1–3, 168n1; collective memory of Canadians at, 58; International Conference on the Indian Residential School Commission of Canada (Montreal), 1–3, 168n1; Truth, Reconciliation and the Residential Schools (Nipissing University), 128. See also Halifax Truth and Reconciliation Commission national event; Indian Residential Schools Truth and Reconciliation Commission (IRS TRC); Inuvik Truth and Reconciliation Commission national gathering; Victoria, BC, Truth and Reconciliation Commission regional event; Winnipeg Truth and Reconciliation Commission national gathering
Coombes, Annie, 7–8
Coqualeetza Indian Residential School, 3f, 154–56, 187n63

National Residential School Student
Death Register, 149
New Credit First Nation, 50
New Future, A (CBC), 44–46, 51, 161
Neyersoo, Richard, 122
Ngugi wa Thiong'o', 46
Niezen, Ronald, 26, 105, 173n36
Nipissing University, 128, 161
"Nitotem" (Halfe), 135–36, 186n38
Nora, Pierre, 132
Nuu-chah-nulth, 169n8

Ojibwe Nation of Credit, 40, 48–50
Oka Standoff, 36–37
Okimaw, David, 34
On Collective Memory (Halbwachs),
    173n37
Osborne, Brian, 131
Ottawa, 54

pamphlets, 30–32, 65–68
Peawanuck community, 149–50
Pelican Lake Indian Residential School,
    3*f*, 149
Peters, Robert, 142, 144–45
Pettipas, Gerard, 113
Pigalak, Edna, 84
Pinney, Christopher, 57–58
Poitras, Jane Ash, 76–77, 78, 178n59
police and military, 24, 36–37, 155
Portage la Prairie Indian Residential
    School, 3*f*, 15, 142–48
Port Alberni Indian Residential School,
    3*f*, 148–49
Porter, Judy, 149
Potato Peeling 101 to Ethnobotany 101
    (Poitras), 76–77
Pratt, Mary Louise, 58
Presbyterian Church: archives of, 15; in
    IRS system, 1, 29. *See also* apologies
Prince, Rufus, 142

Quebec sovereignty movement, 38

Ratele, Kopano, 128
reclamation: of names and identities, 50,
    101, 122; national gatherings and, 50,

105, 124; of sites, 125–26, 142–43,
150, 156*f*, 159; testimonies and, 50,
105. *See also* assimilation of Indigenous peoples; image archive and
photography
reconciliation: critics of, 1, 3, 5, 11–12,
111; future and, 11, 39–43, 53, 118,
158, 159, 165–66; Indigenous and
non-Indigenous (settler) processes
in, 2, 5, 11–17, 21–32, 23–31, 47–48,
111–12; international context of, 8–11,
21, 43, 91, 98, 170n25; language and, 2,
107; meanings of, 1; methodological
approaches to, 15–18, 110; movement
toward, 35–41, 52–53, 82, 114; and
national duty to remember, 41–44;
national memory and identity in, 14,
17, 19, 41–44; tolerance values and,
20; visualities and, 5, 6, 20, 21, 46–53;
as way of seeing, 19–53, 75–76, 160,
183n58. *See also* apologies; assimilation
of Indigenous peoples; image archive
and photography; Inuvik Truth and
Reconciliation Commission national
gathering; tolerance and benevolence: in Canadian national identity;
Winnipeg Truth and Reconciliation
Commission national gathering
Red Deer Industrial School, 73, 150,
187n60
Red Sucker Lake First Nation, 37–38
Ree, C., 127
Reed, Hayter, 70–71
Regan, Paulette, 16, 129
Regina Indian Residential School, 3*f*, 59,
62, 63–64, 68, 72–73
Regina Indian Residential School Com-
memorative Association, 177n40
Remembering Inninimowin (Koostachin),
34, 161–65, 188n5
Remembering the Children Society,
187n60
Renan, Ernest, 41
Right to Look, The (Mirzoeff), 46
Robinson, Dylan, xiii–xiv, xvi–xvii, xix,
115, 168–69n5, 170n32, 180n7, 183n64
Rothberg, Michael, 14–15

Tracing Memory blog (Angel), xii–xiii, 17, 143–45, 151
trauma, ix, x, xii, xiii, 11–12, 13, 21–22, 34, 42, 53, 83, 97–100, 115, 122–24, 129, 170n32, 172n19, 181n30, 181n35, 181–82n37, 182n44
TRC. *See* Indian Residential Schools Truth and Reconciliation Commission (IRS TRC)
Trivedi, Harish, 96
Tr'ondëk Hwëch'in First Nation Cultural Centre, 54
Trouillot, Michel-Rolph, 157
Trudeau, Justin, xvi
Trudeau, Pierre, 35
Truth and Indignation (Niezen), 26
truth commissions: in comparison with Canada, 8–9, 20–21; literature on, 181n36; in memory and history construction, 41–42; religiosity and secularism in, 113. *See also* Australia; South Africa
Tsinhnahjinnie, Hulleah J., 50
Tuck, Eve (Unangax̂), 127
Turner, Dale, 43
Turtle Island, xvi
Tutu, Desmond, 113

United Church: and burial sites, 150; in IRS system, 1, 26. *See also* apologies
United Nations: Declaration on Rights of Indigenous Peoples, xi, 174n61; international year of reconciliation and, 8, 169n16
Unity Riders, 106
US Department of Interior, xii

VanAntwerpen, Jonathan, 113
Van Styvendale, Nancy, 99

Veracini, Lorenzo, 83
Victoria, BC, Truth and Reconciliation Commission regional event, 183n64, 183n66
visuality: colonial frameworks of, 46–47; of tolerance, 5; in truth and reconciliation, 5, 6, 18, 46–53, 76, 129
Vizenor, Gerald, 99
Voudrach, Paul, 120–22

Wakeham, Pauline, xvii
Wallot, Jean-Pierre, 74
Washington Post, xii
Weems, Carrie Mae, 178n59
Wet'suwet'en, Coastal GasLink pipeline and, x–xi
What Do Pictures Want? (Mitchell), 130
"What of the Indian's Future" (Anglican Church), 67–68
Wheeler, Winona, 38
Where Are the Children? (Legacy of Hope Foundation), 62–63
White Calf Collegiate, 3f, 147, 148
Willett, Cam, 12
Williams, Raymond, 98
Wilson, Marie, 16, 40, 174n69, 182n52
Winnipeg Truth and Reconciliation Commission national gathering, xiv, 3, 3f, 4f, 18, 19, 91, 92, 95–96, 97, 98, 102–17, 119, 124, 142
Wolfe, Patrick, 7
Woo, Grace Li Xiu, 134
Wounded Knee massacre, 134

"year of reconciliation" model, 169n16
Yellowquill, Peter, 112
Younging, Gregory, 104

Zimbabwe, 170n25

CPSIA information can be obtained
at www.ICGtesting.com
Printed in the USA
LVHW021239021222
734426LV00012B/392